Another Day's Begun

Another Day's Begun

Thornton Wilder's Our Town *in the 21st Century*

Howard Sherman

methuen | drama

LONDON • NEW YORK • OXFORD • NEW DELHI • SYDNEY

METHUEN DRAMA
Bloomsbury Publishing Plc
50 Bedford Square, London, WC1B 3DP, UK
1385 Broadway, New York, NY 10018, USA

BLOOMSBURY, METHUEN DRAMA and the Methuen Drama logo
are trademarks of Bloomsbury Publishing Plc

First published in Great Britain 2021

For legal purposes the Acknowledgments on p. 261 constitute an extension of
this copyright page.

Cover design: Louise Dugdale
Upper cover image: Deaf West and Pasadena Playhouse production of *Our Town*,
photo by Jenny Graham.Cover images: (top) The Deaf West and Pasadena Playhouse
production of *Our Town*, photo © Jenny Graham; (bottom) The Miami New Drama
production of *Our Town*, photo by Stian Roenning.

A catalogue record for this book is available from the British Library.

ISBN:	HB:	978-1-3501-2344-1
	PB:	978-1-3501-2343-4
	ePDF:	978-1-3501-2345-8
	eBook:	978-1-3501-2346-5

Typeset by RefineCatch Limited, Bungay, Suffolk

To find out more about our authors and books visit www.bloomsbury.com
and sign up for our newsletters.

About the Author

Howard Sherman is a theatre administrator, writer, and advocate.

He has been executive director of the American Theatre Wing and the Eugene O'Neill Theater Center, managing director of Geva Theatre, general manager of Goodspeed Musicals, and public relations director of Hartford Stage, as well as interim director of the Alliance for Inclusion in the Arts. He has also held administrative positions at the Westport Country Playhouse, Manhattan Theatre Club, and Philadelphia Festival Theatre for New Plays.

Since 2012, he has been the US columnist and a feature writer for *The Stage* newspaper in London, and in 2018 was named contributing editor of *Stage Directions* magazine. His writing has appeared in a number of other publications including *Slate*, the *New York Times*, the *Guardian*, and *American Theatre* magazine.

Howard frequently consults, writes, and speaks on issues of censorship and artists' rights in both academic and professional theatre and he created the Arts Integrity Initiative in 2015 to focus on those efforts. He has delivered keynote addresses for, among others, the Educational Theatre Association, KCACTF, Florida Association for Theatre Education, and the Texas Educational Theatre Association's Arts Program Administrators Conference. He was cited as one of the Top 40 Free Speech Defenders in 2014 by the National Coalition Against Censorship and received the Dramatists Legal Defense Fund's Defender Award in 2015.

A native of New Haven, Connecticut, and graduate of the University of Pennsylvania, Howard resides in New York with his wife, producer Lauren Doll.

www.hesherman.com   www.artsintegrity.org

Contents

1

Introduction: This Book Is
Called *Another Day's Begun*

It has become fashionable to knock Thornton Wilder's *Our Town* as sentimental, old-fashioned, golden-hued, sepia-toned, done-to-death nostalgia. It has also become fashionable to write about how *Our Town* is improperly and ignorantly relegated to the status of sentimental, old-fashioned, golden-hued, sepia-toned, done-to-death nostalgia.

It is derided as fodder only for high school theatre. Yet, Arthur Miller's *The Crucible* and Reginald Rose's *Twelve Angry Men* (now often done as *Twelve Angry Jurors*) are less than twenty years younger than *Our Town*, and are also frequently produced in high schools, but it doesn't seem that people feel the incessant need to haul out a narrow set of stereotypes, or anti-stereotypes, which still repeat canards about them when those plays are produced professionally. The former drama may forever be placed in the context of the McCarthy era, and the latter's original white male dynamic will often be explained as a product of its time, but they are more dramaturgical notes than the lede in reviews of productions or the reasons offered as to why the plays should not be done.

Our Town does offer a certain challenge when one looks for an easy way to encapsulate or explain it, since it defies easy synopsizing. It has certainly proved a challenge for many. The poster for the 1940 film version billed it only as "The screen's most unusual picture," in an era when willful misrepresentation in marketing was the norm. In *TV Guide* magazine in 1959, a televised version was described as, "The Stage Manager starts, interrupts, halts and comments on the activities of the players, who represent the residents of Grover's Corners, N.H. A minimum of scenery and props is employed." The website of Concord Theatricals, which licenses the play for stock and amateur productions, offers up, "Narrated by a stage manager and performed with minimal props and sets, audiences follow the Webb and Gibbs families as their children fall in love, marry, and eventually – in one of the most famous scenes in American theatre – die."

To be sure, no one- or two-line precis can possibly do justice to any great literary work. After all, the whole point of synopses is to be reductive, to simplify. But perhaps more so than any classic American dramatic work of its era, *Our Town* proves slippery precisely because it doesn't have a conventional plot, a singular through-line of narrative, only glimpses, out of chronological order, with a foray into fantasy—or is it? It was meta-theatrical even before people spoke in such terms, experimental without being so ostentatiously avant-garde that its innovations have calcified with time. For those who value it, it is remembered not for its story but for its message.

Of the last, there can be no mistake about what Thornton Wilder wanted audiences to receive from attending the play. At its emotional pinnacle—it is difficult to refer to a climax in a play that has no obvious conflict or overt action—the character of Emily Webb, the largest female role in the play, cries out, "Oh, earth, you're too wonderful for anybody to realize you." She then asks the avuncular but ill-defined figure who has narrated the story, through tears per the stage directions in the text, "Do human beings ever realize life while they live it?—every, every minute?"[1]

Almost as if concerned that audiences might miss this essential query, asked to another character onstage but truly meant for the people watching the play, Wilder proffered a series of queries in an essay for *The New York Times* which ran only nine days after the play opened. It was titled, somewhat curiously, "A Preface for 'Our Town.'" It's odd in that it assumes those who will take in the play might need some preparation, not only in its style, but in its philosophy, in the questions that Wilder himself wished to explore. "What is the relation between the countless 'unimportant' details of our daily life, on the one hand, and the great perspectives of time, social history, and current religious ideas, on the other?" he asked rhetorically. "What is trivial and what is significant about any one person's making a breakfast, engaging in a domestic quarrel, in a 'love scene,' in dying?"[2] It is a veritable study guide for the play.

Perhaps in that era, this preface didn't linger, the way it would today on the internet, for every person who sought to see or participate in a production of the play to reference. But Wilder would write a more permanent preface to the 1957 compilation *Three Plays by Thornton Wilder*, which grouped together *Our Town* with *The Skin of Our Teeth* and *The Matchmaker*. In that essay, Wilder devoted one paragraph solely to *Our Town*. "*Our Town* is not offered as a picture of life in a New Hampshire village; or as a speculation about the conditions of life after death (that element I merely took from Dante's *Purgatory*)," he wrote. "It is an attempt to find a value above all price for the smallest events in our daily life. I have made the claim as preposterous as possible, for I have set the village against the largest dimensions of time and place."[3]

In the final revised version of *Our Town*, the standard text for production, Thornton Wilder's nephew, Tappan, literary executor of his uncle's work, offers yet a bit more elaboration on the 1957 preface, drawn from unpublished notes in his uncle's archives. In it, the younger Wilder asserts that the line about "an attempt to find value above all price" is the single most quoted line in theatre programs for *Our Town*. But instead of calling it "preposterous" as he did originally, Thornton would later call the attempt "absurd." Yet he acknowledges in a handwritten note that audiences possess even greater vision than the play's characters, that Emily "learns that each life—though it appears to be a repetition among millions—can be felt to be inestimably precious."[4]

Our Town, it would seem, is about everything, wherever, whenever, and whomever you may be, and for goodness' sake, pay attention.

* * *

Who were the greatest American playwrights of the 20th century? It is likely, were one to take a casual survey among theatre scholars, practitioners, and knowledgeable fans, that the answer would be something along the lines of O'Neill, Williams, Miller, Albee, and Wilson, with apologies for the biases that blinkered who could reach the stage for the majority of those 100 years. But ask about the greatest American plays of the 20th century, and you might hear *Long Day's Journey into Night*, *The Glass Menagerie*, *A Streetcar Named Desire*, *Death of a Salesman*, *Who's Afraid of Virginia Woolf?*, *The Piano Lesson* . . . and *Our Town*.

Yes, that is a generalization, but readers are encouraged to try this for themselves. They are very likely to find some accuracy in this claim, which then leads to why there is this disconnect, which places *Our Town* among the plays but excludes Wilder from the playwrights. Perhaps it is due to the fact that Wilder wrote a great many one-acts, but very few full-length plays, and so his body of dramatic work is viewed as less substantial than the others. There's also the fact that Wilder was equally adept at writing fiction, having won his first Pulitzer Prize (of three) for his 1927 novel *The Bridge of San Luis Rey*, the second of seven novels in total. But the status of *Our Town* is not easily questioned, for its importance in its day, for its influence on writers who would follow and audiences who would see it, and for its continuing place in the modern theatrical repertory in the US and abroad, for professionals, amateurs, and academics and their students.

Edward Albee, never noted as a soft touch when it came to assessing the works of others, often declared that *Our Town* was very likely the greatest play by an American author. Albee didn't say this as an attempt to curry favor when, as a young playwright, he became friends with Wilder in the elder writer's later years. It was in 2011 that he told the National Endowment for the Arts' Josephine Reed, "I think *Our Town* is a masterpiece. I think *Our Town* is probably the finest American play written so far." Elsewhere in the same interview, Albee said, "It's one of the toughest, saddest, most brutal plays that I've ever come across. And it is so beautiful, and when it is funny, it's gloriously funny. There are times, there are scenes in *Our Town* that it's hard for me to think about without wanting to cry. It's that beautiful a play."[5]

Albee went on to declare that the play carried the same meaning Wilder had intended back in 1938, saying, "When it is done properly it makes us understand that if we don't live our lives fully and completely, we've wasted everything we have."

*   *   *

What is there to write about a play more than 80 years old, produced countless times throughout the world, that hasn't already been said? There have been multiple biographies of Wilder—the gold standard is Penelope Niven's from 2013—and an array of academic papers on Wilder's writing, in general, and on aspects of *Our Town*, specifically.

But, by and large, those many valuable and learned works recount the life of the man or offer scholars' literary analysis of the text. They rely on historical sources or personal analysis. Yet plays are meant to be performed, and outside of feature articles about this production or that, there seemed to be a disproportionately small number of works which featured the voices of the artists who have brought this play to life since the turn of the current century, that is to say, since January 1, 2001.

What is it to live in Grover's Corners eight times a week? What is to think about the Mind of God every night, to bid farewell to the living at student matinees? How does it feel to step back in time while making certain the work speaks to audiences today? What are the stories that surround the making of *Our Town* productions in this particular era, about theatre, life, family, career, language? Those are the conversations that underpinned the more than 100 interviews that make up the majority of this book. The productions spoken of herein were selected for their variety of approach, their geography, their impact in various communities. Nothing should imply that these have been found to be the best productions of the past generation, though surely there are advocates who might feel that way about one or more that they may have seen from within this group, and nothing should dissuade them from their enthusiasm.

The voices in this book also don't agree on everything. They have found different things in the play, conceived of different backstories for the characters, chosen to emphasize different qualities in the staging. Because the goal was to elicit why and how this play speaks to our present day, or our relatively recent days, every interpretation is deemed valid. For a reader, it provides different perspectives. For people contemplating or doing the play, it offers interpretive alternatives that are by no means exhaustive or definitive. At the same time, there are stories that repeat across chapters, across an ocean, across years, even as certain elements of *Our Town* seem immutable, no matter how they are embodied.

By concentrating the majority of this book on recent productions, there was the opportunity to speak first-hand with the artists, rather than to rely on past interviews or accounts that had already passed through the filter of another writer and their editor or editors. Some of the voices in this book may have told their stories before, but they told them anew for this volume, so they may have even evolved their thoughts—or forgotten things. The majority of the people, both veteran actors and uninitiated amateurs, have likely not been interviewed before about this play, and there are a number who have never been interviewed before in any context. These narratives are preceded by a short history of the play in its early years and a survey of its numerous inroads into American culture.

In a conversation with Gregory Mosher, who directed the 1988 Broadway production of *Our Town*, which falls outside of the time frame of this book, he drew distinct parallels between Wilder and Samuel Beckett, between *Our Town* and *Waiting for Godot*. "Wilder anticipates the deaths of 60 million," said Mosher. "Beckett responds to the deaths of 60 million people." He went on to further illuminate the connection, first by quoting Beckett: "'They give birth astride of a grave, the light gleams an instant, then it's night once more.'[6] That's the plot of – to the degree that there's a plot, which isn't much – of *Our Town*." Mosher went on to call *Our Town*, "A shocking play. Deeply shocking play. The greatest American play, perhaps. Because of what it takes on." Mosher elaborated, observing, "If one of the questions of the play is not only people die, but that civilizations die, 2020 seems like a very good time to be doing the play."

What are the many reasons why we keep returning to this barest sliver of life at the turn of the 20th century? How does a play set in in what was most assuredly an all-white, patriarchal, Protestant, semi-rural small town in New England manage to speak to audiences more than 80 years on? "It ain't houses, and it ain't names, and it ain't earth, and it ain't even the stars," wrote Wilder. Perhaps, "that something has to do with human beings." For this most produced of American classics, there is always another day begun, and another truth to be discovered.

2

Building Grover's Corners

On February 3, 1938, a new play opened on Broadway. Its subject was mortality. In a bucolic setting, it explored the implications of death in life, and ended with its leading characters departing their human existence. It was a hit, playing for over 300 performances and closing in November of that same year. It would be quickly made into a film and later receive multiple Broadway revivals.

The play in question was *On Borrowed Time* by Paul Osborn. *Our Town*, which in very general terms tackled not dissimilar themes, and had a comparable life on Broadway, on tour and in the movies, opened on February 4. More than eight decades later, *On Borrowed Time* is rarely seen, while *Our Town* seems omnipresent. But while, then as now, themes in Broadway theatre arise by accident and coincidence rather than coordinated planning, certainly the New York theatre critics and avid first-nighters must have wondered what was in the air creatively and philosophically at the mid-winter point of 1938.

Playing concurrently with those plays on Broadway were *Amphitryon 38*, S. N. Behrman's adaptation of Jean Giraudoux; Ed Wynn in *Hooray for What!*; George M. Cohan in *I'd Rather Be Right*; John Steinbeck's *Of Mice and Men*; Gertrude Lawrence in *Susan and God*, a comedy about faith; *The Cradle Will Rock* by Marc Blitzstein; *The Women* by Clare Boothe Luce; Kaufman and Hart's *You Can't Take It With You*; and Orson Welles' *Julius Caesar*, the last of which, like *Our Town*, did not have any scenery to speak of. There was one other production on Broadway at that time worth noting: the ninth Broadway iteration of Ibsen's *A Doll's House*. Why does one of many *Doll House*s merit a mention? Because, in addition to Nora being played by the indefatigable Ruth Gordon, it used an English version by a classicist, novelist, and educator named Thornton Wilder.

A Doll's House is a reminder that by the time *Our Town* debuted, Wilder was hardly an unknown figure in American letters. He published his first novel, *The Cabala*, in 1926 and followed it quickly the next year with *The Bridge of San Luis Rey*, which received the Pulitzer Prize for literature in 1928, when Wilder was only 31. He had already begun writing for the theatre, with *The Trumpet Shall Sound* having been produced Off-Broadway in 1926. His collection of short plays *The*

Angel that Troubled the Waters and Other Plays was published in 1928. *The Long Christmas Dinner and Other Plays*, more one-act works, would follow in 1931, a volume that included *Pullman Car Hiawatha* and *The Happy Journey to Trenton and Camden*. These plays would build an appetite for Wilder's theatrical work and were widely produced by schools and "little theatre" groups in the days before regional theatre had coalesced as a professional alternative to commercial theatre. They were also evidence of Wilder's experiments with spare staging and time-compression.

Wilder's literary success also brought financial success, and he used his newfound income to build a house for his mother and siblings in Hamden, Connecticut, just outside New Haven, which would remain the family home until his sister Isabel passed away in 1995. It was his home base as well, though he was frequently absent. Wilder could be called a citizen of the world, having been schooled for a portion of his youth in China while his father was in the US diplomatic service there, and having begun regular travels to Europe as an adult that would continue throughout his life. His fame and travels in the US and abroad brought him quickly into a circle that included F. Scott Fitzgerald, Pablo Picasso, Max Reinhardt, and Gertrude Stein, the last of whom became his close confidante until her death in 1946.

He published two more novels in the 1930s prior to *Our Town*: *The Woman of Andros* and *Heaven's My Destination*. His adaptation of *Lucrece* played a brief Broadway run in late 1932 and early 1933, produced by and starring the distinguished Katharine Cornell. A short Hollywood foray in 1934 included work on a never to be produced movie about Joan of Arc for Katharine Hepburn.

So while *Our Town* may have been Wilder's first multi-act original play to reach Broadway, he was already famous, and the announcement of the work generated immediate press interest. He promised the play to his friend, producer-director Jed Harris, who carried out those duties on *A Doll's House* as well. Three years Wilder's junior, Harris had already had a string of Broadway hits, most notably with Ben Hecht and Charles MacArthur's *The Front Page*.

A play which began as *M Marries N*, then *Our Village*, was one of the projects Wilder was pursuing in 1937, writing first at the MacDowell Colony in New Hampshire. After serving as a delegate to a League of Nations conference in Paris, he settled in to work further on what had evolved into *Our Town* in Salzburg and Zurich. This writing period coincided with the depths of the Depression and the rise of the Nazi Party in Germany, important contexts to a play set prior to World War I. He also cited numerous influences in the work, as summarized by Penelope Niven: "Ibsen and Nestroy, Dante and Molière, Gertrude Stein and Alfred North Whitehead, Alexander Woollcott and Mabel Dodge Luhan, Fred Astaire and Ginger Rogers on the movie screen, his mother and his father, Rome and New Hampshire, Paris and Zurich."[1] His staging ideas were drawn from multiple forbears, including Greek and Asian theatre.

By mid-September, Wilder wrote to Stein about *Our Town*, saying that her own work was a strong influence on him, going so far as to say that she was "in a deep knit collaboration" with him.[2] Just two weeks later, he would write her again, mentioning "an influx of ideas that make my little play the most beautiful one you can imagine."[3] The play had its first reading in Paris in November. Late in the month, at Harris' behest, Wilder returned from Europe to work further on *Our Town*, although he was isolated by Harris in Old Brookville on Long Island to focus on the play while Harris himself saw to preproduction matters. The play went into rehearsal in late December, with Frank Craven as the Stage Manager and his son John as George.

For a play in which there is no overt plot, let alone conflict, *Our Town* did not have an easy birth. Wilder and Harris fought one another tooth and nail. As Wilder wrote to Stein on January 12, 1938:

> As you predicted Jed got the notion that he had written the play and was still writing it.
> As long as his suggestions for alterations are on the structure they are often very good; but once they apply to the words they are always bad and sometimes atrocious.
> There have been some white-hot flaring fights.[4]

Harris had, in fact, asked for co-author credit on the play, which Wilder had denied.

There was certainly no dispute about the bad blood between the two men. Referring to Wilder's dissatisfaction with the production, Harris wrote in his memoir:

> He did not merely dislike it, he detested it. And his detestation reached such shrill heights on the opening night in Princeton that all further communication between us lapsed. The author was not even remotely in my confidence while the show was in Boston.[5]

During rehearsals, two actresses playing Emily were fired in succession. Martha Scott, who would ultimately have a great success in the role, joined the company only eight days before its first public performance. *Our Town* debuted in a one-night out-of-town engagement, at the McCarter Theatre in Princeton, New Jersey, on January 22, 1938. The review in *Variety* was harsh, opining, "It is not only disappointing bur hopelessly slow," and while, the cast was praised, the critic identified as Rosen., decided, "it will probably go down as the season's most extravagant waste of fine talent."[6]

While originally slated to open immediately in New York, *Our Town* instead traveled to Boston for a two-week engagement. There has been some dispute over the play's reception on Boston, suggesting it had been panned. While sales were weak, leading to the run being trimmed to only a single week, critical response was certainly encouraging:

Frank Craven and Martha Scott (foreground) in the original 1938 Broadway production of *Our Town*. Photo courtesy of Photofest.

The acting is excellent throughout and it is not at all improbable that this highly unusual and thoughtful drama, in a season when the theatrical nabobs are busy breaking new trails, may become a hit.[7]

Peggy Doyle, *Boston Evening American*

It is written with sympathy and feeling and in spite of the unusual presentation of the story of Grover's Corners, it compels attention.[8]

Mordaunt Hall, *Boston Evening Transcript*

He has recorded his impressions with evident savor of New England character into a fantasy that dips gently into comedy and sentiment and turns at the end into a comforting species of allegory.[9]

unbylined, *The Boston Globe*

That's not to say there weren't mixed responses as well:

The playwright's excursions into the life after death are a little fumbling and uncertain, though he makes almost unbearably touching the attempts of the dead girl to revisit the past and her realization that her spirit can find peace in forgetfulness.[10]

Elinor Hughes, Boston Herald

In summing up the overall response, *Variety* cited "wonderful backing from reviewers" and, jointly referring to *Our Town* and Orson Welles' *Julius Caesar*, said that they had "enthusiastic raves from the local press."[11] Oddly, as if to diminish the entire Boston engagement, a *Variety* piece written only seven days later out of New York remarked of *Our Town*, "Show had been panned in the Hub [Boston]."[12]

Wilder's close friend, Alexander Woollcott, to whom the play is dedicated, supported him with frequent letters. On January 26, Woollcott wrote to Wilder, "I have an abiding faith in this play of yours and others that you are going to write."[13] Just two days later, Woollcott wrote, "Good for you! Stick to your guns. But not to the last ditch. After all, what matters most is that the play, as published, be the way you would have it. That is the form in which it will be read in years to come and from which, in years to come, revivals will be made."[14] Playwright Marc Connelly and *New York Times* critic Brooks Atkinson both visited Boston to see the show and provided strong encouragement. Connelly reportedly asked Harris, "You are worried about a show like this?"[15]

However, Wilder continued to pour out his unhappiness about the play to friends, writing to Stein on February 1, "It's been one long fight to preserve me [sic] text from the interpolations of Jed Harris, and I've only won 50% of the time ... The play no longer moves or even interests me; now all I want out of it is money."[16]

With the play closed a week early in Boston, Harris had to make a rapid decision about Broadway, and without a solid theatre booking, he opted to present the play at the Henry Miller's Theatre, which he could only have for ten days, due to a prior commitment for the venue. Following the shortened Boston run, and with only four days to prepare it in New York, *Our Town* opened on Friday, February 4, 1938.

The reviews ran the gamut of opinion. There were those who saw *Our Town* as a major achievement, but some were mixed, and the occasional notice didn't seem to think much of it at all:

Probably the majority of playgoers are in so great a hurry to see life that they will be impatient with 'Our Town' on the ground that it slows them up. They shouldn't. It's really very fine.[17]

Arthur Pollock, Brooklyn Daily Eagle

The author's running comment and philosophical flights of fancy, voiced by the ever-present Mr. Craven, are of the sort to which one listens with respectful attention and polite interest without hearing anything to stir the imagination unduly, even on such a fascinating subject as life after death.[18]

Wilella Walford, *New York Post*

Under the leisurely monotone of this production is a fragment of the immortal truth. 'Our Town' is a microcosm. It is also a hauntingly beautiful play.[19]

Brooks Atkinson, *The New York Times*

It is a poet's conception; but in the eyes of this regretful reporter it is not quite a poet's achievement ... One wishes in an admittedly inexplicit way that the drama, so spacious in conception, could be more tightly knit within that space.[20]

John Chapman, *Daily News*

"Our Town" is beautiful and touching. I suspect it of being merely pretentious in its occasional outbursts of cosmic brooding ... Clearly "Our Town" is one of the events of the season, and, while it is likely to prove greatly disappointing upon occasions, it is almost invariably stimulating.[21]

Richard Watts Jr., *New York Herald Tribune*

Overall, the play was deemed sufficiently successful, so it ended its brief run at the Henry Miller's Theatre on February 12, and Harris moved it to the Morosco Theatre, where it reopened on February 14 and would remain for the rest of its run.

One of the most surprising reviews came not from a theatre critic, but rather from the First Lady of the United States, Eleanor Roosevelt, who had obviously caught the play in the first few weeks after opening. Writing in her daily syndicated column "My Day," Mrs. Roosevelt opined, "When I went to see 'Our Town,' I was moved and depressed beyond words. It is more interesting and more original and I am glad I saw it, but I did not have a pleasant evening."[22] Mrs. Roosevelt also questioned the type of work theatre critics were championing, prompting a flurry of essays by critics defending their opinions and profession against this slap from the president's wife.

A counterpoint to Mrs. Roosevelt's critique was provided by Kate Smith, a popular singer and radio host who became beloved in the era for her rendition of "God Bless America." On her radio show in April 1938, Smith spoke passionately about Wilder's play, telling her listeners, "I loved every minute of 'Our Town,' and I wept all through the last act, at the simple, fragile beauty of an almost perfect piece of work."[23]

In record time, *Our Town* was published on April 2, 1938. The text was, per Wilder's nephew Tappan, a transcription of what was seen on stage on Broadway in 1938, complete with some of Harris' unasked-for interpolations. As *Variety* had noted immediately following the Broadway opening, "Prior to the premiere there was a dispute between the manager and author over lines which Harris inserted. Instead of holding the producer to the terms of the Dramatists Guild contract, which gives the author full control of the script, Wilder decided not even to speak to Harris."[24] This version persisted in use for a number of years, with Wilder's revised and preferred version published beginning in 1957, with further reconstruction decades later from Thornton's own notes.

The varied critical reception was a harbinger of the New York Drama Critics Circle Awards, where Best Play went to John Steinbeck's *Of Mice and Men* in mid-April, with 12 votes for *Mice* to *Town*'s four.[25] However, the tables turned at the beginning of May when *Our Town* received the Pulitzer Prize for Drama.

The play's outward success did nothing to assuage the conflicts between Wilder and Harris. Come the summer of 1938, Harris was seeking to have Wilder accept a reduction in his weekly royalty on account of what he characterized as the production's financial position. Wilder fired off a telegram to Harris, saying, "You so resent the Dramatists Guilds [sic] effort to be fair that you threaten to close the play now unless a hundred dollar difference in the minimum is closed Stop Ugly cheap shrill blackmailing methods the consternation of everyone who has tried to speak up for you."[26] Wilder's attorney wrote to him, saying that he had not necessarily characterized the situation with full clarity, yielding detailed correspondence from Wilder, which prompted the attorney to say, "I did not realize that you had so many reasons to be irritated at him and can understand your desire to terminate diplomatic relations."[27] The royalty reduction was ultimately granted in the fall, but only a few weeks before the show closed.

On the matter of having some text corrections made in the Broadway production as requested by Wilder, Harris wrote to Wilder, "I received your latest communication and like all others I ever get from you it is a characteristic blend of fatuousness, vanity and superb unconscious buffoonery."[28] The back-and-forth relationship between the pair continued for years, with Harris writing to Wilder in 1942: "It is simply this I would prefer that we do not communicate with each other about anything whatever am sure you understand."[29]

Possibly spurred by a rumor that Harris wished to take on the role of the Stage Manager during a two-week vacation that was owed to Frank Craven, Thornton Wilder joined Actors Equity and stepped into the role for two weeks in September; Wilder donated his salary to The Actors Fund. The press came to see him, even with such a short run, with a critic from *The New York Times* writing, "Being a lecturer of some renown and having been at one time a schoolmaster, Mr. Wilder has, as they say, stage presence . . . He warmed up as the evening went along, and by the final curtain was jaunty."[30] Wilder was much in demand as the Stage Manager subsequent to this, and he would frequently perform the role at benefits in cuttings of the play, in addition to appearing in the full show at summer theatre companies between 1939 and 1959, making his final appearance in the role at the Williamstown Theatre Festival in Massachusetts.

The Broadway production of *Our Town* came to a close on November 19, 1938, having completed 336 performances, a strong run for a play in that era. Harris sent the play out on tour almost immediately, with Frank Craven reprising his role; the tour played such cities as Washington, Philadelphia, Cleveland, and Columbus, before being shut down in February in Chicago by Harris in what several press accounts described as surprising and which some attributed to a dispute between Harris and Craven. Harris remounted the production once more in April in Los Angeles (it would also play San Francisco), while a separate company led by Eddie Dowling as the Stage Manager concurrently played several engagements in the northeast, including a return by the play to Boston.

The stock and amateur rights for *Our Town* were released in April of 1939 through Samuel French, to overwhelming demand, yielding 658 productions in the United States in the first 20 months that it was available. Even as war was brewing, international productions sprang up, including both in Zurich and Rome in 1939. The Rome production was not without controversy: at its opening, as reported in a letter from Isabel Wilder to her brother Amos, "a leading Fascist politico tried to stop the performance, he and his group in the audience starting catcalls and speeches."[31] Actress and producer Elsa Merlini responded, saying that she had received approval from the Fascist authorities, and that, "this play is art, not politics." When she asked the audience if the play should go on, the consensus was that it should, and it did.[32]

World War II unsurprisingly slowed the play's spread, although amateur productions continued. Perhaps the most unexpected of these took place at Japanese internment camps in 1943, among them a high school production at the Topaz War Relocation Center in western Utah and a "little theatre" production at the Tule Lake War Relocation Center in the northeast corner of California. The reports from the internment camp newspapers carry no commentary about the productions, only notices about them taking place. From a 21st-century vantage point, one hopes that these unjustly imprisoned Americans found some comfort in this new play, rather than feeling a particular template of American life was being forced upon them.

There were also productions by those serving in the war, not just of *Our Town* but of other American plays as well. However, the servicepeople participating in the Allied Force Headquarters' production of *Our Town* in 1944 had a most surprising guide to the play: Thornton Wilder. While he had volunteered for service right after the opening of *The Skin of Our Teeth*, Wilder had not seen combat, and his wartime work took full advantage of his theatrical experience. As he wrote to his mother and his sister Isabel, speaking about the many productions underway, "All this requires a lot of coordination and committee and club meetings, and is accompanied I'm sorry to say with a lot of underground politics and some very bitter feuds. I'm getting out of the chairmanship as soon as I can and will restrict myself solely to overseeing the Our Town."[33]

Our Town also received its first professional Manhattan revival during World War II, when Jed Harris remounted the play for a January 1944 run at City Center, with Isabel Wilder on hand representing her brother. Playwright Marc Connelly took on the role of the Stage Manager with Martha Scott once again playing Emily and a young actor named Montgomery Clift as George. The limited run played for 24 performances.

While production planning had certainly begun while the war was still underway, with VE Day declared on May 8, 1945, the May 9 announcement of 18 US plays that would tour military bases in Europe under the auspices of the United Service Organizations (USO) seemed impeccably timed. *Our Town* would ultimately go out to military bases with Raymond Massey, already famous from the films *Abe Lincoln in Illinois* and *Arsenic and Old Lace*, the biggest name in any of the companies; he stepped in at the last minute for the novelist Christopher Morley, who was unable to pass the required physical.[34]

The production played for 70 performances in Europe, but Massey noted in retrospect that the selection of the play was not without its detractors. Officials at the American Theatre Wing, which was working in concert with the USO, expressed concern, per Massey, "on the astonishing grounds that it would induce homesickness in the troops." Massey responded, saying, "Do you think they're not homesick now?" before going on to assert, "One reason I suggested *Our Town* is that it will be a good dose of what's eating them, a kind of life and home most of them are longing to come back to. It will be that catharsis that psychologists are always bleating about, a kind of release."[35]

Our Town was the first American play to be produced in Berlin after the war, in 1946, but once again the play engendered conflict. Having been mounted in the Russian portion of the divided city, it was quickly shut down and moved to the US sector. There was never a determination on precisely what precipitated such a reaction. A report from the Associated Press said the Soviets canceled the play "on the grounds that the drama is too depressing and could inspire a German suicide wave."[36] However, a report in *The Billboard* said the Russian shutdown of the play came "because it upheld family life."[37]

In the wake of the war, the Department of State worked vigorously to have American plays, including *Our Town*, produced in both Germany and Japan. A program was set up to license the plays in those countries directly through the US Army, with the Army negotiating rights directly with the playwrights (rather than their agents) and overseeing the translations to ensure no hidden messages were slipped in. The German productions of *Our Town* happened rapidly, with *Variety* describing the intent as "using theatre as a means of bringing democracy to presumably truth-starved German teen-agers."[38] The Japanese productions didn't begin until 1948.

With life in England having begun to work its way back towards normalcy by 1946, *Our Town* made a belated English debut with a tryout in Liverpool in April.

The Stage said, "the reception which the play received at the close of its first performance in Liverpool indicated that its success in this country is likely to equal that achieved on the other side of the Atlantic."[39] The production, with Marc Connelly and Martha Scott paired once again, moved to London in early May, but *The Stage*'s enthusiasm was not to be borne out. *Variety* wrote, "Despite good notices here, Jed Harris production 'Our Town' has failed to catch on and is expected to shutter shortly."[40] It was gone by the beginning of June.

* * *

The proliferation of productions of *Our Town* is simply too vast to recount in detail. While World War II may have slowed its spread for a few years, it has been widely and continually produced throughout the world in an array of languages. In the United States, it has been revived on Broadway three times since the 1944 City Center production: in 1969, with Henry Fonda as the Stage Manager; in 1988, with Spalding Gray under Gregory Mosher's direction; and, in 2002, with Paul Newman. According to the Educational Theatre Association, the organization that created the International Thespian Society for high school theatre, the play has been one of the six most popular high school plays every decade since the 1940s, topping the charts in the 1950s, 1960s, and 1990s.[41] In 1967, *The New York Times* reported that *Our Town*, at that point almost 30 years old, was the highest-grossing title for licensing house Samuel French.[42]

While the population of Grover's Corners in the early 1900s would likely have been predominantly, if not entirely, white, productions of the play have been, by dint of the show's international popularity, performed by actors of every race and ethnicity. In the US, *The New York Times* took note of an "integrated" *Our Town* at the Inner City Cultural Center in Los Angeles in 1968, detailing its diversity, referred to as "novel and startling," as follows: "Emily Webb, the girl, is being played by a Negro, her father by an Apache Indian, her mother by a Russian-American and her brother by a Mexican-American. George Gibbs, Emily's sweetheart and young husband, is being played by a Japanese-American, his mother by a Negro and his sister by a Chinese-American." The director of the production, C. Bernard Jackson, told the *Times*, "What Wilder did not do is write about a New England community in that era which we love to call the age of innocence. We assert that it was written with a universal scope which knows no boundaries; it transcends time and space and place."[43]

The gender construct of *Our Town* began to be altered in the 1970s, as productions started to feature women playing the Stage Manager. Many accounts report that Geraldine Fitzgerald was the first woman to play the Stage Manager, at the Williamstown Theatre Festival in 1976, just a year after Wilder's death. But she had at least one predecessor, of whom Wilder was unquestionably aware, as shown by surviving correspondence with the production's director. In 1972, a production which dedicated the new Ida Green Communication Center at Austin College in

Texas featured a guest artist as the Stage Manager: Ginger Rogers. Flash forward to the summer of 2019, and the opening event of the Pride Plays, a series of readings at the Rattlestick Playwrights Theatre in Greenwich Village produced as part of the 50th anniversary of the Stonewall Riots, featured *Our Town* with a cast made up of transgender, non-binary, gender nonconforming, and gender-fluid actors populating Grover's Corner, proving that in each generation, there is a place for everyone in the community Thornton Wilder created.

3

Expanding Grover's Corners

*George Gibbs is one of those extreme individualists. Oddly enough, it
makes George Gibbs the best soldier because he values all of the acquired
liberties of civilian life and yet resigns them – proudly and knowingly – for
one great end.*

from *Act 4 of Our Town*

The immediate fame of *Our Town* upon its premiere, and its legacy over the years,
would play out in a wide variety of adaptations, homages, response works, parodies,
and excerpts from the play in other media. While Thornton Wilder opted not to
have an official hand in those subsequent or derivative works, there was one
exception, and he was among the first to expand upon the world of Grover's Corners.

Following his enlistment in the military in World War II, only ten days before
he would age out of eligibility for active service,[1] Wilder reported for training in
Miami, Florida, on June 27, 1942, having completed the screenplay for *Shadow of a
Doubt*.[2] In what was surely a most unusual training exercise, Wilder quickly
participated in what was referred to as "Act 4 of *Our Town*" for the program
Contact, broadcast out of WKAT in Miami on July 8.

Wilder was designated as "Soldier of the Week" on the program, and he engaged
in prepared chat with one of the hosts, who prompted him to muse about how war
might have influenced his earlier works. After saying that he would have written *The
Bridge of San Luis Rey* "differently," Wilder said, "*Our Town* could provide a fourth
act, showing the characters of that New England village living under a state of war."

Wilder proceeded to introduce a brief coda, largely narrated by him, essentially
taking on the role of the Stage Manager. Set contemporaneously in Miami, listeners
heard Corporal George Gibbs being awakened by a sergeant before Wilder whisked
them back to Grover's Corners. He spoke of the special independent qualities of
both New Hampshire and Vermont boys—no concern about the source of out-of-
state marble rivalry here—which made George "the best solider."

He would go on to note that Captain Ezra Hawkins of Grover's Corners—
perhaps kin to Shorty—had been captured by the Japanese and that town folk had

trouble wrapping their heads around such a fact. Another local boy, Chet Foster, who flew a B-17 in the Pacific theatre, had landed in the water, and was presumed lost. A parson character, rather than Wilder, repeated the speech from *Our Town*'s Act III about the Grover's Corners boys who fought and died in the Civil War, and Wilder reminded listeners that George was just one of 11 million soldiers, "a speck", who hopes the war will "be thorough and quick, and on that he's centered every part of his mind and body."[3]

A *Variety* review said the piece was "highly articulate" in its portrayal of "the physical and psychological effects of the war on the citizens of Grover's Corners."[4]

This was not even the first time that Wilder participated in a spin-off of the play. While no authorship is cited, the *Brooklyn Daily Eagle* reported on a benefit for the New York and Brooklyn Federations of Jewish Charities in November 1939, which featured a one-act play called *This Town*, drawn from the themes within *Our Town*. The cast included Eddie Dowling, who had toured in *Our Town*, cast members from the then current Broadway production *Time of Your Life* (which Dowling starred in and had co-directed with playwright William Saroyan) . . . and Wilder himself.[5] In his remarks that evening, Wilder spoke in "an epilogue of his own writing" of "gallant company in every town and city, who, while the majority continues daily rounds, feels prompted not only to give to the needs of the community, but to go out and call the attention of the rest of us to the organization that ministers to our less fortunate neighbors."[6]

While seemingly a work that was uniquely suited to the live theatre, *Our Town*, nonetheless, worked its way into the American consciousness not only through its myriad stage incarnations, but also through electronic media. It was taken up almost immediately, and those who didn't easily have access to a local theatre, professional or amateur, or who couldn't afford it, still had a chance to be introduced to *Our Town* without buying a theatre ticket.

Direct adaptations

The broadcast of *Contact* was not the first time any aspect of the story of *Our Town* had been electronically disseminated. The very first national version of the play had debuted on radio's Campbell Playhouse, Orson Welles' successor to the Mercury Theatre, on May 12, 1939. Welles himself played the Stage Manager, and his already standard repertory company, including Agnes Moorehead, Ray Collins, and Everett Sloane, were among the denizens of New Hampshire, joined by the original stage George Gibbs, John Craven.

The Campbell Playhouse *Our Town* set a pattern that would hold true for many of the radio adaptations of *Our Town*, in that it pared back the play to under an hour, in order to make room for an introduction, ads, and even a "next week on" segment. Despite the presence of the wunderkind Welles in the role, the character of the Stage Manager—who is never identified as such—was trimmed significantly. Though the Babylon speech remains, the community background by Professor Willard and Mr. Webb is absent.

In other variations from the stage script, Welles interrupts the acts not for people to stretch their legs and have a smoke, but to make way for messages about Campbell's Soup; Welles does not step into the role of Mr. Morgan in Act II and it is played by a separate actor; and Simon Stimson is wholly absent. Without the visuals of the stage, some sound processing is employed to differentiate between settings, most notably in Act III, when the voices of the dead are noticeably tinnier than others. Welles, however, retains his basso profundo, as if he is narrating his way through the act with Emily, rather than joining her in the afterlife.[7]

On May 6, 1940, *Our Town* was once again on the radio airwaves, this time under the auspices of the Lux Radio Theatre, which specialized in radio versions of forthcoming and recent films. Cecil B. DeMille was the program host, though unlike Welles, he did not play a role. DeMille's fulsome introduction emphasized the nostalgic qualities of the play, putting on one of those early layers of sentimentality cited by fans and detractors alike:

> Many of us who live in big towns reserve a corner of our hearts for some small town. For the schoolhouse on the hill, the elms that line the streets, sound of familiar church bells on a Sunday morning. Wherever it is, in Indiana, Idaho or New Hampshire, each one of us goes back to his hometown tonight, as we listen to the play called *Our Town*. Most of us will feel right at home in Our Town, because it contains at least part of everybody's story, of growing up and falling in love, and making a living, and all the things that make up our own absorbing everyday drama.[8]

The cast was that of the film that would be released only two-and-a-half weeks later, including Frank Craven and Martha Scott repeating their stage roles, and William Holden as George. However, in this version, the Stage Manager is now Mr. Morgan of Morgan's Drug Store fame, and he specifically notes that the broadcast and therefore his narration is taking place in 1940. Also reduced to less than an hour, there's room, nonetheless, for Simon Stimson, and for Mr. Webb talking about the town and responding to audience questions. But the Act I closing with Rebecca speaking about the address on Jane Crofut's letter is gone.

The film of *Our Town*—the only theatrical film of the play to date—opened on May 23, 1940, and was overall well received. As presaged by the Lux Radio version, the Stage Manager is again Mr. Newton Morgan in the film. The empty stage and minimal-to-imaginary props of the theatrical production were rendered fully physical in the film, save for the afterlife scenes in Act III, which exist in an undefined and ethereal place, where viewers see headstones transformed into the seated figures of the dead (via cutaway edit, rather than a magical dissolve).

For those who knew the play, or even the Campbell Playhouse version, the film diverges from the text in one very significant way, as previewed in the Lux broadcast, in that Emily does not die. Her difficult childbirth gives way to a dream of a possible afterlife, a feverishly imagined death and conversations with others who have passed on, right down to the flashback to her birthday. However, after asking whether "any human beings ever realize life while they live it," instead of pleading to be taken back to the afterlife, Emily declares, "I want to live! I want to live!" which yields the response, "Of course you do, Emily," the sound of a baby crying and the silhouetted shadow image of Dr. Gibbs, slapping the bottom of a baby held upside down by its feet.[9] George then peers in soulfully from the cracked bedroom door and shares a solemn but loving look with his wife.

Purists certainly took—and take—umbrage at this denouement, so much happier than the play and so reminiscent of the "There's no place like home" ending of *The Wizard of Oz*, released just a year before. However, the source of this much debated decision was the one person who deserved the final word, and it was neither producer Sol Lesser nor director Sam Wood. Thornton Wilder himself made the determination.

While Wilder had declined to write the screenplay, which was turned over to Frank Craven and Harry Chandlee, Lesser constantly sought his advice and Wilder engaged in significant correspondence about the direction of the screenplay between October 1939 and March 1940. Discussions about the adaptation and the letters pertaining to it proved of such interest that a number of the missives between the two men were collected and published in *Theatre Arts* magazine in November 1940.

The final letter from Wilder in that exchange, in response to a March 21 letter from Lesser in which he was still equivocating about the ending, having shot it both as fantasy and as an actual death, read:

> In the first place, I think Emily should live. I've always thought so. In a movie you see the people so *close to* that a different relation is established. In the theatre they are halfway abstractions in an allegory; in the movie they are very concrete. So, insofar as the play is a generalized allegory, she dies–we die–they die; insofar as it's a concrete happening it's not important that she die; it's even disproportionately cruel that she die.
>
> Let her live—the idea will have been imparted anyway.[10]

By the time the film was released, the play had already had a Broadway run, a national tour, been licensed for stock and amateur productions, been heard twice on radio, and been seen in productions around the world. Nonetheless, the film was likely consistently available to many people in the US and abroad for the first time in this bowdlerized version, albeit one with the playwright's stamp of approval. It and the linked Lux Radio edition would be the only major versions of the play to employ this ending. Wilder received a screenplay credit, even though he had officially declined to work on the film; Lesser was so pleased with the finished product that he gifted the playwright with a new car at the end of 1939.[11]

In addition to the prolific Lesser, the creative team behind the film of *Our Town* was very solid. The director, Sam Wood, had directed the Marx Brothers in *A Night at the Opera*, as well as the original *Goodbye, Mr. Chips*, before heading to Grover's Corners. Production designer William Cameron Menzies had taken on the same task on *Gone with the Wind*. The score of *Our Town*, which has proven more durable than the film, was by Aaron Copland, only his third time composing for a movie, and written shortly before his creation of *Rodeo, Appalachian Spring*, and many other revered works. The film was populated by some of Hollywood's most familiar character actors of that era, including Fay Bainter, Beulah Bondi, Guy Kibbee, and Thomas Mitchell; the last three had been seen just a year earlier in Frank Capra's *Mr. Smith Goes to Washington*.

Our Town took to the radio airwaves once more in April 1944 as the debut episode of *Arthur Hopkins Presents*, broadcast on the NBC radio network from 11:30 p.m. to 12:30 a.m. Eastern time, allowing audiences nationally to hear it after work and dinner (and perhaps bedtime). Frank Craven returned to his signature role, joined by several members of the original Broadway company, including Helen Carew, Phil Coolidge, Thomas Ross, and Evelyn Varden, with newcomers Mary Patton as Emily and John Thomas as George. As was the standard in radio versions, pieces of the show were cut, in this case such scenes as Mrs. Gibbs and Mrs. Webb's morning chat in Act I, Rebecca's speech about Jane Crofut's letter, and the elimination of the character of Sam Craig.

Post-war, *Our Town* would reach the radio yet again in 1946, still compressed into an hour. Produced as part of the US Steel–sponsored *Theatre Guild on the Air*, this version had a distinction of its own: Wilder served as the Narrator, again with no reference to a Stage Manager. The Emily Webb was Dorothy McGuire, who had succeeded Martha Scott in the original Broadway run; James Dobson played George. The beginning of the show provided a very different start than the play, as Wilder said:

> This broadcast is going to be about a town called Grover's Corners. Grover's Corners, New Hampshire. The first act will show a day in our town. Today is May 7, 1901. You know a broadcast like this would seem mighty strange to the folks of Grover's Corners just those few years back. But think: it'll be heard in our 48 states. People of other countries will hear it. So here's our chance to give 'em an idea of the people in our town, how they lived in and the changes they've gone through. Seems like a good idea.[12]

Before commencing with the story proper, he called out, as if checking to see that they were ready, "Miss McGuire? Sound effects? Music?"

The Babylon speech came at the very top of this version, with the breakfast scenes entirely cut, jumping directly to George and Emily coming home from school and George speaking with his father about the chopping of wood. In Act II, the Narrator did not transform into Mr. Morgan (that role went to future patriarch of *The Waltons*, Will Geer), though the Narrator did deliver the pre-wedding speech, while another actor played the minister for the ceremony. Act III generally followed the dramatic line of the play, though it ended a bit sooner, finishing Emily's journey with her cry of, "Oh, earth, you're too wonderful for anybody to realize you." Wilder then wrapped things up with a terse, "Well that's the story, friends. That's what we wanted to tell you about our town."

By the time of this fourth radio broadcast, Wilder had already played the Stage Manager in a range of stage productions. In those cases, it was the complete play. His participation in the radio broadcast, and surely his knowledge of the earlier ones, affords an implicit approval of the cuttings—all done by different writers. There's no question that adapting a play for another medium requires adjustments, as Wilder himself acknowledged in regard to the film. But it's somewhat surprising to have an author actively participate in a nationally broadcast version of their own work which essentially cuts it in half.

The same year that her understudy was playing Emily on radio in the US, Martha Scott reprised the role in England for BBC Radio in September 1946, several months after the close of the London stage production. Stanley Maxted played the Stage Manager and William Eythe was George. The adaptation was by Cynthia Pugh, with Val Gielgud, brother of John, producing.

The 1946 US radio script by Erik Barnouw would be used once again by Theatre Guild on the Air in March of 1950 for a return engagement of *Our Town*. Walter Huston, who won an Oscar in 1949 for *The Treasure of the Sierra Madre*, took over the role of the narrator, while the Emily was the future Oscar winner and tabloid fixture who had already been seen in *National Velvet* and *Life with Father*—Elizabeth Taylor.

The changing political tone of the era and the gathering Red Scare, a persecution wholly out of step with Wilder's environment, was evident not from the text or messages from the cast, but rather in the two commercial breaks. In the first, US Steel's spokesman George Hicks begins an account of the life of a US Steel employee by saying, "I think [*Our Town*] would be a mighty good story for the youth of Russia to hear too. Why? Because it shows so clearly and simply how rich the opportunities are in our free American way of life." At the top of the second commercial break, Hicks opens with, "Most of us Americans insist on getting the facts before we form our opinions on anything. That's fortunate, because in this great democratic nation of ours, it is we the people who finally decide what is truly in the public interest and only that which is in the best interest of the public can long endure in our American way of life." The commercials seemed to press Wilder's humanistic tale even more fully into being a symbol of America and ostensibly of American values. It needed no such emphasis.

In 1957, *Our Town* was back on radio, courtesy of Voice of America, the government broadcaster originally founded to provide US messaging in Europe and Asia during World War II. For this version, Marc Connelly and Martha Scott returned to the roles they had played on stage at City Center and in London. It was the most complete US radio version of the play to date, totaling one hour and fourteen minutes of playing time. The notable omissions from the play are at the top of Act III, with the Stage Manager no longer speaking about the Grover's Corners boys who died in the Civil War and the characters of Joe Stoddard and Sam Craig completely absent, their pertinent plot information given to the Stage Manager. Added were stray mentions that seemed slightly modern even for 1912, with the Stage Manager telling listeners that the young people in Grover's Corners liked to spend their time at "the moving pictures" and wanted to emulate the fashions they saw on screen.

Later radio versions include *Bonanza* patriarch Lorne Greene playing the Stage Manager in a 1983 version for the Canadian Broadcasting Company, directed by Joseph Ziegler, who would go on to stage the play three times for Toronto's Soulpepper Theatre. BBC Radio revisited the play in 1993 with Ed Bishop as the Stage Manager and Barbara Barnes as Emily, but it is a singularly bland and uninvolving iteration, despite keeping a great deal of the play intact thanks to a 90-minute running time.

While there is only the one film of *Our Town* itself, there is a closely related film worthy of note. *OT: Our Town* is a 2002 documentary about a school in Compton, California, that staged a play for the first time, choosing *Our Town* as its inaugural production. In a school with limited resources and no theatrical tradition, a racially mixed cast from economically distressed families made a place for Grover's Corners in a community which seemed inhospitable to the performing arts, let alone *Our Town*. Yet, within the film, the directors of the production and the students in it often ask themselves the same questions and face the same challenges as those in the productions profiled in the ensuing chapters of this book.

Our Town on television

Even as radio broadcasts of the play continued, *Our Town* was also taken up by the new medium called television. In its formative days, all broadcasts were live, which led to a play as popular as *Our Town* being done three times on TV by the end of 1950. Unfortunately, very little remains of these programs, because Sol Lesser released the rights to TV with the stipulation that no kinescopes be made of the broadcasts, lest they interfere with future earnings of the film.

The earliest television version, broadcast on June 6, 1948 on NBC, featured Raymond Massey as the Stage Manager, the role he had already played on stage; he was joined by original Broadway cast members Billy Redfield, who had played Si Crowell, as George, with Helen Carew reprising her role as Mrs. Webb. The script used was a variant of Erik Barnouw's radio script from 1946, though this television version ran slightly more than an hour. Some surviving rehearsal photos indicate that a realistic set was employed for the production, with the kitchen of the Webb house looking like a somewhat spiffier interior of the Kramden kitchen on *The Honeymooners*. When Emily and George had their homework tête-à-tête, they did so from fully built dormer windows, even showing a bit of wood-shingled roof and the silhouette of a tree between the two houses.

In his autobiography, Massey wrote of the production that it was "well done by the Guild, faithful to Thornton's text but, I think, unfair to the play itself. Thornton's play stubbornly resists film and television presentation. Most of the charm and simplicity of the stage play are lost in the embellishments of the screen and the box."[13]

The next *Our Town* broadcast was part of the anthology series *Robert Montgomery Presents*, aired on April 17, 1950, just a month after the second Theatre Guild radio incarnation. Dean Harens was George, Jean Gillespie was Emily, and Burgess Meredith, a stage stalwart perhaps best known at that time for the film role of George in *Of Mice and Men*, played the Stage Manager. Meredith found the production insufficiently important to warrant much mention in his memoir, save that rehearsals interfered with his ability to attend Kurt Weill's funeral.[14]

A different version of *Our Town* was offered on *Pulitzer Prize Playhouse* in December of that same year, with Laura Weber as Emily, Biff McGuire as George, and Edward Arnold, a film veteran familiar from Frank Capra's *Mr. Smith Goes to Washington* and *Meet John Doe*, among many others, as the Stage Manager. Of this broadcast, a *Variety* review noted, "Use of overhead shots, split-screen, dissolves, etc., eliminated the need for sets and made the show as much an appreciated experience for viewers as the Broadway production was for legit goers."[15]

Such was the demand for *Our Town* on TV that an ANTA-produced variety program called *Show Time* aired a 10-minute version of the play in May 1951 on the DuMont network. Intriguingly, it was not one of the more idyllic sequences, but rather a condensed version of the play's Act III. Wilder himself played the Stage Manager. An extant script for this truncated bit of the play notes, in Isabel Wilder's handwriting, that this version was comparable to the version Thornton had performed in previously at a benefit.[16]

After three TV *Our Towns* that were not preserved for posterity, fortunately the fourth was saved—although it's not a straightforward *Our Town*. When the lights came up on *Producers Showcase* on September 19, 1955, Grover's Corners had gained an orchestra, because this was the first musical version of the play, with a script by David Shaw and a score by the team of Sammy Cahn and Jimmy Van Heusen. The George and Emily were rapidly rising stars: Paul Newman and Eva Marie Saint. The program's headliner, as the Stage Manager, was Frank Sinatra, just two years after his career was revitalized by *From Here to Eternity* and a year after his first album release on his new label, Capitol Records. Newman didn't speak much about the production as his career flourished; James Naughton, who directed Newman as the Stage Manager in *Our Town* in 2002, said that the actor was embarrassed by it.

Because this version aired only once, with no original cast or soundtrack recording or video in official release, and because this version cannot be licensed for production, it has achieved a somewhat legendary status among musical fans— at least those who have heard of it—but also a reputation as rather poor. The latter is not the case. In contrast to the earlier radio versions, there were 90 minutes afforded to *Our Town*, and the play's plotline and structure are retained. Save for one unexpectedly lively dance sequence called "Wasn't It a Wonderful Wedding" that echoes the work of Agnes de Mille, the play's assets remain in place. Staged in a large studio that allowed the cast to travel from location to location, and with scenery that was predominantly framed outlines of buildings with translucent scrim walls, it's more defined than the original stage directions demand, but vastly less realistic than the sets from the 1940 movie.

As the youthful leads, Saint at 31 and Newman at 30 were both older than their characters ever appear in the play, and neither have strong voices (Saint had the

Eva Marie Saint and Frank Sinatra in the 1955 television musical version of *Our Town*. Photo by John Swope/The LIFE Images Collection via Getty Images/Getty Images.

edge), but Cahn and Van Heusen seem to have anticipated that. The heaviest lifting in the music department was left to Sinatra, in great voice. Thanks to Sinatra later releasing his songs commercially, the show yielded one standard: "Love and Marriage," sung at the top of Act II, with Sinatra even giving a verbal cue to the band leader that signaled we weren't necessarily in New Hampshire at that moment. It lives on, given life again 30 years after it was first heard, when it became the ironic theme song of the brash sitcom *Married with Children*. Act III of this version had only a single song, sung after Emily asks the Stage Manager to take her back following the return to her twelfth birthday; "Look to Your Heart" was first sung by Sinatra and, rather shortly thereafter, reprised in an even more melancholy tone by Saint.

Variety wrote of the musical version, "For Sinatra and Miss Saint it was their shining hour on television, a cameo of bright etching that must have gripped every set-sider with the powerful impact of their pretending." The review finished by saying, "Were 'Our Town' filmed instead of being televised live, it would join the perennials of TV."[17] That was not to be.

Four years after the musical, *Our Town* was back on television once more, *sans* music. José Quintero, having directed a successful Off-Broadway revival of the play at Circle in the Square, was the director when it was featured as one of the *Art Carney Specials*, an intermittent series of programs that demonstrated the range of Jackie Gleason's *Honeymooners* sidekick. Carney played the Stage Manager, with Clint Kimbrough as George and Kathleen Widdoes as Emily. Some members of the cast were repeating their Off-Broadway roles. Photos from the broadcast reveal that it was done in accordance with Wilder's stage directions—only chairs, ladders, and a black background can be seen. An effusive *Variety* review praised the program extensively, saying, "the 90-minute dramatic special reiterated the fact that occasionally video is still capable of doing something worthy and upstanding," while diminishing the play itself as "as entertaining a piece of literary cornball as one could find." It went on to finish, "In sum, the mastery of Wilder in treating almost pure sentiment so tastefully in the first place, the mastery of Quintero in treating Wilder in like fashion, and the general acting performance made this a potent whole."[18]

After an 18-year hiatus, NBC TV gave a prime-time slot to the play on May 30, 1977, with a cast made up of familiar, veteran actors who weren't necessarily stars. Hal Holbrook made his first appearance as the Stage Manager; he would go on to perform the role on stage in 1988 at the Long Wharf Theatre and in 2007 at Hartford Stage, both in Connecticut. In an odd casting coincidence, the fathers were played by Ned Beatty and Ronny Cox, who had shared a hellish canoe trip in the 1972 movie *Deliverance*; the mothers were Sada Thompson and Barbara Bel Geddes, the former a year into playing the matriarch on *Family* and the latter a year away from playing the matriarch on *Dallas*. Charlotte Rae played Mrs. Soames and John Houseman had an appropriately ponderous cameo as Professor Willard. George and Emily were played by the young romantic duo of the day, Robby Benson and Glynnis O'Connor, previously paired in the films *Jeremy* and *Ode to Billy Joe*.

The simply designed production was clearly meant to look like it was backstage at a theatre or a studio. Over the opening credits, an announcer informed the home audience they would see "a drama that has been performed more times than any other play in the history of the American theatre," while the cast mingled and greeted one another as if on the first day of a rehearsal period. Once the show began, the language was just as Wilder's script had it, although as Holbrook began describing the town, he had a small painted scene of the town he could point to, though it wasn't a map. But overall, it was a faithful representation of the play.

Our Town would appear in two more television versions in the US, but in both cases they were TV adaptations of productions created for the stage: Lincoln Center Theater's 1988 production, directed by Gregory Mosher, with Spalding Gray, Penelope Ann Miller, and Eric Stoltz, and the Westport Country Playhouse/Broadway production, directed by James Naughton, with Paul Newman (see Chapter 5). Among many international versions, Germany had a televised *Our Town* in 1954 and England had it in 1957 on the series *BBC Sunday-Night Theatre*; later foreign television versions include France in 1959, Italy in 1968, and Norway in 1982.

* * *

There were other efforts to bring *Our Town* to radio and television, but in series form. The only one that made it to air in any significant way was part of a radio variety show that debuted in July 1942, *Camel Caravan*. The *Caravan* included in its retinue what *Variety* described as "a sample of Main Street folksiness based upon and following the rambling narrator-into-illustration style of Thornton Wilder's 'Our Town' (and so billed)." The premiere episode featured Edward Ellis in the Frank Craven role and involved a shy solider and a girl. The review went on to say that the characters "seemed overdrawn to the verge of caricature and they ended by being more silly seeming than heart-tugging. Yet despite this hoked up treatment, there were other lives and characters that hit the ear as sincere and true."[19]

In response to inquiries that began as early as 1939, Wilder delegated oversight of all radio and television projects to his sister Isabel, and the result was an array of treatments, scripts, and multi-episode outlines, exceedingly few of which came to fruition. But the various writers who tackled the project contemplated entire episodes based on both the main characters from the play, as well as subordinate characters—or folks merely spoken of—from the original play. One extant script for radio is the story of Simon Stimson, but as it wasn't developed by Wilder himself, let alone produced, it's certainly not canonical.

An unsold pilot of an *Our Town* radio series was broadcast on CBS in January 1947, with Ralph Bellamy, identified only as himself, as the Stage Manager-like host, who guided the story through its present-day, past, and future time frames. The plot concerned the efforts of Mr. Cartwright to have Grover's Corners renamed Cartwrightsville (shades of Pottersville in *It's a Wonderful Life*), given that he owned two-thirds of the town's real estate. Much hubbub accompanied the return of Cartwright from New York to Grover's Corners, but also great consternation over his plan. As Bellamy told listeners, "In some countries when people get riled up, they start a revolution. In Grover's Corners, they call a town meeting." He would later interrupt the meeting to make explicit the kind of ideas that were more subtly woven into Wilder's play, saying, "This is self-government, friends. This is our town looking to the business of our town. This is for the people, by the people, and what's most important, of the people."[20] Because the unsold pilot had no advertising in its breaks, the program featured a fake sponsor not entirely out of step with Wilderian philosophy, perhaps more suited to *The Skin of Our Teeth*: the Incognita Corporation, which, as audiences were told, didn't actually have any products yet, but had "great integrity."

Other *Our Towns*, other stages

The television musical of *Our Town* was quite anomalous, considering that Wilder had already made his feelings about such adaptations known. In 1950, Wilder denied a request from Aaron Copland who, having written the film score, now wished to transform it into an opera. Wilder explained his reasoning by letter, writing, "I'm convinced I write a-musical plays; that my texts 'swear at' music; that they're after totally different effects; that they delight in the homeliest aspects of our daily life; that in them even the life of the emotions is expressed <u>contra musicam</u>."[21]

While the television musical of *Our Town* was seen only once, the relative dearth of television programming even in 1955 meant that it had an audience in the millions. A second musical adaptation of the play, created for the stage in the mid-1980s by Tom Jones and Harvey Schmidt, strutted its brief hour upon the stage to a smaller audience in the latter half of the 1980s as *Grover's Corners*. It premiered at the Marriott Lincolnshire Theater outside Chicago in 1987, with Jones himself as the Stage Manager and Schmidt serving as the onstage pianist.

Its early reception was encouraging. Sid Smith writing in the *Chicago Tribune*, said, "Wilder took the mundane and genuinely made it monumental. Maybe that is why 'Our Town' plays like music—he found a way in drama to do what the big numbers are supposed to do in musical comedy." Further on, he wrote, "'Grover's Corners' succeeds as well as it does mostly because Schmidt and Jones wisely surrendered. They serve mostly as illustrators, never quite soaring to heights in their own work, but never sullying the good, either."[22] Smith also said that the score was reminiscent of the work of Samuel Barber and Aaron Copland. David Richards of *The Washington Post* wrote, referring positively to the portion of the intermissionless musical that corresponded to the play's Act III, "Half of the musical is so lovely, so deeply in tune with its source that you can only wish a rosy future for the show."[23]

There were plans for *Grover's Corners* to take to the road in 1989, touring with Mary Martin as the Stage Manager, however those plans fell apart when Martin fell ill.[24] Schmidt and Jones' rights to the play lapsed and as of 1996, Jones philosophically told Richards, "It's hard to imagine *Grover's Corners* in a world where *Rent* rules supreme."[25]

While the two musical theatre works drawn from *Our Town* are no longer in general circulation, an operatic version is significantly more accessible. After the 1955 version on TV, Wilder resisted all overtures to musicalize the play in his lifetime—having had no such issue when he allowed *The Matchmaker* to become *Hello, Dolly!* in the 1960s. But his nephew Tappan did give the go-ahead to an opera. Composer Ned Rorem, working with librettist J.D. McClatchy, created a faithful rendering of the play, with the libretto at times drawing directly from Wilder's prose. There are some divergences, allowing for the difference in form. The most notable is almost immediate, in that the opera opens with a funeral, without revealing who it is for until the opera reaches Act III. Many of the facts about Grover's Corners, significantly trimmed to begin with, are not sung, but rather projected, as are scene locations and dates. Sam Craig and Joe Stoddard have been excised, leaving the Stage Manager to inform the audience about the nature of Simon Stimson's death.

The opera premiered at Indiana University Opera Theater using a cast and orchestra of students in February 2005. The professional debut came in July of the following year at the Lake George Opera in New York state, when it was also presented by Aspen Music Festival in Colorado. Subsequent productions include Festival Opera in 2007, Juilliard Opera Center in 2008, Baldwin-Wallace College Conservatory in 2010, and the Guildhall School of Music and Drama in 2012. Despite not having played any of the world's major opera houses as of yet, and with many of its productions taking place in academic settings, the Rorem/McClatchy opera shows all signs of maintaining a place in the operatic repertory.

Our Town has been told through dance as well, thanks to a 1994 eponymously named ballet choreographed by Philip Jerry. Jerry's version was set to existing music by Aaron Copland, including not only his film score but such works as "Fanfare for the Common Man." Jerry created the work while a student at Princeton, which followed his career as a principal dancer for the Joffrey Ballet. Upon its premiere in New Jersey, Jennifer Dunning of *The New York Times* wrote, "The piece is also based on a play that develops slowly and is full of nuances of a sort not easily expressed in ballet. Mr. Jerry's dance, dedicated to his mother, is filled with the spirit of the Thornton Wilder classic, but it also succeeds in dramatic and pure dance terms."[26]

Paying homage

Set a play in a small community, and, almost inevitably, someone will liken it to *Our Town*. Stage a show without scenery and someone is bound to say it evokes *Our Town*. Exaggeration? In reviewing Will Eno's *Middletown*, *Chicago Tribune* critic Chris Jones described it as, "a piece reminiscent of *Our Town* if it had been penned by Dr. Seuss and edited by Samuel Beckett."[27] Taking its cue from a reference in Laura Collins Hughes' *New York Times* review of *America is Hard to See*, a documentary theatre piece about ex-cons who had served time for sex crimes, the headline read, "An 'Our Town' with Sex Offenders."[28] The numbers of plays that in some way evoke or are reminiscent of *Our Town* are surely legion, while often being entirely subject to individual perception.

Other plays are forthrightly modeled *Our Town*, some going so far as to often name a character the Stage Manager, and calling young paramours George and Emily, deploying direct address, presenting scenes that are fragmentary and sometimes out of order. The style of *Our Town*, and the collective consciousness of *Our Town*, makes it a point of reference from which playwrights can create different stories or riff on Wilder in new ways, often to comment overtly on present-day societal issues and problems that may have been only glancingly referenced in the original play, or perhaps not at all.

In Susan Miller's one-act *It's Our Town Too*, many new characters are mixed with the Stage Manager, George, and Emily, but the play doesn't posit that George and Emily end up together, even for a short time. Miller gives Emily a romantic partner named Elizabeth and George has a lover named Louis; the play dates to the early 1990s, when marriage equality was not yet legal. The couples each have children, Chance and Molly respectively, and that's the pair to be married in this play. While the depiction of stable gay households with children may have been quite topical in its day, the short play also brings in the aspect of loss that suffuses *Our Town*, but in this case not through childbirth, but rather random gun violence.

Darrah Cloud used the *Our Town* template to examine an incident from her youth, specifically the Nazi March in 1977 in Skokie, Illinois, a national story that pitted the right to free speech against the intentionally inflammatory actions of the American Nazi Party in targeting a town with a strong Jewish community as a place to air their hate. In Cloud's *Our Suburb*, there is a Stage Manager narrating the play, but in this case, she is very clearly depicted as a modern stage manager, complete with headset and calling lighting cues. The play examines the impact of the march on two neighboring families, one WASP (with a child named Thornton) and the other Jewish. There's also a young African-American grocery delivery man who shuttles between the families, as an analogue for Howie Newsome, but significantly more involved in their lives. The Skokie of *Our Suburb* is decidedly fragmented, depicted in contrast to the equanimity of Grover's Corners while facing many more issues than Wilder ever raised in his play.

While Cloud notes that *Our Suburb* is an homage, Casey Llewellyn's *O, Earth* is rather more of a riposte to how people with modern sensibilities may be inclined to view the 85 percent Protestant, 86 percent Republican, entirely white heterosexual community of Grover's Corners. Llewellyn refracts the play through a prism of race and gender, making George a transgender male, Emily a questioning woman, and the Stage Manager a Black queer woman, adding Wilder as a character and having him step into the role of Simon Stimson as required. Elsewhere in the mix are celebs Ellen DeGeneres and Portia de Rossi, as well as transgender activists Marsha P. Jackson and Sylvia Rivera. In this accepting but re-envisioned Grover's Corners, even the Stage Manager questions their role in the metatheatrical play, speaking personally in a way that Wilder eschewed for his narrator:

> I want to be able to be neutral. But also a person! Like if that old white dude neutral, I can be neutral. But I don't want to be a function . . . I can't get the lines out. I want to talk to people! From my own perspective! I know it's a play, but like my own thoughts. My whole self.[29]

In Llewellyn's view, the characters are grappling with their roles in life, as well as their roles in the play.

In *Ripe Frenzy*, Jennifer Barclay imagines a New York state high school so dedicated to *Our Town* that it has staged the play annually—39 previous productions and in progress on the 40th during the action of the play. The play's Stage Manager equivalent, Zoe, who also serves a bit like Professor Willard at the start, is a mother who had played the Stage Manager in her high school years. She's now helpful drama mom for the new production. However, the progress of the show is increasingly disrupted as news of an out-of-state school shooting is followed by both parents and kids, with Zoe trying to shut out the horror and proceed with the play, until violence begins to manifest itself in her home auditorium.

Kaela Mei-Shing Garvin uses *Our Town* as a touchstone in *Corner's Grove*, but is less beholden to many of the specific of the play, preferring instead to mix and match elements in order to tell the story of a very different small town on the West Coast, set in 2008, 2011, and 2012. There are familiar names like George, Emily, Rebecca, and Simon, but all of the characters in the play are, when we first see them, teens, separated in age by no more than two or three years. There's still romance, a wedding, and a funeral, and a young man who dies in battle, but in this case it's Afghanistan. There's a teen named Julia Gibbs and another named Melissa Cartwright. At the beginning of the script, Garvin asks that the play be cast to reflect ethnic diversity, even suggesting that character last names can be changed as needed. Overall, the play's main theme is to question the wisdom of staying put in one's home town as opposed to moving away to start life on one's own and by the end, most of the Corner's Grove kids have opted for the latter.

A campus shooting has devastated a college production of *Our Town* at the very start of the musical *Our (New) Town*, by Gabriel Jason Dean, Jessie Dean, and David Dabbon. As a result, *Our Town* is more spoken of than depicted or commented upon by the musical, but it serves as a symbol of innocence destroyed. Destruction is also on the mind of the surviving students in the musical, who have gathered without permission in the shuttered performance space. Their aim is to memorialize the lost castmates and students in the audience in the waning hours before the theatre is to be torn down, because it is too painful to contemplate asking audiences or students to attend anything there again in the wake of the carnage.

While *Our Town* may prompt viewers to wish they could visit Grover's Corners, Brian James Polak's *Welcome to Keene NH* will not be endorsed by that community's tourism board anytime soon. Audiences are guided through the present day vicinity, where the mill became a mall, by a Mexican-American woman parking officer. The intertwined lives of the characters include a youth-molesting tennis coach, alt-right community members who interrupt a wedding with an anti-government protest, and the closeted Korean-American owner of a Chinese restaurant. Gun violence rips through the community as in several other homage plays.

Jacqueline E. Lawton's *Freedom Hill* uses the structure of *Our Town*—an omniscient narrator, a close-knit community, a young woman dying in childbirth and returning from the afterlife to revisit a day from her past—in service of a very different narrative. The small town of Freedom Hill, North Carolina, is part of the American historic record; it was founded by freed slaves in 1865 and was the first self-governed Black town in the United States. The play imagines life in that community, refracting *Our Town* through a decidedly different lens, one where remembering an earlier time means remembering life under the injustice of slavery and where men who died in the Civil War are just a few years gone, some still presumed to be only missing. The play's Stage Manager equivalent, Earnestine McKnight, informs the audience at the start, "This play is an homage to another play actually called *Our Town*. Playwrights are sometimes in conversation with each other many years apart. It's a kind of communing."

Our Town in other mediums

An empty studio, the ground plan of a town taped out on the floor. Ask those familiar with Lars von Triers' *Dogville*, and they'll be quick to liken it to a particularly dark version of *Our Town*. After all, the opening lines, in starting to describe the film's Rocky Mountain community, note, "The residents of Dogville were good, honest folks and they liked their township. And while a sentimental soul had once dubbed their main street Elm Street, though no elm had ever cast its shadow in Dogville, they saw no reason to change things." This possibly elegiac opening is quickly dashed by the very next lines, "Most of the buildings were pretty wretched; more like shacks, frankly." A Grover's Corners spirit is evoked, only to be immediately undone.

Critics writing about the film made the connection repeatedly. "*Dogville* playfully alludes to Thornton Wilder's *Our Town*," wrote Peter Bradshaw in *The Guardian*.[30] An unsigned introduction to a revisit of the film in *Rolling Stone* called the movie a "warped *Our-Town*-through-a-glass-darkly parable,"[31] while Christopher Orr in *The Atlantic* described it as, "*Our Town* as the Marquis de Sade might have staged it."[32]

Novelist George Saunders has acknowledged the influence of *Our Town* on his novel *Lincoln in the Bardo*, which significantly consists of conversation among those who have died, a link to *Our Town*'s Act III, but he also nods, as did Wilder, to *Spoon River Anthology*.[33] In an as-told-to essay in *The Atlantic*, Tom Perrotta, who wrote the novel *The Leftovers* and co-created its television version, made his debt to *Our Town* quite clear. For his story about those left on earth after two percent of the world's population inexplicably disappears overnight, Perrotta spoke of an issue central to Wilder's seemingly laid-back play: "To write dramatically about any group, you need some kind of conflict and division. A sub-culture, even a cult of some kind, that threatens the dominant way of thinking. In *Our Town*, that division occurs between the living and the dead." Perrotta also characterized the temporal conceit within the play: "*Our Town* captures the cruelty of time's brutal swiftness in a way I think is singular."[34]

In the realm of Young Adult (YA) fiction, a production of *Our Town* in a school on the moon in 2057 is a central plot point in Paula Danziger's *This Place Has No Atmosphere*. While the novel's setting is the stuff of science fiction, the production of the play—well out of copyright at that point—seems no different than it might have been at a school in 1940 or 2020. The book's 15-year-old protagonist Aurora, like so many before her, dreams of playing Emily, but settles for being Mrs. Gibbs, and comes to terms with being happy in the role. Literally more down to earth is *Our Town*'s appearance in a subplot of another YA novel (and subsequent film) *Wonder* by R. J. Palacio, about a boy with Treacher Collins syndrome, which causes facial difference. The boy's sister, Via, has competed with her best friend, Miranda, for the role of Emily in *Our Town*, and while Miranda wins the role, guilt over other matters prompts her to fake an illness at the last minute so that Via, her understudy, can perform instead. Via is, of course, triumphant.

Lampooning *Our Town*

It certainly didn't take long. Keeping in mind that Wilder's play opened on February 4, 1938, the appearance of a cartoon in the February 28 issue of *Life* magazine that clearly poked fun at *Our Town* was surely among the first instances where the play's minimalist aesthetic came in for a ribbing. Admittedly, it was not alone, as the cartoon appeared in an article which included other comparably spare productions: Orson Welles' *Julius Caesar* and some plays that were performed without sets by circumstance rather than intent, including *The Cradle Will Rock*. In the one-panel gag, three society matrons (signified by the furs they wear) stand at a box office window and inquire via caption, "Does this play have scenery?"[35] Later that summer, Orson Welles, a year before he would play the Stage Manager on radio, incorporated a spoof of *Our Town* and his own *Caesar* into the brief run of his adaptation of William Gillette's *Too Much Johnson*, seen at the Stony Creek Playhouse in Connecticut.[36]

Opening six years after the original Broadway production closed, although just weeks before the play's first New York revival, a sketch by George S. Kaufman for the 1944 revue *The Seven Lively Arts* relied on the audience's familiarity with *Our Town* for one of its better jibes. In "Local Boy Makes Good," a stagehand named Spike (played by Bert Lahr) tells a producer about the pleasures of his job:

Spike Did you catch me in *Our Town*?
Martin *Our Town*? Yes, I saw that.
Spike Great show! No scenery. Didn't have to do nothing. I hate scenery. Fellow named Frank Craven or something—actor—he moved all the furniture. Great show. Played cards down in the cellar all season . . . I made a 450 pinochle hand in spades during the third week . . . Great show![37]

The British critic Kenneth Tynan parodied *Our Town* in service of panning the Royal Court Theatre's production of William Faulkner's *Requiem for a Nun*, adapted for the stage by Ruth Ford. While frequently deploying terms that were as racially offensive then as they are now, Tynan offers a brief preface, in which he acknowledges that the review is meant to be consumed as if offered up by the Stage Manager:

Anyways, a lot of things have happened since the curtain went up tonight. Six billion gallons of water have tumbled over Niagara Falls. Three thousand boys and girls took their first puff of marijuana, 'n' a puppy dog in a flying coffin was sighted over Alaska.[38]

As celebrated as Tynan's takedown was in its day, its full ugliness is best left in the past.

In 1962, columnist Art Buchwald utilized the *Our Town* structure to give a Grover's Corners flavor to then present-day Washington, DC. He imagined the Stage Manager chatting up Lyndon B. Johnson, Bobby Kennedy, and Earl Warren. The column ended with the Stage Manager saying:

Well, it's getting on to bedtime. There's a party going on over there at the French Embassy, the Shrivers are having a cookout for the Peace Corps, and the Kennedys are having Leonard Bernstein and the Philharmonic orchestra in for a quiet evening at home. Outside of that most people in our town are tucked in for the night after another uneventful day.[39]

Leaping forward to more recent days, and back to the stage itself, just as *Our Town* inspires and influences new works, it remains a choice parodic target. In 1998, Dutton Foster wrote *Our Rotten Town*, a short mash-up that blended *Our Town* with Shakespeare's plays, thus killing two high school staples with one act. Save for a Stage Manager, Foster deploys major characters from *Hamlet*, *Macbeth*, *Othello*, and *Romeo and Juliet* in a town he dubs Bard's Corners:

That's Ms. Macbeth's garden over there . . . Dewdrops clinging to the poison ivy. Sunlight striking the belladonna. Amanita mushrooms poking their lethal little heads out of the rotten log. And over here's Ms. Gertrude's yard. Roses. Nothing but roses. Bard's Corner is a very simple, very plain little town. It's so simple . . . that it's invisible. So we didn't have to build a set![40]

Dad's Garage in Atlanta was home to a semi-improvised show called *Invasion: Our Town*, devised by Travis Sharp. The premise was that a cast of eight have rehearsed a rough approximation of the original play, but that every night, without their knowledge, a ninth character would be tossed into Grover's Corners onstage, with the first eight actors having no idea who or what they might encounter each and every performance. Two examples cited in reviews were a patent medicine salesman and a person dressed as a chicken; one advance report suggested that action icon Mr. T might visit New Hampshire.

Though it didn't manage to make its presence known in the play's title, *Death of a Streetcar Named Virginia Woolf*, conceived by Tim Ryder and Tim Sniffen and written by Sniffen, tossed Grover's Corners into its blending of classic dramas, all played for laughs. In its own way, it reaffirmed *Our Town* in the pantheon of iconic 20th-century works. With sequences set on a fire escape, a bowling alley, and on a train to New Orleans, one scene of the multi-targeted parody was specifically set in Grover's Corners. Its 21st-century comedic sensibility offered a George who bounded out of the family home declaring, "Gosh, masturbation's tricky. Hi, Mr. Webb!" and the transition from the soda fountain to the wedding to the funeral was collapsed into:

Emily   Gosh, George, I've got dreams of my own! I want to travel. I want to see a minority. Getting married would mean giving up everything that's important to me!

Stage Manager   So Emily and George were married. [Serves as priest.] Thank you for gathering here today. George, do you take Emily to be your wife?

George I do.

Stage Manager Emily . . . you get the idea. By the power vested in me, I now pronounce you husband and . . . dead.[41]

In the era of *28 Days Later* and *The Walking Dead*, *Our Town*'s journey into the afterlife certainly was ripe for a collision with the undead as they're known today, and John Geoffrion obliged with his travesty *Our Town . . . with Zombies*, which delivers exactly the story promised by its title, blaming the cause of the outbreak of ravenous corpses on a new chemical devised by Professor Willard and introduced into the ground of Grover's Corners by the industrialist Mr. Cartwright. Sam Craig returns to Grover's Corners not because he had business in the area, but in response to a telegram from George, reading, "Dear Sam, stop. Please help us, stop. I know who killed Wally, stop. They're after me and Emily, stop." Suffice it to say that when both Emily and Wally return to visit their family, things don't go well at all.[42]

Our Town infiltrates television culture

Our Town has clearly served as a touchstone for many people who would go on to create an array of television series, sometimes explicitly and sometimes as Easter eggs for those in the know to discover. Episodes of the sitcoms *The Nanny*, *Cheers*, and *Growing Pains*, as well as the drama *My So-Called Life*, centered on the characters played by series regulars being involved in productions of Wilder's play—all presupposing that the viewers had some knowledge of *Our Town* itself. Unlike the present-day's niche TV audiences fragmented across broadcast, cable, and streaming, these shows were broadcast at a time when it wasn't uncommon for *Growing Pains* to reach 13 million viewers a night, while *Cheers* could draw 19 million. It was especially important that network broadcasts didn't get too obscure or risk stumping a mass audience.

All of the theatrical action in the *Cheers* episode "Two Girls for Every Boyd" remains offstage, but the friendly, if slightly slow-on-the-uptake, bartender Woody Boyd talks about his participation in an amateur *Our Town* and its progress to his pals at the eponymous bar. He hides this from his fiancée Kelly, who suspects Woody is having an affair. But one line that is likely best understood only by those who know the play comes when Woody describes why he's keeping Kelly in the dark, telling the bar's regulars, "This play has a lot of stuff like kissing and homework and dying. Believe me, *Our Town* isn't the kind of play you want to take a nice girl to."[43]

On *The Nanny* episode "Fashion Show," the irrepressible and often garishly attired Fran Fine takes over the costuming of a benefit performance of *Our Town* being produced by her employer-paramour Maxwell Sheffield, albeit with the help of her cousin "Toddy," revealed to be the real-life designer Todd Oldham. Summing up her approach to the project, Fran drops such theatrical insight—quite antithetical to what the play demands—as, "Your dead ingenue, Emily? You know she's on stage every minute so she's really gotta pop. And like my cousin Toddy says, 'If you're gonna be dead, be drop dead.'"[44]

Growing Pains took a somewhat more level-headed look at the play, as Mike, the somewhat irresponsible oldest child in the Seaver family, surprisingly takes on the role of George, albeit primarily to get close to leading lady Monica Shackleford. There are brief snippets of real Wilder dialogue sprinkled throughout, and an impassioned introduction to the play's author—"This is *Our Town*," says the exasperated Carol Seaver to her brother, "by Thornton Wilder, an American genius."[45] The circumstances surrounding the production are more farcical: Mike's failure to learn his lines; his friend Boner's misguided attempt to use a cassette recorder as backup should he forget his lines as Mr. Webb; the fact that the gym coach is directing the play, in his standard gym uniform and deploying sports terminology.

What's odd on the *Growing Pains* episode, to anyone who has ever seen the play: Dewey High School manages to put on the show with only eight students, all the more surprising because it's made clear that Carol Seaver is playing Rebecca Gibbs and Ben Seaver is playing one of the Crowell boys, but not both, as it's evident he has only a single line. As is often the case with family sitcoms, the episode delivers a message, about Mike needing to buckle down and do his work in order to achieve something. It echoes both Dr. Gibbs' heart-to-heart with George in Act I and Emily's conversation with him in the lead-up to the soda-fountain scene.

Messages are heavy in the "Betrayal" episode of *My So-Called Life*, where *Our Town* is being offered up by the high school drama club just as the series' lead teen character Angela Chase has a falling-out with her best friend Rayanne over—what else—a boy. This threatens to scuttle Rayanne's performance as Emily, which she has modeled on the less worldly Angela. Rayanne initially disdained the play, saying, "*Our Town*, what's that? It's a town. It's ours. End of story." Once again, Wilder's actual dialogue is heard intermittently, the delivery of which has been aided in rehearsal by an insightful director, Mr. Katimski. Advising Rayanne to drop her affected style, he counsels her, "Stop acting. There's really no need for it. You see, Emily is dead, the life she had is over. That's a pretty big deal. I mean oh gee whiz, she is just now realizing how precious every moment of that life really was and that she never fully appreciated what she had. Just imagine what that must have felt like, Rayanne."[46]

The deepest TV homage was the episode "Their Town" from the final season of the hospital drama *St. Elsewhere*. Abandoning its usual medical setting, the entire episode was set in New Hampshire, and it found regular character Dr. Donald Westphall narrating, *à la* the Stage Manager, an account of a visit to his home by some of his friends from St. Eligius Hospital and his family, as various rivalries and resentments simmer. While there were very slight quotations from Wilder, the majority of the dialogue was evocative rather than borrowed. Westphall, in direct address to the camera, said mid-show:

> The truth is our lives are made up of little unextraordinary activities like taking a hot bath or wearing a new coat, eating peach pie. They are wonderful, but they go by so quickly we hardly notice.

He finished the episode with a monologue that most closely overlapped the play:

> This business of living: it's confusing, it's exhausting. And that struggle, that strain, is going on in every house in our town, our planet. It can be so hard that sometimes all you can do is lie down and take a rest.[47]

More recently, an episode of the ribald comedy *Children's Hospital* called "Children's Hospital: A Play in Three Acts" reframed the show's arch tone as an *Our Town*-style tale, draining the settings of their usual color and detail and introducing an unnamed narrator, outfitted in a brown tweed three-piece suit and talking in a homespun manner—albeit with the show's usual naughty tone lying just underneath. The Narrator began simply enough, laconically telling viewers, "Lend me your patience, for a spell, I'd like to tell you about a little place called Children's Hospital. It's a whole day's ride from the big city. Things move a little slower here." But the show quickly took a turn towards the subversive and somewhat crude, as the Narrator introduced one physician by saying, "Dr. Valerie Flame. Now normally when you're in bed and there's something on fire, you're going to want to put that fire out. But in the case of Dr. Valerie Flame, this is one fire you don't want to put out—you want to have sex with it."[48] Clearly viewers were far from the hospital named for Dr. Gibbs.

In 2017, *Riverdale* show creator Roberto Aguirre-Sacasa wasted no time invoking *Our Town* in his dark riff on the *Archie* comic books. The first words heard on the first episode of the series had a decidedly Wilderian feel, as a voice, which viewers would later learn to be that of Archie's sidekick Jughead, introduced the series with, "Our story is about a town, a small town, and the people who live in the town. From a distance, it presents itself like so many other small towns, all over the world. Safe. Decent." For those who might have missed the subtlety of this Grover's Corners allusion, later in the episode, Aguirre-Sacasa gave Veronica Lodge the throwaway aside of, "I feel like I'm wandering through the lost epilogue of *Our Town*."[49]

Perhaps the most out-of-left-field evocation of *Our Town* came in the final episode of the comedy *30 Rock*, when, caught up with emotion in the countdown to the final episode of the show within the show, cynical network executive Jack Donaghy suddenly exclaims:

Beloved co-workers: Oh life, it goes by so fast we barely look at each other. I didn't realize all this was going on. Goodbye, goodbye world, goodbye long hair guy, goodbye Richard Esposito. Go home to your wife and eight beautiful children. You're all so beautiful.[50]

An unlikelier Emily Webb is hard to imagine.

Keith Randolph Smith and the company in the 2017 production of *Our Town* at Miami New Drama, directed by Michel Hausmann. Photo by Arnulfo Maldonado.

Our Town
Production Oral Histories
2002–19

4

The David Cromer Productions, 2008–14

Considering that David Cromer would have preferred to direct a Tennessee Williams play for the Chicago theatre troupe The Hypocrites in 2008, it's very fortunate that the company's artistic director Sean Graney was ultimately insistent on *Our Town*, telling Cromer that he could either direct the Thornton Wilder play or someone else would be found. From the initial production in a tiny basement space at the Chopin Theatre, the production would be seen a number of times over the next half-dozen years.

Following its original spring run in the Chopin's basement, it returned in the fall in the venue's larger space. In early 2009, the production, with many of the original company heading to New York, moved to the Off-Broadway Barrow Street Theatre in Greenwich Village, where it played for a year and a half, the longest continuous run of an *Our Town* production in Manhattan. It was subsequently seen, with a variety of casting changes over time, at the Broad Stage in Santa Monica in early 2012, later that same year at the Huntington Theatre Company in Boston, in 2014 at the Kansas City Repertory Theatre in Missouri, and almost simultaneously in 2014 at the Almeida Theatre in London.

In multiple runs, Cromer also played the Stage Manager, shepherding his actors through Grover's Corners on a nightly basis. Over the course of the New York run, he was succeeded in the role by, among others, Michael McKean, Michael Shannon, and in a stroke of casting that brought renewed attention to the already hit production, Helen Hunt. Hunt had previously appeared in *Our Town* in New York on Broadway, succeeding Penelope Ann Miller as Emily in Gregory Mosher's production. She would reprise the Stage Manager role in Santa Monica, while Jeff Still, who had played Dr. Gibbs at Barrow Street and at the Broad Stage, was the Stage Manager in Kansas City.

As simple as Wilder had asked the setting to be, Cromer's production made much that came before it look opulent. The actors wore what appeared to be nothing more than modern street clothes, and the small stage used only tables and chairs; even ladders seemed too extravagant for Cromer. In New York, the seating was arranged on three sides of the playing area, though Barrow Street's wide but shallow balcony afforded space for Simon Stimson and his choir to practice,

David Cromer in *Our Town* at the Huntington Theatre in Boston in 2012, directed by David Cromer. Photo by T. Charles Erickson.

and for musical director and composer Jonathan Mastro, who played Stimson, to provide intermittent underscoring. The production was done largely without the benefit of standard theatrical lighting, providing minimal delineation between the start and end of each act, save for the departure of the actors from the stage.

In its utter simplicity and lack of artifice, Cromer successfully, albeit invisibly, was preparing the audience for a single brief *coup de théâtre*. When it came time in Act III for the Stage Manager to take Emily back to her twelfth birthday in 1899, the actor playing the role suddenly drew back a heavy black curtain at the back of the playing area, revealing a detailed vintage kitchen, with a heavy cast-iron stove, on which real bacon was frying, its smell wafting through the house. A single window revealed the sunrise on a snowy morning, vividly lit in yellow and orange hues; Mr. and Mrs. Webb appeared in period clothes. At the conclusion of the brief scene, the Stage Manager drew the curtain across the tiny set, cutting the audience and Emily off from her memory and her life for good.

Cromer's production was not the first to alter Wilder's outline of the look of the show; by way of example, in a production at Dallas Theater Center in 2002, designer Michael Yeargan created a clear wall that physically separated the living and the dead in Act III. But Cromer's innovation certainly was the most widely seen and written about so far this century, and likely had a prominent effect on liberating *Our Town* from its original conception, while staying entirely true to its spirit.

In this chapter:

David Cromer, director, also Stage Manager in Chicago, New York, Boston, and
    London
Laura Elsworthy, Emily Webb in London
Anna Francolini, Mrs. Webb in London
Heather Gilbert, lighting designer for all productions
Jennifer Grace, Emily Webb in Chicago, New York, and Santa Monica
Helen Hunt, Stage Manager in New York and Santa Monica
Jonathan Mastro, music director of all productions and Simon Stimson in Chicago,
    New York, Santa Monica, and London
Michael McKean, Stage Manager in New York
Lori Myers, Mrs. Gibbs in Chicago, New York, and Santa Monica
Jeff Still, Dr. Gibbs in New York and Santa Monica, and the Stage Manager in
    Kansas City

David Cromer People remember *Our Town* as sentimental based on nothing.
Every time they actually see it, they go, "Well, this is gorgeous. This is devastating
and it speaks to me." But then you leave and someone says, "Well, it's about a small
town." There's a thing that you think about *Our Town* when you're not watching it
that's wrong. It all is agonizing to think about, because it's important that everything
that's happening right now is the most important thing in the world and this is the
harshest time. There's just a coldness to the story that I think is hard for people.

Michael McKean It's something that really grew out of this country, and this
notion. What he says about the Civil War soldiers is so deep and true, where he says
they're Grover's Corners guys who went off to fight to preserve something. "All they
knew was the name, friends – the United States of America. And they went and died
about it." It's this little dew drop of a town, but it's also the universe, it's also America.

Jonathan Mastro At a party, David was talking about *Our Town*, specifically about
the moment in which Simon is just staring at Editor Webb and the Constable, and
they're not saying anything. He's this catatonic drunk, and David used as an
example a mutual friend of ours, who had a serious drinking problem, so I'd
recognize the intensity and the kind of person that he was imagining. I remember
thinking something to the effect of, "That's in *Our Town*?"

Jeff Still I'm sure you could argue that it is the best American play of all time. And
I think I would get that message no matter who was doing it—if sixth graders were
doing it.

*   *   *

Jennifer Grace I was a company member of The Hypocrites. The Hypocrites had been looking for an opportunity to work with David for a long time. I remember when the play was suggested as part of our season. The way that we used to do it was all of the company members, there were about 15 of us, were encouraged to read the plays that were suggested and then to come back with thoughts about whether or not we felt like it was a good fit for our company. The Hypocrites had a reputation for being a bit edgy, a bit avant-garde, which was part of what drew me to the company.

David Cromer Sean Graney said, "Well, we're going to do *Our Town* and I'd like you to do it." I said, "Okay, but I want to play the Stage Manager." It really came out of my mouth without thinking about it too hard. I realized down the line that impulse buys were going to be my friend on *Our Town*. Sean said, "Great." Because Sean's a theatre director in every sense of the word—I would say he was always bolder in choice and more avant-garde and extremely iconoclastic—he said, "Don't be afraid to change everything or anything." He didn't mean the play. He just meant to be bold.

Jeff Still Part of the brilliance of his concept for *Our Town* was it's gotten too sentimental over the years. Let us strip it of the sentimentality. He's not forcing a harshness onto it, he's just laying out the ingredients and saying, "You guys make the meal. Here is what it is." Have a sentimental reaction to it if you like, but we're not going to string that along by crying, or doing something that's not appropriate.

David Cromer I had an understanding of the Stage Manager as someone who should be at a remove from the play. If I was going to play the Stage Manager, I had to figure out why. Sometimes when you're directing you have to make up a justification for something, but then also ask, "Okay, well why did I have that impulse?" or "What good does it do us?" I knew that the Stage Manager has a cooler reserve, removed from the play, than we traditionally think, based on Spalding Gray and Gregory Mosher's understanding of it. That's when I understood, "Oh, it's not that he's not reliable, but he has a separate agenda. He's not here to gently take me through the meaning of the universe."

Helen Hunt When I got offered the opportunity to step into Gregory Mosher's production [as Emily], I remember where I was when I read it. I was in Northern California and it was familiar, but not really. I got to the goodbye speech and went, "Oh wait, this is bigger than I knew."

David Cromer When I would teach directing, I would try to explain to students what I thought the role of the director was. I would say, "The director stands in between the actors and the play and helps move them towards each other. You have a production and then the next phase of the directing job is you stand between the audience and the production and you coax them towards each other and then get out of the way."

Jonathan Mastro At Columbia College, you had enormously talented people, and people that were just lost, and they're in the same class, and sometimes they were the same person. The way that I worked with these folks was to try to bring the best out of them as much as I could, and sometimes that had a certain degree of . . . I don't want to say violence, but I pushed them to the limits of what they thought they could do and to a place that was further along than when they started. It was intense. That's why he cast me. We did a Simon Stimson version of what that was. What is it that Simon wants to do? He's always trying to restrain his rage, but it sometimes spills out.

David Cromer I realized the reason I want to play the Stage Manager is because hiring an actor to pretend he's controlling the evening when, in fact, I am the person who is most truly controlling the evening would be false. My justification for playing the Stage Manager was I was separate from the actors, which meant that I didn't have to be good. I was fine, I liked my performance very much. I could be utilitarian and I could be truly serving the function that I was setting things up to happen in front of the audience at a certain time. Then suddenly the thing had verisimilitude. The audience were really an audience, the cast was really in a play, and I was a separate entity. You had those three forces as opposed to just the two.

Anna Francolini I did a production of it when I was at secondary school. I would've been about 14. Also, I did it at my youth theatre when I was about 15, 16 maybe. I played Emily Webb twice. I knew it very, very well. I quoted from it in life, I still do. I'm always saying, "Good-by, Grover's Corners … Good-by to clocks ticking," and things like that. It becomes part of little things that you say in life. I don't remember an occasion where people have noticed it. You just wait, because you kind of want them to go, "Oh, yeah. I love it, I love it." It's your own little secret theatre.

David Cromer I used to really hold very, very passionately to the idea that I had not really changed anything, that I was going with intent. It's not exactly true, especially in Chicago. There were things I didn't want to do. I didn't want to hear the accent, because I thought it was too much work to get the audience past the accent. They automatically think the characters are dumb, folksy, simple, pure, generally sweet, if you have that Pepperidge Farm accent. Spalding has it in the Gregory Mosher production because that's his accent. Well, his is Rhode Island.

I made a choice in London that some people were really bothered by, which was everyone spoke in their own accents. They didn't have American accents. Accents are such a big deal over there. George was from Liverpool and Emily was from Hull. Some people were just outraged. They couldn't possibly live next door to each other because their accents were from different parts of the country. Didn't bother anyone that nobody was the right age or that no one was actually related in real life, you know what I mean?

Anna Francolini It helped you be simple, because you weren't trying to plug into another era, or plug into a specific person. You were just being a human being. To be honest, it's how I genuinely would like to think I work anyway. It's not Hedda Gabler, for god's sake, it's just another woman.

David Cromer One of the challenges of period costumes is always that an audience has one layer of "I don't know enough about that person based on those clothes, because I don't know that that means that they love their body or that they hate their body," in the way we do now. I said, "Okay, I don't want the accents and I don't want period costumes." My justification for that was that in the first line of the script—his notes, "No curtain. No scenery."

Helen Hunt What I found such a relief, when I saw David's play, is that there is a sense, in many productions I've seen, that this takes place in the olden days. Even with actors who are super-immediate, there is a sense in the way they speak and the way they carry themselves and just by definition of the costumes. With Cromer's production, I felt very at home, because I felt liberated from that. He never changed a syllable of the piece and in the same way that I liked André Gregory's *Vanya*, I thought, "This is what I like. I don't know that this is called, but this is what I like."

Lori Myers He is so fucking funny. He is like a laser beam. I prefer acting that is unadorned and it's simple and it's direct. David is very much about, "Look at somebody and ask a question. And you expect an answer. If you don't get an answer, you have to ask it again. You may be asking in a different way." He doesn't mess around with a whole lot of frilly garbage that is not on the page.

David Cromer I was thinking about the experience of watching it in 1938, not knowing what was going on, not knowing what was going to happen. The question was, because it's so known, or because everyone thinks they've seen it or thinks they know it, how do you have the experience of making it, for want of a better word, seem a little hip? All that stuff which was innovation has now become standard vocabulary. We're used to a flashback, we're used to breaking the fourth wall, we're used to stopping the action, we're using all that stuff that would make a Broadway audience in 1938 go, "What the hell's going on?"

Jonathan Mastro There was something about the way the music functioned in that show. It felt to me that the presence of music in that production served as a counterweight to the perceived sentimentality of the play.

David Cromer It says the Stage Manager looks at his watch. I would hold my phone up, which was my watch. "You need to turn your cell phones off." Then the show was going to start and the lights would never go down. Now, all that was false because Heather Gilbert, the lighting designer, she figured out, "Well, what if we just don't use theatre lights?"

Heather Gilbert We ended up using hanging lighting fixtures, regular incandescent light bulbs because if you want to go to the width of that space [Chopin Theatre in Chicago, the first venue], it's the only thing you're going to be able to do. You end up having to light with whatever you can. The fact that that became our hard and fast rule came later.

David Cromer We were in this tiny room in a basement. She created something that looked as if it was house lights but wasn't, because the room didn't have that. It was all just clip lights. It covered the space. So, the audience never got the separation of darkness, a clear demarcation. They were already confused.

Heather Gilbert I scattered different color-temperature light bulbs throughout the space. If I used different color-temperature light bulbs between the inside and the outside, it was easier to look through all of that light and focus on the other side. There was actually a lot of really specific technical thought put into these very incandescent light bulbs. There's some really long cues in that show, like 10 minutes long and 7 minutes long, in order for people not to realize.

Helen Hunt Cromer is the one who didn't add anything, didn't change anything, just simply turned the lights on for me about very immediate issues in the marriages and the growing up that would be true today—is true today, all the time.

David Cromer I looked at the script and there's stage directions that say, "George and Emily grab their books and leave." Then it also says, "George and Emily enter carrying imaginary books." Doc Gibbs is not carrying a doctor bag, he's carrying an imaginary doctor bag. But he takes a real handkerchief out of his pocket, so what are the rules? He keeps changing the rules, so we started changing the rules.

Sometimes the Stage Manager's wrong. We were tracking all that. Let's not take Act III for granted. Let's say, "What would it be like in 1938 when you saw Act III?" You'd go, "What the fuck's happening? You killed the main character, you're describing what the afterlife is like, you've done this strange avant-garde thing where the dead sit in chairs and stare off into eternity and wait for their flesh to burn, wait for all their earthly concerns to burn away so that they can move on."

Also, flashbacks were not a particularly known theatrical device that I'm aware of. We started talking about how is that one different? If you're stretching a rubber band, at one point the rubber band's going to snap. When you're working on something, you're always stretching a rubber band, trying to create a certain amount of tension as it goes on.

Heather Gilbert Wilder's point was to strip away artificiality, and in doing so, created this style of theatre which people now do all the time. David really wanted to go back and to do the same thing that Wilder had intended, as opposed to do what people now do. He knew he wanted to strip away artificiality. He knew he wanted to put the experience of the kitchen at the end of the play. We didn't know how to do that.

David Cromer We have to treat this like it's never happened before. What's it look like? What would it be like if you were in your mother's kitchen when you were 12? What does the clock look like? What do the counters look like on a cold morning and you have to go to school and it's still dark outside? For good or ill, that's pretty evocative. We were trying to figure out, when should it be? What would it be? Would it be just a couple years ago? We said we'd manifest the kitchen in a very real way, but then we didn't know what period to set it in.

We were going to cut it and we did maybe our first preview and there were only 20 people there. At the end in the blackout, Jennifer Grace, who was playing Emily, and I heard people laughing. We were, "Fuck! What the fuck, fuck them!" The lights came up for curtain call and they were just projectile bawling.

Laura Elsworthy The trick at the end of David's *Our Town*, I always thought it was more for the actors than the audience. Because I turned around and I watched the curtain go, and every night I was hysterical. Without fail. I would turn around and after all the silence and the black box and everyone in their normal everyday outfits, I'd turn around and he would do the curtain and I would be really upset. I defy anyone to be playing that part and not be really upset when you are suddenly pushed in your face with all this light and smell and love and snow and the actors that you loved working with.

David Cromer I don't know if I ever meant this, but one of the things people said is that the impact of the Act III reveal was, to my understanding, going back and seeing everything, it articulates the idea in the play which is that you don't notice things while they're happening. We didn't say we're justifying this line. It just sort of happened. If you think of an average production of *Our Town*, there was no more or less design in ours than in any other one. We just crumpled it all up and put it in one scene.

Helen Hunt It was the icing on a cake that he built and the cake was all those other things, all those performances, all that unsentimental work. All that deep look at the play. That kind of X-ray vision that I think he had into the play and this idea that your senses are going to get flooded just as you have to say goodbye to all those things. It was just a super brilliant grace note.

* * *

David Cromer I don't often think with a standard issue play like that, that there'd be multiple versions. There's the multiples of Shaw, because he kept rewriting, and there's multiples of plays that playwrights would keep rewriting. [Our text, from 1941] was the one I copied because I pulled it off my shelf. I did not know there was a different script, but I also cut some things in Chicago.

The idea that I was somehow behaving with great purity towards it is a little bit of a self-sustaining myth. I cut things I felt were pious or overly religious. I wanted to keep it tough. I got rid of things I thought were cute. "Wherever you come near the human race, there's layers and layers of nonsense," and, "Look how stupid they all look. They don't have to look like that."

Simon Stimson, when he's talking to her, "Now you know, now you know." At the end of it, he said, "Did you shout to 'em? Did you call to 'em?" She says, "Yes, I did," and he says, "Now you know them as they are." Which is just so brutal. He tried it, too. He begged for help and no one would help him, which is fairly significant.

What did I cut? I cut something about eternity. I did something very controversial, that a few people complained about. "Do any human beings ever realize life while they live it? Every, every minute?" I said, "No, maybe some," instead of "No, the saints and poets, maybe—they do some," because I thought that was a little sweet.

I thought, obviously they're going to want this super-cool production to play in New York and so Tappan [Wilder] will agree and I'll get my way. As I kept talking to him, I realized that I'm just not getting my way. I was very threatened and very uppity and very upset and very raging and things like that, but he said, "Look, my job is to represent what I feel are my uncle's intentions and I don't think those are his intentions." So, that kind of shut me up.

* * *

Jennifer Grace When I was pitched the idea of *Our Town*, my immediate response was, "No. No way. I don't want to do it. I don't know why anyone wants to do it." I never saw a production of *Our Town*. I had read it in high school and I don't think I even had a memory of reading it. The way that I recalled *Our Town* is it seeping into our cultural subconscious, probably on *Growing Pains*.

David Cromer I knew these actors. I'd seen them but I didn't have a strong feeling about it. I used members of the company, found out who else was available. I asked some friends to be in it.

Jennifer Grace Maybe David's memory of this is different than mine, but I would not have considered us friends before we worked on this show. I had met him once or twice casually. It never occurred to me that he remembered me in any of those meetings.

David Cromer I said to a friend, "Of these three actresses in the company, who would you cast as Emily?" He said, "Jennifer Grace," so I said, "Okay, Jennifer Grace." The only interesting thing I can think of about casting that show was that Jennifer Grace as Emily was so uncompromisingly what is on the page. As opposed to like a princess. She defined the style for the rest of the thing.

Jennifer Grace I'm pretty sure I was home alone. My fiancé at the time was wherever. I remember reading it and having the sensation that this is not at all what I remembered because I was just reading the words and there were no famous faces or old-timey costumes attached to it. By the end of the play, I was wrecked. I was crying in my bathtub. I decided then that I love the play. It's a beautiful play. There's no place for me in this play, but we should do this play.

Cromer called me and he said, "Hey, listen. You know I'm doing *Our Town*. How do you feel about playing Emily?" I said, "Well, I'm too old to play Emily." At that point, I was 32 or 33, which now seems ridiculous that I thought I was too old. I always looked young and people always treated me much younger than I look and I hated that. Him saying, "I want you to be Emily," was affirming a thing that I didn't want to be true about myself, the youthfulness which now I really wish I had back.

I said, "I don't think I'm right for Emily." He said, "Hear me out." This is a very David Cromer thing to say. I love David. He can be an asshole without meaning it. He said to me, "Hear me out now. They talk a lot about how Emily is the smartest girl in town. First of all, it's not a very big town and also no one ever says she's the prettiest girl in town," was what he said to me to convince me that I was right for the play, which I perceived as, "It doesn't matter that you're not particularly pretty or smart. You can do it."

David Cromer I think it was just her instincts as an actor, which were, "This kid's a pain in the ass." On paper, she is a pain in the ass. "Walk simply." "I'm the brightest girl in school for my age." Attacking George for his behavior, having this sort of breakdown. It's not a negative. She's a teenager. She's just ordinary. And a mess. The way people are. A temper and a lot of emotional turmoil that she doesn't really understand.

Laura Elsworthy The main thing I responded to, and I remember really clearly was, "Mama, am I pretty?" I was 23 then, and didn't conventionally look like an actress or the actresses that we see. Had a bit of an accent. Was a little bit rough around the edges. To read a story with a leading part that was about a girl who was questioning herself, it wasn't the stereotypical leading part for a girl my age. It was just nice to read a story about a girl trying to find her way through.

Anna Francolini I remember what we were told for the audition, the very first one. It was telling us how to act, basically. David was like, "I don't want anyone to come in and act. I want you to do the lines as if you've just sort of thought of them, as if they're just sort of coming out naturally." I remember that, thinking, "I'm an actress. This is what we do. What are you talking about?" The more we lived with the play, I realized it was something beyond that.

Laura Elsworthy It was very hard to be simple. I'm an actor because when I was a kid, I was a massive show-off. I wanted attention all the time. To do nothing, to have 400 people watch you do nothing, is really difficult. You want them to like you or to be following the story or to be in it with you. If there's nothing really in the text that's showy or you can't do that, you've got to trust that they are interested enough in it and that they're following it.

David Cromer The original Chicago cast was not wildly diverse, because, at the beginning, I thought that doesn't matter. When I got to New York, I never said, "Well, we're all the same." I liked the verisimilitude of, "It's going to be a super white, super homogenous, little suburban community." I know I'm saying it's universal, but I want it to be super specific. The play supports the idea there are others and they're on the edges. I set out to say, "It's just a bunch of flailing white people." That started to become impractical. Then I also found out that the verisimilitude of that did not actually matter.

I wish I had not done that. I wish I had not limited the way I approached the show when it got to New York. I probably will never do that again. London was where it was aggressively diverse. People like me have to evolve faster. I didn't think of myself as someone who was denying access. But you wake up one day and realize you're old fashioned and yes, you are doing that.

* * *

David Cromer I think the Stage Manager is always struggling to be explicit and I don't think he always succeeds. What I was trying to say was elusive, so I just embraced the idea that he was failing, he was struggling. He says it's early afternoon. "No, sir. It's later than I thought. There are the children coming home from school already." Why doesn't he know what time it is? He doesn't have all the power.

Jonathan Mastro Textually, in the first days of rehearsal, I apologized to the cast in advance and said, "I'm just going to bully you guys. Don't take it personally." A lot of the cast weren't singers, they admitted to not being singers, and they were scared to sing. I was forcing them to sing harmonies, but the way in which I would do it, I'd be a little bit of a dick to them.

David Cromer Narrators in plays are notoriously difficult. Tom Wingfield seems to be in a theatre. The Stage Manager seems to be in a theatre. Other narrators aren't in a theatre. Who are they speaking to? When are they? This one comes the closest to being purely, "I am in a play."

Jeff Still When the play was written, and they're doing a flashback, it would be like a play now going back to, maybe, the 1970s or the 1980s. It wasn't a great deal of time ago for those audiences first seeing *Our Town*, but the play became this quaint thing the further back 1900 got.

David Cromer Why is Editor Webb suddenly in 1938? Why does he come out and talk to this audience of New Yorkers? The play's written, I noticed, specifically to be speaking to New Yorkers. It's speaking to the Broadway audience. "This is the way we were in the provinces north of New York."

* * *

Jennifer Grace In many ways, the version of Emily that I ended up crafting is very close to who I grew up being. I grew up in a very small town, a town the size of Grover's Corners more or less in small-town Kansas. So, a lot of that experience of feeling very small, not as worldly as people around me. I think this play was a perfect place once I had the guts to go there, to strip off acting and be that version of myself.

Laura Elsworthy David could tell a bit of shit acting. He could tell when you were lying and he wouldn't fall for that. Because he's an actor as well. He could tell the tricks you were playing to try and get the scene to finish or to get through it and he wouldn't stand for it.

Anna Francolini I loved the fact that we were all just ourselves. It was really far more intriguing, and interesting, and satisfying than I anticipated.

Lori Myers If you're going to spend time getting an audience to listen to, "Gosh, I really would love to go to Paris," over and over again, it's obviously important to her. David and I worked together on, "How do we keep exploring that?" I think he found that pretty interesting. "You want something more than what you have." What we worked with in the New York production was, I got married to the doctor because of my parents. The possibilities of things that you don't get to do. The whole poetry of time and time passing and things left unfulfilled or unaccomplished was there.

Jonathan Mastro I think the walls of the town are closing in on him. His ambitions for something more, or bigger, or more pure, and his inability to transcend that. I think Simon talked about himself when he said, "To go up and down trampling on the feelings of those . . . of those about you." I think that's also crucial to him. I don't think he's talking about other people trampling on his feelings. He talks about his own awareness of the way he's treating other people.

Helen Hunt My friends will tell you, I'm always the one saying, "We should get together, we're all going to be dead soon. Let's celebrate, let's all be together. Don't blow it off, it could happen at any moment." I am usually the voice of that and I wouldn't dare to put my own words into the speech he has at the beginning of the third act—it's some the most meaningful writing I've ever read in my life. He's basically dancing around the idea of, "What is there that we can't see?" He's not selling a religion or a faith, he's not telling you it's all going to work out, he's simply saying it's an unnameable something that has something to do with human beings.

That's about where I land. I don't really line up with people that are a 100 percent sure there is nothing after we die and I don't line up with people that say, "I know exactly what it is and this is what it's called and this is how you have to behave to be invited into its club."

Jennifer Grace My way into that was probably dangerously closely aligned with my own personal arc. It shifted as I aged. When Cromer offered me the job, I was engaged. There was a break in-between productions in Chicago, the two productions. In that break, I got married. When I came back to do it again after having gotten married, the energy that I felt doing the wedding scene was very different.

Jeff Still David and Lori Meyers had done it before. They had painted a picture that was forcing me to look at Doc Gibbs in a different light than I saw him. They were saying, "The guy said he was going to take her to Paris and he never did. No, you're not going to kiss her when you come home from work. There's no touching, there's no kissing." I just didn't see it the same way. I invented something to help myself get through it, which was that Doc Gibbs, being a doctor, knew there was a little something wrong with his wife. That physically she really wasn't up to that kind of travel. He was frustrated because he didn't know enough to be able to fix it as a doctor, but he knew that she couldn't take a big overseas trip. That was the reason, because Lori seemed so harsh to me.

Jennifer Grace I'm a mother of a young son now and I recall not being a parent and hearing friends talk about the experience of being a parent. You get a portion of it intellectually, of course. But there are things you know in your gut and in your body on the other side of life experiences that you can't know.

David Cromer The only thing I might have figured out utterly accidentally, and found a way to recreate over the couple of years I kept having to direct it was: you need every second of it. That's not a great observation, that should be true of any play. But in order to say anything about it, you have to experience every little bit of it. The boring parts need to be boring.

Jennifer Grace Here we are in this sacred place, the theatre, and we're choosing not to put the lights down on you and pretend that you are not here. We are here because you are here. Perhaps you don't have lines, but this is *Our Town* and you belong the way that I belong.

David Cromer I think a lot of times we all think we need to show our work. How will you know I'm sad if I don't act sad? How will you know I'm sad if I don't cry? You don't have to. I always said the first big, real, true gut punch of my life was when my father died. Luckily, it happened much later in life, but when my father died, I walked around saying, "My father died." The fact that it was true was as sad as it needed to be.

Michael McKean He's the Stage Manager. I think he belongs to the play, which informs him about belonging to the town, but he only knows of this town because he's the guy they hired to be the Stage Manager. I don't think he is a deity. I don't think he is an unblinking eye in the sky. I never felt much of a compulsion to make him anything more.

Jennifer Grace In the third act, I had ceased to be Emily and I was myself onstage. I think the thing that made me urgently want to do the show when I read it was the third act. The way that it took my breath away because it spoke to something very lizard brain in me, very primal and urgent, which I suspect is a pretty universal feeling, which is that I do not want to die.

I don't know what death is. I'm so scared of that thing I don't know. So, those first two acts felt like, for me, an exercise and meditation on what it means to be alive. But in the third act, having the opportunity to just sit and be quiet in a chair for a few moments and listen to the world around me, to feel the light shift, and then to have my own meditation on death meant that when I did pop up and speak to the Stage Manager, those were all honest questions. It was all very real.

The thing that's so magnificently written about the third act is how well it speaks to something inarticulable. I know that it has to do with something larger than us.

*   *   *

Michael McKean Plays are not made of words, they're not even made of emotions, they are made of actions that contain words, or that utilize words, and the emotions come out of the actions, the achievement of goals, the frustration in the achievement of goals.

David Cromer All of the people who played the Stage Manager are unarguably stronger and more experienced actors than me. All of them. With more facility with language, more grace, more charisma with an audience, all those things. I felt bad only because I was really struggling with the idea that sometimes I was trying to get them to do something I had done. It was awkward. It was never intended for anyone to play it other than me.

Jennifer Grace I love David, but honestly, he had his notebook. He took notes during the show. At intermission on the stairs down to the green room or to our dressing rooms, he would give notes. That's not appropriate. In a normal run of a show, the director stops giving you notes after the show is in performance. He never stopped. In the moment sometimes it could be really frustrating. I think that it was, again, these are all elements to this desire to take the screen away. The process was laid bare and it felt very honest.

Jonathan Mastro If the director's not there, and you're doing a regular show, at the intermission the actors can bitch about the audience. In this show, if Cromer is there as one of the actors, he's dealing with it, but the actors also know that you can't just hide behind, "Oh, the audience is dead today." You know that David sees it, and that David knows your bag of tricks. So, there was a cleansing purity that his presence in the show gave, and it wasn't because he was a hard-ass, it was because he has so much integrity, and so much insight.

David Cromer People were different. Michael Shannon was like Atticus Finch as the Stage Manager. You just wanted to sit up and behave when he was on. Helen was great. Helen was great because Helen's just like a brain on a stick. Her intelligence absolutely radiates. But audiences aren't as used to it unless she's given all of this language and all of this strange subtle insight to these strange little double-meaning plates to spin.

Helen Hunt The Stage Manager talks about all the things I care about. Period. So, I just was very grateful to get to walk under it. It took a toll—I don't know how Jennifer turned in that performance year after year. But at the end of these three acts, I felt affected by it and what it talks about. What it means to say goodbye, what it means to realize that there is no way to quite be grateful enough for each day. You can't do it. Maybe a little for a minute, that's it. That's a devastating fact. I was reading through it with a friend and she pointed out at one point—this is a life-long friend of mine—she just turned to me and said, "You know one day one of us is going to say goodbye to the other." That's just true. So, how that informs how you live each dumb day is interesting to me.

Jennifer Grace Helen is the only woman that I ever worked opposite in the role of the Stage Manager. It was a much richer and more nuanced experience in terms of what I heard and the information that she and I exchanged, maybe because we're both women. Helen played Emily, for not as long as I did, in the Spalding Gray production. She and I spoke about that at length. It felt for a few different reasons like there was a kind of a mentorship, a direct line between Emily and the Stage Manager when I got to work with her. That could just be how I feel about her as a person. There could be something biologically about either honestly seeing a nurturing quality or by nature of her being a woman, expecting more of a nurturing quality from a Stage Manager who's a woman.

David Cromer The show was sort of intentionally conventional in its casting prior to Helen. The men who played Doc Gibbs were in their forties and looked tired and frustrated or overworked or preoccupied. It was conventional in that way and I thought, "Oh, isn't it written as a man? Isn't it written in a man's voice?" And I don't think it was.

Lori Myers Helen just had a such a good energy. She's very concise and clear. She loves the play and she loved the production so much, she wanted it brought to LA for people to see it and it really, I think, resonated in her performance. I think initially Cromer had said, "Oh, there's never going to be a female Stage Manager, no." But then she came along and you're like, "Well, how do you not let her do it?"

*   *   *

David Cromer If you're just going to say, "Isn't it sad that we don't realize life while we live it?" you could just say that at the beginning of the play and everyone could go home. But Wilder's really roundabout. The Stage Manager had to say, "I kind of know what I want to say at the end, but I don't know how exactly I'm going to say it."

Michael McKean David's only overriding note was, "This is not a play that's happening to the Stage Manager, this is a play that the Stage Manager is facilitating. He's doing his job."

Jennifer Grace It's strange to me how this play came into my life and how it consumed the better part of several years of my life, but also the ripple effects that it has had after in beautiful and complicated ways. I spent a number of years in therapy after *Our Town*, just trying to figure out how to tease Emily and I apart. In some ways I think in service of trying to give Emily everything that I had, I wasn't quite conscious enough of how much I was absorbing in response.

Laura Elsworthy I remember speaking to a therapist once and he said, "Your body doesn't know when you're crying that it's not real crying. Your body is physiologically still doing the action of producing tears, isn't it?" It's a draining thing to do it on stage. I remember being really tired. But I also remember going out every night and having a lot of energy as well, a weird kind of boost from doing the show.

Michael McKean There was the moment in the homework scene, when Emily says, "If you hold your breath, you can hear the train all the way to Contoocook. Hear it?" Some nights, four or five anyway, we could hear the Sheridan Square subway going by. When that subtle thing goes rumbling through, it was like, "Man, New York City is playing along with this."

Lori Myers I feel that the writing is not only just intensely beautiful, but like Cromer said, actionable. It goes back to any single solitary man, woman and child. Any being can pick something from that play and it relates to them. You could argue it's non-inclusive. This is a very non-inclusive hetero play, but what stands up is just the beauty of the script and the power of the structure and the concise nature in which the production executed *Our Town*.

Helen Hunt How could you see a play like this and not have it speak to your right now? Your right now is all you have, every audience member. How many people have you lost? How many parents are still living? Have you lost a daughter? I just can't imagine seeing anything, particularly this play, and not having it be affected by where you are in your life.

David Cromer It was the first time in many years, and the last time in any of the years since then, that I lived in a community consistently that was supportive and entertaining and fun and that you could count on this giant group of people. It was an idealized version of Grover's Corners.

That sounds cutesy. I was patient when I was playing the Stage Manager. I was unperturbed by things, I was philosophical about slights or upsets or disappointments. I'd go, "Well, okay. It's going to be okay. We'll move on from here." I didn't realize that this had had this effect on me until I wasn't playing the part anymore and I just found myself getting frantic and shrill and childish and petulant about things. Then, when I played it again, I relaxed.

Laura Elsworthy I've got a bit of a difficult relationship with my dad. He came to see the play and I remember desperately thinking, "This is it. This is when he realizes how special," not because of acting, but because of Emily's journey and what it means. I think he found it very hard to watch. He didn't stay after it. He left. I don't think he could compute it. Which I suppose is a good reaction in a way, because at least there was a reaction.

My mom, who I've got a brilliant relationship with, really didn't want to watch it again. She said, "I'll come and watch the first two bits." My mom's a teaching assistant and I still don't think she can quite separate that what I'm doing is not real. She was like, "I just can't watch the last bit again. It's too hard."

Jennifer Grace I went to a tattoo parlor and I got "Every Minute" tattooed because I wanted to hang onto the thing that is unhang-on-able. It's a thing that David would talk about all the time, that you cannot live life and appreciate life at the same time. It's not possible. You will be insufferable if you walk around appreciating every moment. I think that's part of the beauty of the play is that it does go so fast, by design. It must. I'm a big believer that happiness is a sensation that we feel in retrospect. It's not a thing that exists as you do it.

I think now that were I to play Emily would be very, very different because through the course of doing that play, I worked through all of those milestones. The falling-in-love, the marriage, the having the baby, the death. I have a different sense of it from that junior in high school who read it and didn't remember it. But I will say, too, that the beauty of the way that *Our Town* stays with me is that when my husband died, he'd been sick for a while. He was supposed to be getting better, so it was unexpected. We were at Mt. Sinai and when I got word that things had shifted and it was going to be that day, the waiting room was filled with people from *Our Town*. They came.

As a widow, I feel profoundly that there are times that I can look back to and say, "Yes, that was," and know that it will happen again. *Our Town* has changed my life fundamentally in huge ways. When my husband died, our son was a toddler. Basically, it was the ending of *Our Town*. I had spent all of these years and this time feeling like death was so scary and that I was so scared to do it, to be embraced by it, never once entertaining the possibility that perhaps I'm not Emily, but George.

Heather Gilbert We have such a long experience with all these people. The babies that were born. We've had engagements. We've had people break up. We've had deaths within our family. It's huge, all of the things that we've experienced. In *Our Town*, that's what you track. Just a few weeks ago, I was like, "David, we could do the play again." He's like, "We're not the same people." I'm like, "I know, but that's the point of this play. We're not those people. We're the next step on these people's lives."

Helen Hunt I remember my dad came to the Gregory Mosher production and his wife said he had to be carried out of the theatre. It's a bit cruel and unusual to make a parent watch their kid play Emily. My daughter played Emily two years ago. She was so beautiful and simple and true.

The play takes flight if you're in the eighth grade or you're David Cromer. These 13-year-olds heard it, they really did. Are they going to hear it in a different way when they're 45 and sit down in a production and have daughters of their own? Yes. But that doesn't mean that they're not hearing it now.

David Cromer I could look right at the audience and people just looked like, "What the fuck is going on?" which I took as a little badge of honor, because they were seeing *Our Town*. There was one performance it in Chicago with a little old lady who talked about what she thought about it all the way through. About halfway through, she goes, "This is the weirdest play I've ever seen."

5

Westport Country Playhouse and Broadway, 2002–3

It's been said many times: the events of September 11 make us realize the value of what we have. For this, at least, we are grateful. Those events have taught us to honor the legacy of the past, and to respect the efforts of those who have gone before.

from "Dear Theatregoer" letter in the Westport Country
Playhouse program for *Our Town*, signed by Elizabeth Morten,
President of the Connecticut Theatre Foundation, and
Joanne Woodward, Artistic Director

Located on a busy commercial stretch of Route 1 in Westport, Connecticut, the Westport Country Playhouse's name seems a bit incongruous for a venue located in such a highly developed part of this Long Island Sound shoreline community. But in the 1930s, when Lawrence Langner and Armina Marshall of New York City's The Theatre Guild converted a 19th-century barn into a theatre with a Broadway-scaled stage, Westport was still quite rural. In the ensuing years, even as the community grew, Westport gained a reputation as a semi-pastoral retreat for New York artists, only a short train-ride away from Manhattan.

The Playhouse operated for decades in the classic mode of summer stock theatre, offering a different production every week between June and August, appealing to locals and weekenders alike. It was not uncommon to find famous actors both treading the boards and watching from the pew-like bench seating. When the Langner family opted to relinquish ownership of the theatre in the mid-1980s, James B. McKenzie, who had been operating the theatre as producer for 25 years, organized a group of investors to purchase it and ensure its continued life.

Upon McKenzie's retirement in 2000, he was succeeded by longtime Westport resident Joanne Woodward, the Oscar and Emmy Award-winning actor. Woodward took the title of artistic director and gathered a team to reimagine how the company would produce. Her model was that of American regional theatres, with multi-week runs of fewer shows, spread throughout the year, however to do so meant a reconstruction of the one-time barn, which had never been intended for (human) winter use. Woodward used her considerable charm and fame on behalf of the theatre's fundraising efforts, often enlisting the help of her husband, the Oscar-winning film star and charity-food entrepreneur Paul Newman, for events and benefit readings.

Our Town was an ideal show for Westport, not least because Thornton Wilder had been of the opinion that the play belonged in a great big barn of a place. While there was an intimacy to the old Playhouse, it was inarguable that it was, or at least had been, a barn. Wilder performed as the Stage Manager at the Playhouse in 1946, a particularly convenient spot for his summer barnstorming because Westport was located only a bit more than 30 miles from his home in Hamden. The fact that the theatre's stage house was little changed since its original conversion to a theatre lent verisimilitude to the proceedings, although designer Tony Walton created a more explicitly vintage setting for the production.

While impetus for the 2002 Westport show was to produce the play as a balm for the southern Connecticut community in response to the attacks of 9/11, there is no question that the main event was Newman's return to the stage in a full production. Newman was no stage novice, having acted in the original Broadway

Paul Newman (foreground) in the 2002 Westport Country Playhouse production of *Our Town*, directed by James Naughton. Photo by Joan Marcus.

productions of *Picnic, The Desperate Hours*, and *Sweet Bird of Youth*. He had performed for years in benefits supporting The Hole-in-the-Wall Gang camp he had founded for seriously ill children in Ashford, Connecticut, however *Our Town* would be his first true stage appearance since his Broadway run, with Woodward, in the forgotten 1964 play *Baby Want a Kiss*.

Ticket demand at Westport was sufficient to prompt the Playhouse to self-produce *Our Town* on Broadway later in 2002 for a limited run. That engagement formed the basis for a televised version, filmed by the Showtime cable service, later broadcast on PBS. The new playhouse opened in 2005.

Our Town would be Newman's final stage appearance. He passed away in 2008.

In this chapter:
Jayne Atkinson, Mrs. Gibbs
Frank Converse, Dr. Gibbs
Jane Curtin, Mrs. Webb
Jeffrey DeMunn, Mr. Webb
Alison Harris, executive director
Anne Keefe, associate artistic director
Maggie Lacey, Emily Webb
James Naughton, director
Paul Newman, Stage Manager
Stephen Spinella, Simon Stimson

Anne Keefe Joanne did it absolutely without question as a response to 9/11. It's a play that's always been a favorite of hers. We talked a lot before all of us actually got involved with the Playhouse about the things we wanted to do. We wanted to put it on even before 9/11, but it was so big that we thought, "Okay, well there will always be a time to do it." Then, once 9/11 happened, Joanne said, "This is the time. This is the time, we'll figure out how to pay for it, but this is the time to do this play. If ever it was needed, it's now."

Frank Converse We had a meeting after 9/11, about what kind of season they would have at the Playhouse, in memory of or respect of 9/11, to reflect what was happening, what the theatre could contribute to the sense of mourning.

Jeffrey DeMunn It was just in everybody's blood, as you know. It was in every breath you took, it was that the world had changed in a massive way. This little play was still relevant.

Anne Keefe We'd put *Our Town* on the program, and we were still finishing the scheduling for the rest of the season. The phone rang. My husband said, "Joanne's on the line." I picked up and she said, "Listen, there's something I want to run by you. Paul and I were talking about *Our Town*, and he said, 'What would you think if I played the Stage Manager?' I paused and said, 'Gee Paul, you know it's been like 32 years since you've been on stage, and it's an awful lot of memorizing, and neither of us is as young as we used to be.' So, he said, 'I tell you what, give me a couple of hours.' He went into the study and he closed the door." Joanne said that two hours later, he came out and he had committed to memory half of the opening speech. So, she said, "Before I tell him yes, I just wonder if you think it's a good idea?"

James Naughton I'm probably one of the few American actors who had never been in a production of it or had never worked on it, or had never seen a production of it, before I worked on this. Joanne called one night and said, "Jimmy, you know how I've always wanted to do *Our Town*?" We'd been friends for a couple of decades and she'd always talked about it since she had taken over the Playhouse. This was after 9/11, and she said, "Well, I think now is the time when we all could use it." She said, "You won't believe this, but Paul wants to play the Stage Manager." Now, she and I had been after Paul to try to do something on the stage probably for 15 or 20 years.

Anne Keefe It was a very communal and collegial decision, as were all the designers that we chose. Because they were all people that we knew and felt comfortable with and knew they would deliver.

James Naughton Joanne and I talked about it and I said, "Well, I think it'd be great if we could cast this from our town as much as possible," because we've got a bunch of wonderful actors in our town. Frank Converse lives in Weston and Jayne Atkinson, who's one of my favorite actresses, lived then in Weston. Jane Curtin lives just up the road, up Route 7. Jake Robards grew up in Southport. Then we cast the rest of it basically from town.

Emily came down to two people, Maggie Lacey or Anne Hathaway, and I couldn't figure out which way to go. I asked Joanne to come in and she sat in on an audition with me. When they got through, she said, "I don't know, Jimmy, I don't know. Your choice." Maggie was quite wonderful.

Anne Keefe Joanne and Paul were local celebrities, and you did run into them in town. There was this ethos that nobody asked them for autographs, nobody intruded on their privacy when they ran into them. It was just a local, unwritten law of courtesy. I think everybody has, still to this day, a Paul Newman story or a Joanne Woodward story. So, this was pretty big news, and very big news in town. We got a little piece in *The New York Times* in "Arts Briefly," an announcement about Paul.

Alison Harris The opening day that we put tickets on sale, there were these incredible lines at the box office.

Anne Keefe A line like we haven't seen before or since, it was incredible, snaking all the way down to the Post Road, with people waiting to get tickets. There were literally people from London, and Tokyo, and Germany—people buying whole subscriptions just so that they would have that seat to see Paul Newman do *Our Town* up here in Westport. That was sort of a stunner.

James Naughton I decided it would be a really good idea for us to rehearse, if we could, not on a taped-out floor someplace, but in a theatre, because Paul hadn't been in a theatre, and there's a big difference. I thought to make him as comfortable as possible, so we rehearsed at the White Barn Theatre. That was a delight to go over there and for us to be in that place together, that company.

Anne Keefe Look, Paul's no dummy. In spite of the fact that he hadn't been on stage for years, that's where he started. He understood that dynamic as well as anybody. I think everybody was in full support of that, not actively, but everybody wanted to be their best self.

Stephen Spinella My first thoughts about the play was that it was a horrible, just awful reactionary play about these people who don't want anything to change.

James Naughton On that first day, the little kids might not have, but everyone else knew who Paul Newman was. Maggie and those guys did, and Jeff and Frank and the Janes and Mia Dillon. Everybody was aware of it.

Anne Keefe It was a very collegial company. People with enough sense to understand what they were, where they were, were sort of in awe. But for the most part, these are people with huge careers of their own.

Jane Curtin There was a sweetness in the theatre. We were working with retired teachers. We were working with people who had grown up in Westport all their lives. They weren't actors, they were people from the town. So, we became a town and it was a sweet town. It was just that overall feeling. Paul set the tone and you were just drawn in.

James Naughton They knew that Paul and I were friends and that was obvious, because our rehearsal would be interrupted constantly by, "Jimmy, Jimmy, Jimmy, Jimmy!" And he'd say, "What about if, how about if, we do this?" Then he'd come up with some terrible idea, I mean really off the wall, and I'd say, "Well, I thought about that. That's a possibility, but here's what I want to do and here's why." And then he'd go, "Oh, okay. Good, that's good." He always was one of those guys that always thought outside the box.

Jayne Atkinson He had such a spirit of what I would call young at heart. He lived a lot of life and he had decided some things that made his life work for him that were pretty extraordinary. He threw away all his suits and he had a couple pairs of khaki pants, a couple of white shirts, I think Docksiders, and that's what he wore. He came to rehearsal completely memorized which was astounding, and he said, "Look kids, this is not because I'm trying to impress you, it's because if I didn't come here memorized, we'd all be up shit creek without a paddle."

Anne Keefe They wanted not to let Paul down, because they understood what Paul was doing by taking this on. I think everybody was really trying to be the best they could be across the board. He certainly set the tone. When the leading man works that hard, everybody else damn well better.

James Naughton Paul's a very generous guy and a very shy person, so they saw that, but I think there always was kind of a separation, too.

Jayne Atkinson One day, one of the kids brought a scooter and one of the young girls, Kristen Hahn, she played my daughter, was a little nervous to get on the scooter. Paul took the scooter and shot across the stage on it and shot back and he said, "You just can't be afraid," and got her on it. He kept the tone for the entire thing along with Jimmy. He just was easy and funny and so that quality morphed into his narrator and it all became—I guess the word that I want to use is that they became precious.

Jane Curtin Paul was a movie star, but Paul wasn't an ego. Paul was very much of an actor. He represented himself as one of us. We were all in the same boat. We were out here to do this little play in Westport, where Paul and Joanne loved this little theatre and we're doing this because we love to act. He played with all of the kids in the production. Of course, they had no idea who he was, but he made them all feel great. He was a guy who just was so happy being an actor and loved being around other actors.

Frank Converse He was kind of a contrast. There was a wicked little boy inside him, but then he was also so closed up, so very, very private. Mostly it was about the work. From the first day I thought, 'Well, of course I might say this, but he's perfect.' But then I also say Hal Holbrook is perfect, so that's not a very good statement. The cliché is, he's very comfortable in his own skin on and off-stage. What I found out later from Naughton was, "I have trouble getting him to come forward, to come below proscenium line." He's afraid of falling and yet outwardly, he seemed to have all this confidence.

James Naughton It makes me crazy when directors get in there and their work becomes evident, making a statement or a concept. I like it when the director's work is really strong and good and invisible. I was trying to do something for my friend Paul, to bring all of the elements of what Wilder wrote, what he meant, to bear. I said to Tony Walton, "I want this to be beautiful, because I think that the message is heartbreakingly beautiful, so let's try to be subtle, but go for that."

Jane Curtin People are people and people can be funny. That's another thing about how you approach these things. You cannot treat everything as sacrosanct. People have flaws. They have different interpretations. Some people laugh inappropriately. Some people cry inappropriately. People in general are all very unique. So, you can't have everybody say the speeches the same way because they're all unique individuals.

James Naughton One of the things that I came to really respect in what Wilder accomplished was the scene where there two young people meet, Emily and George. It's a compression. What he does is he compresses a whole couple of lifetimes into this two-and-a-half-hour play. He goes from George tossing a ball, and Emily's there, and then he comes down and they have this little conversation and she tells him she thinks he's stuck up and she gets upset and he sees that and he apologizes to her and he tries to make it up for her. He consoles her and he says, "Can I buy you an ice cream soda?" They go into the soda shop and by the time they come out, they're going to get married. The compression of things, the life moments, in a 10-minute scene. That is art, and when that happens, if you take that ride with them, then you're giving them your heart.

Maggie Lacey Jimmy gave me a note in the audition that sort of liberated me throughout the process, which was don't think about her age, especially at the beginning. Don't think about her needing to be 14, or you needing to do anything. I think I set out not to do that. But there's something, maybe, that just sort of bubbled up.

Jeffrey DeMunn *Our Town* doesn't arm-wrestle anybody, it doesn't push you into a position, it doesn't demand that you feel one way or another. It says, 'Here,' and it lays out its story. If for you it's sentimental, then it's sentimental. I think if you're saying that *Our Town* is a sentimental play, then that's talking about you.

Jane Curtin It is sentimental and there's nothing wrong with being sentimental. It's old-fashioned in the sense that it deals with basic beliefs about what it is to be a human being and what it is to live in a world with other people. That's the simplicity of it and that's what makes it old-fashioned because it's dealing with just the basic principles of humanity. There's nothing fancy about it. There's nothing forward-thinking about it. It just talks about who we are and how far we've come from who we should be. I think the Grover's Corners people are who we should be.

Jeffrey DeMunn I'm not sure how much anyone ever gets the Amerindian comment from Professor Willard. I think you have to spend a lot of time, a lot of investigating, to find out the horrible thing that happened there. It gets pretty glossed over.

Stephen Spinella I remember going, "Oh, my god. I was so wrong about this. This is not reactionary. This is not about wanting to go back to a previous way of living. This is about people struggling to hold onto their lives which they find be very beautiful, and the impossibility of that." It's the opposite of reactionary. It's that you can't hold onto the past, that the past is constantly driving you into the future. You're constantly moving into the future and there's no way to get out of that.

Anne Keefe It was a treat to watch Paul turn himself into a theatre actor again, to play with the scope of not playing for a camera, to be playing for bigger space, and watching him just embrace it and get better and better.

James Naughton When it came to directing him, my job was to get him to look up a little bit, because he was shy. He was afraid he was going to make eye contact with somebody in the audience and that that would freak him out. In the beginning, he was kind of behind his eyes scrolling through his lines and I just kept talking to him, going up to him, saying, "You know, you can look out there at the Playhouse."

Paul Newman I think there's a great deal of envy in today's audiences for that kind of life. It's slower and a real sense of completion and a great sense of simplicity. The lack of acceleration of time and place. I would certainly recommend it. There's too much going on now, to have the luxury of a much slower pace. It's a luxury, indeed.

James Naughton I spent a lot of time working with Maggie on trying to get that third act stuff, because what happens is we all work really hard and then we hand it off to Maggie. "Save it, save it, save it, save it. Save the emotion." Yeah, she's hopeful. She wants to go back. Then she goes back and then she realizes, and it's heartbreaking for her. "Do human beings ever realize life while they live it?" "Saints and poets, maybe." Then she's got to bring it home.

Stephen Spinella Maybe he's gay, maybe he's not. He doesn't even understand what that word means. Maybe he has feelings, but there is no event onstage that allows that to be expressed. It all stays kind of amorphous.

Jane Curtin Break it down into its simplest form. It's easy to understand. You just have to be kind to each other. You just have to look at each other's eyes and see that there is a human being there. You have to look up in the stars. What do you see there? I mean how does it affect you? It's all very simple.

Maggie Lacey Emily was a better student, academically, than I was growing up. I did fine, but I think it wasn't hard for her. I loved getting to pretend to be that person, who just would have no qualms about doing her homework. I don't think she was vain when she's talking about how good she is at it. I think it's just straightforward in that New Hampshire way.

Once I got to work with Jane Curtin and Jeffrey DeMunn, I could really expand an image of her based on her relationship with those two particular people. Jane was not giving her daughter an inch, as far as coddling or telling her she's pretty. But that doesn't diminish Emily's confidence. Then Jeffrey—I could imagine so much, just fully, about her relationship with her father and having it be a really a progressive relationship in that day and age.

Frank Converse My *Our Town* score is two Holbrook, one Newman. I did one with Hal at Long Wharf, and then, in '07, we did it again at Hartford Stage. With Hal, I always played Editor Webb. With Paul, I was the doctor. Thanks to Jeff DeMunn, who played Editor Webb in the Newman production, I found out where the laughs were.

Jeffrey DeMunn I think Editor Webb considered himself a bit of a leader, because the newspaper, it's a natural position, I guess. An observer of the town. Maybe I thought of him as one of the town councilors, one of the people making decisions and running the place.

Paul Newman When Wilder wrote the play, we were still pretty much in the center of a depression, and yet it's interesting that the possibility of something like that economically happening to either one of those families was never even hinted at.

Stephen Spinella Simon Stimson was somebody who really should've gotten out. I just felt like he's one of the people that needs to leave, that needs to go find a bigger place. I don't really know what Simon Stimson's problem is. I don't know why he was a drunk. He's the unhappiest person in the place, so you feel Wilder nudging you in that direction. More than a nudge. He says it. Then you build an internal life based on those kinds of things.

He drinks for a reason. You have to figure out what that reason is. In the choir scene, he constantly drives the women to be better, and better, and better. He's a perfectionist. Perfectionists need to be surrounded by people who are willing to work towards that perfection. He is not. He's surrounded by amateurs.

Paul Newman I don't think as the Stage Manager looking at this play that I concerned myself with all of the interactions and reactions. He was simply the engager, he simply engaged the people in this play. That was his job. To comment on the times, more than the absolutely minute interactions between the characters.

So, as an actor, I didn't think that it was my obligation to examine those things as minutely.

My job was simply to find the way to create the narrative of the play, and I gave myself one word: which was to seek. To seek the expression, to seek the vocabulary, to not have the language available to me as a kind of recitation. To give the audience possibly even the idea that his narration would change every night, depending how things struck him in a scene, or to tell the story differently or to have a different emphasis.

Jeffrey DeMunn I would never leave the wings. I stayed in the wings and watched the play every night. I would watch Paul working on a section, night after night, and it would just get better and better, until it was perfection. Then the next night, that whole route that he had carved in the snow, in the mountain, or however you want to picture it, was thrown out, and he started all over again. It was an amazing lesson in never repeat, don't try to do the same thing twice, because that's dead theatre.

James Naughton That 10-minute transition scene, when they go have a soda and then they get engaged, was just so beautifully written and constructed, so that if you don't lay too much on it, don't impose anything on it, let it happen, it can be sweet and beautiful. We set you up for caring at the end when she dies. Talk about being manipulated, right?

Paul Newman When I say seek, I meant he didn't seek what he was going to say, he had to seek the way he was going to say it. It was much more of an acting task than it was a comment on the times or comment on that character existing inside the play.

Jeffrey DeMunn To me, all the subtext and all the other things come straight from the audience, both with Shakespeare and with *Our Town*. The audience brings it, and you're just laying out the stuff. It's the words, just say the words and move on, and it gives the audience an opportunity to participate in a very different way.

Frank Converse I think that Editor Webb is a deeply sardonic and very wise guy. I don't mean in the gangster sense, but he is a very sensible, sophisticated man. He enjoys teasing George a bit. I think actually I preferred playing the doctor. I found that the doctor is a very no-nonsense fellow. I do not say he's sour, or that he's humorless, but maybe as a physician in a little town that he's hard pressed. He's delivering children for impoverished people. He's probably one of the go-to guys in town. I don't think he can relax.

Stephen Spinella One of the most beautiful moments in the play is when George says he wants to stay, he wants to figure out a way to stay. He doesn't want to go to agriculture school, and everyone's telling him he should. These people who try to hold on to something they can't hold onto. The whole play opened up for me in this completely different way.

Jane Curtin I'm a New Englander. I was born in Massachusetts and I live in Connecticut. I can't get it out of my system. It's in my DNA. All of my relatives, they're New Englanders and there are quirks to being a New Englander. It was my take on this New Hampshire woman because of my New England roots.

I think she was a pretty woman who married a man who married a pretty woman. I think she was a little vain. There were disappointments in her life, but she was okay. There was an air to her that didn't belong there a little bit. I think she thought a little much of herself, but within the confines of this tiny place, it didn't really affect anybody but her.

Jeffrey DeMunn The play shows you yourself, and if you're 26 years old doing a part in it, or a 66-year-old doing a part in it, it just reflects back to you. It talks to all different generations—astounding to me—and all different times. It is no less relevant now that we've got the rather twisted and horrific situation that we have, than it was back in earlier days. If anything, it's probably more powerful now.

James Naughton Joanne left us alone. Paul went home every night and I'm sure he was reporting to the artistic director, but everybody was happy and he was happy. She was always supportive of him and of us, I mean the whole company. I think she was delighted.

Jeffrey DeMunn Up at Westport, she'd be just sitting in the audience knitting. Just listening, without even watching, just listening when he did a section of the play. She would laugh at each of the funny things, as if she'd never heard it before. It was beautiful, it was beautiful. The two of them, holy cow, we should all aspire to have such a beautiful relationship.

Jayne Atkinson You just felt that Joanne was quietly watching her man, supporting her man, supporting the show, probably giving some notes to Jimmy. Watching and guiding. Guiding Paul. I'm sure that, besides Jimmy, the person he trusted most was her and she knew this was a big deal for him. She was going to make sure that he felt good, felt strong, and had her support, but she was great with all of us. It was just so wonderful to have her around. The knitting made everyone feel relaxed. It can't be too bad if she's back there knitting.

Maggie Lacey I always felt his support. One of the beautiful things about being an actor, is that you're often in a play with people of an age very different from your own, very far away in one or the other direction. I was always aware, which I think led to my shyness a little bit, of the stuff that they could perceive that I couldn't yet perceive. Not in a mean way. But those things where, "If I could just tell her this one thing, I could probably help her." I've worked with older actors, who I could tell were watching me. And it kills it. He was never like that.

Anne Keefe Paul would tell these stories when we were fundraising about being able to see daylight through the walls of the barn, and never really able to get a blackout in a matinee because there was so much light coming in through the chinks. Then the rain on the expensive seats, and the fact that in order to get from one side of the stage to the other, you could give yourself a concussion.

Jane Curtin There were breezes blowing through the clapboards. It was just fun. It was, "Hey kids, let's start a theatre." You know, we were Judy Garland and Mickey Rooney and, "Gee, I guess Pauline, you'll have to do the costumes. Greg, you can do the hair."

Broadway

Jayne Atkinson We had more time with it. I think it deepened and I think we all felt the import of the Great White Way. But I think that the seed of the beauty of what we had started in Westport moved to that theatre. The journey from Westport to New York brought us closer, we were like in camp. We were all together all the time, and I think that camaraderie and the excitement deepened our relationships to each other on stage, deepened our relationship to our characters, deepened the work. It just grew and expanded and got better, being able to have that next part of the journey together.

Jane Curtin It made me sad that we moved from Westport to New York just because we lost the town. The town became a little bit of a suburb. Just in the sense that it was the space. It was just what was surrounding you. Even though the production didn't change in any way, the idea of it did.

Jayne Atkinson I think when you would bring a play to New York you are facing a more critical audience. I wouldn't use the word sophisticated, although I might be tempted to, but you are going to be having people come to this play who see it as the iconic play that it is and are looking for notes. They're looking for are we getting it right? What is there new? What isn't new? Did we get it?

Jane Curtin Sometimes with New Yorkers, or with a Broadway audience, they're there with their arms folded and they've got this little look on their faces going, 'Okay, what have you got?' I never felt that in Westport.

Jeffrey DeMunn It was a less quiet conversation we were having with the audience. It was not huge, it was that beautiful little Booth. It was still a small theatre, but you lose a little bit of intimacy when you upsize like that. The job became to keep the intimacy going, at the same time as you're grabbing that whole house, because you've got to get right to that back wall and bring them all along.

Alison Harris Paul ssaid, "The reason I'm willing to do this, to go to Broadway"— because he wasn't terribly enthusiastic about it, certainly not for himself personally— "is because I want to put Westport on the map." The Booth, what became the theatre choice, was small and charming and it made Jimmy comfortable, but it had this huge electric billboard. Paul said, "That's where we're going to say, 'This is the Westport Country Playhouse production.'" Any listing of the cast anywhere was alphabetical or in order of appearance, but never was it going to be "Paul Newman as the Stage Manager in."

Anne Keefe At the end of the day, he did it for Joanne.

Alison Harris For him, the Westport Country Playhouse was Joanne.

Stephen Spinella We spent a week filming it for Showtime. They built out the stage to put the cameras on, and they had a little video village down audience right in the Booth, with the monitors and all that. One day, I was down there sitting about eight or nine rows back from the cameras and the monitors. Paul was sitting there—or Joanne, I can't remember which was there first—but the other one came and sat down and leaned over and whispered something and they just started laughing and laughing. This went on for like ten minutes. Them just enjoying each other's company with such complete youthful abandon. It was so beautiful. Unobserved, completely unobserved. They thought they were alone, and I'll never forget it. You long for those kind of relationships.

Jayne Atkinson One of the most difficult things I have ever done in my life is sit in that chair and be dead and not speak. Make no mistake. That is one tough job. For the entire act to be sitting there and still and looking up and staring in intention, you know they say there's not small parts only small actors. It wasn't a small part but this was intense to do. I will tell you, one matinee, I had fallen asleep and I woke up in the middle of a scene. It is one of the most terrifying moments. It's one thing to lose your line, that's terrifying. It is another thing to be sitting on Broadway in the front row as a dead person in *Our Town* and fall asleep.

Frank Converse There was an issue about [Paul's] voice, his projection, and so he was miked. He was the only miked actor in the company. Then, one day, he started doing the monologue before the beginning of the third act, where he says now the play's going to change—I'm paraphrasing—'Now the play is going to be about death.' He talks about the Civil War soldiers. Even to think about it to try to paraphrase it makes me choke up, about these boys who've never been more than four or five miles from home. Paul's demeanor and attitude went through this shift. It's necessary there. All of a sudden, he's talking like Orson Welles. You hear this tone and this delivery. DeMunn and I talked about it a lot, because we loved hearing him do that speech. I know at least once we said to each other, "Here we are in an A-production on Broadway, because of Paul and Thornton Wilder."

Jayne Atkinson We didn't have to worry about reviews, we were sold out. We knew we were having an experience that we would probably never have again.

Filming

James Naughton One time the camera comes up behind him and alongside him and then discovers him in front. I just thought it was a nice, an artful way to tell the story and to involve the audience, a couple of people or a family sitting in their living room. It was interesting, because the book on acting is that you do less in front of a camera than you do on a stage, but Paul did much more in front of a camera.

Alison Harris He could go back to just being a soft-spoken film actor and communicating beautifully that way.

James Naughton I said to him afterwards, "You were actually bigger in front of the camera than you were on the stage. Now, tell me, what's the story?" He'd go, "Gee, I don't know. I just thought I have to do something." It was antithetical to everything we think we know about how actors should work in front of a stage, on a stage or in front of a camera. I think that what he does in the third act, on the screen, is just some of the best acting I've seen, some of the best acting he's ever done.

Jayne Atkinson As an actor on stage you have to emit this large beam of intention. But when a camera is there you don't have to work as hard and it captures these nuances between characters and I was flabbergasted. I was so moved by that. Seeing it filmed was another version that was so rich and tender. Of course, when you're on stage, you're not watching it.

Frank Converse We were doing the TV version. There's a bit of blocking where the doctor comes in in the morning in the first scene and he crosses through that trellis as he enters, goes into his home. That was down near the right proscenium, and Newman would be standing down there and I would pass very closely to him as I made the turn into the house. When we were doing the TV, we had a little stop one day while they were doing that set-up and we had just worked over that movement. He said to me, which surprised me because he was always very quiet, just doing the business: "You know, I should tell you that I don't mean to be so close to you there, but I've always felt that it shows the thin line between the Stage Manager, the storyteller, and the characters in the story. It's a very thin line. So that's why I'm always so close to you when you go by there."

Jane Curtin I don't know how people would respond today. I have no idea because I honestly don't know who we are anymore. It seems as though we've lost our innocence. There was an innocence before 9/11, and that's gone. 9/11 took some of it away. Current events have taken most of it away.

Jeffrey DeMunn I don't know what it is about that play, but it sure speaks to people in a very deep manner, people of all ages. You're giving a tool to each audience, each generation of audience, a tool for them to look at their own lives, look at their own world, and to reflect on the good and the bad.

Frank Converse It always impressed me how the play endures. There never were such towns as Grover's Corners. Wilder got to know some New England types, and so he made this broth. He puts in some heartbreaking historical facts. The business of the sacrifice of the young men from the town, in the Civil War. It deals with these issues, and the family relationship and marriage and sacrifice for one's country and of course youthful teenage infatuation and impulsiveness. Those things are so poetically and so poignantly created in this play. I don't think it will lose its attraction to audiences.

Paul Newman I would like to know what that play would look like today, if Wilder were writing today about the average American experience in a small town. I have no idea where that would go now. It would certainly be something different.

Royal Exchange Theatre, 2017

On May 22, 2017, a suicide bomber detonated an explosive vest outside the arena in Manchester, England, during a concert by the pop star Ariana Grande. This resulted in 22 deaths and hundreds of people being injured, a terrorist attack and human tragedy. On September 14, less than four months later, Manchester's Royal Exchange Theatre began performances of its production of *Our Town*, which was programmed in response to the emotional and physical toll the bombing had taken on the city, located some 200 miles north-northeast of London.

The Royal Exchange building was constructed as the city's cotton market, the third structure to serve that function. It operated in that capacity, with its vast open hall designed to accommodate traders, from 1874 to 1968. After five years of dormancy, a theatre company began performing in the space in 1973 and officially established itself as the Royal Exchange Theatre in 1976.

The main auditorium of the theatre is rather unique, in that it is constructed in the center of the hall and resembles something built from a giant erector set or vintage Tinkertoys. While it hasn't the same lightness, the presence of this quasi-spheroid metal construction in a vintage building can easily put one in mind of the lunar-landing modules of NASA, while the contrasting styles suggest that some imagined H. G. Wells vehicle was real—and inexplicably transported to Manchester.

While the 2017 bomb did not inflict physical damage on the Royal Exchange building, the space was no stranger to violence. It was first damaged by a bomb during the Blitz in World War II, and an IRA bomb was detonated just outside the building in 1996. The concert bombing, which visited physical and psychic violence on the Manchester community, was an ugly echo of the explosions that had rocked the Royal Exchange twice in its own history.

The interior of the Royal Exchange's module is a theatre in the round, with several levels of gallery seating above the main floor. There are multiple entrances to multiple aisleways on the first level, all leading to the stage. Actors make their entrances and exits through those portals as well, from the open hall, where the theatre may set up quick-change booths, space for an orchestra, or whatever a production may require. As there are no conventional wings or a backstage, actors must cross a distance in the hall to reach the actual dressing rooms and the rest of the theatre's facilities.

Upon entering the theatre for *Our Town*, patrons encountered preset, nondescript tables and chairs in the stage area. Some audience members were invited to abandon their assigned seats for the first act of the play and take a place at the tables. During the pre-show period, they were seated with members of the cast—who didn't reveal themselves to be actors unless pointedly asked. Their true identities were only revealed to the full audience when the Stage Manager began his litany of, "In it you will see," with each actor standing as their name was called. The actors all wore modern dress throughout and spoke with their own regional accents, save for Youssef Kerkour, an actor who attended college in the US, who used an American accent. Kerkour was the only actor who didn't mingle with the audience at the start, entering only when it was time for him to declare: "This play is called *Our Town*."

During the second act, the space was arranged for a traverse staging, and in the third, the cemetery was indicated not by the sequential rows of chairs as directed in the script, but rather by chairs around the perimeter of the stage. The chairs were occupied by characters designated to be part of the scene, but also by members of the theatre's Elders Company. As Emily prepared to return to her twelfth birthday, snow began to fall, covering the stage and even falling on the seated actors. When the full return to 1899 began, a platform holding a kitchen setting descended from the flies to the ground level, its cables garlanded with sunflowers. Writing in *The Guardian*, Lyn Gardner called it, "A late coup de théâtre [that] feels entirely earned."[1]

In this chapter:
Patrick Elue, George Gibbs
Sarah Frankcom, director and artistic director
Carla Henry, Mrs. Gibbs
Kelly Hotten, Mrs. Webb
Youssef Kerkour, Stage Manager
Nicholas Khan, Dr. Gibbs
Norah Holden Lopez, Emily Webb

Sarah Frankcom Our programming decisions start with a conversation about, 'Is what we're making relevant to the city?' Or, 'What's happening in the city that we need to find and create a program to respond to?' The thing that was very particular about the arena bombing was how the city responded to it afterwards, in that some people felt it really brought the city together, which I think it did in some very big public ways. The square outside of the theatre became the focus for people to come and meet and lay flowers and be held. A lot of the street pastors used the hall of the theatre to take people and to look after people. We were, as a building, involved in that very particular aftermath of the event.

Norah Lopez Holden What ties the whole thing together, was, on the night that it happened, the help of the people around, and the feeling of absolute community in that city, which is quite hard to feel a lot of the time when you live in a big city. Everyone in the surrounding area was willing to give up their flat for anyone who was outside, who was struggling to get home. It was amazing, in such a tragedy, the wake of togetherness and communion. I think Manchester really made a name for themselves on that night. When I read the play, that's what I was thinking about. That feeling of this small town within this city, that when one person's hurt, everyone's hurt.

Kelly Hotten I had this little job in a deli round the corner and parts of the play reminded me of the sense of community you'd feel working in this place. Across the road from the deli—a family lived there who lost their son in the arena bomb. This guy [Martyn Hett] was well known, because he was quite busy on social media and was a superfan of *Coronation Street*, a very popular soap opera that's filmed in Manchester. The parents came into the deli quite regularly, and everybody in the community was just getting together to look after them. The sense of community that you feel in the play absolutely makes me think of that. Did I take it into rehearsals? Yeah. I think there was this feeling in Manchester at the time, and I think it is still here, that people were more open with each other. People were very patient and kind and honest and calm.

Sarah Frankcom The real trigger for it was spending a bit of time with our Young Company. The theatre has a very big Young Company, about 150 members of it at any given point. The location of where the bomb had happened was a place people associated with family trips and rites of passage—that there's a point where you could go there on your own to see a concert. It's a staging post in adolescence. It has maybe shattered something, shattered a kind of confidence. It felt like it had done something to create an uncertainty really, really deep down, an anxiety in young people.

Nicholas Khan In 1996, I got a fantastic job at the Royal Exchange doing *Animal Crackers*. I got the job and remember thinking, 'I'm going to miss out on playing in that theatre,' because an IRA bomb had just gone off. That glass shell had been destroyed by an IRA bomb. We performed the play in a mobile theatre. Since '96, I'd been up for lots of plays at the Exchange, but it just didn't work out. So, when *Our Town* came up, the main reason for Sarah wanting to do it was to acknowledge the bereaved community of Manchester, and to acknowledge the humanity that people have experienced through this loss. My experience of the Exchange was bookended by bombs, by death and life.

Sarah Frankcom I had not been intending to do *Our Town* in that slot at all. I was supposed to be doing another show. It became increasingly clear that we needed to find material that brought people together, that started a conversation around community and life cycle and was as interested in the beginning of life and the end of life. I actually found a way of framing the difficult things that can happen to people, that would allow audiences to maybe understand a little bit of what the year had been about.

Youssef Kerkour I knew the name *Our Town*, because there was always some production going on somewhere. But I'd never actually delved into it. In retrospect, I'm wondering if I knew a little bit. Because it's so pervasive, I would have heard a few lines here and there over the years, and definitely things pinged out during rehearsal, when I thought, 'God, I know that line. I've heard that before. People say that. I didn't know it was from this play.'

Sarah Frankcom *Our Town*'s a play that I'd never seen performed. It's a play that I've used a lot to teach playwriting because I think it's one of the greatest plays ever written. In its form, it's a radical play. It's totally radical piece of art.

Nicholas Khan I couldn't believe what I was reading. It was almost like a hymn that I'd never read, or some kind of song, a higher text that I'd never received before.

Norah Lopez Holden I told a couple of people that I was auditioning for it and was met with the response of people being, like, "Oh, god. *Our Town*, yes. Thornton Wilder. He's amazing, amazing." I pretended to know who he was. It was only as we started doing it that I started to realize the legacy that the play held, amongst writers and creatives.

Kelly Hotten I was immediately hooked. I read it in one and was on a high for about three days after reading it, this weird kind of emotional and spiritual high. As an actor, it was pure theatre and that really excited me, so going from thinking I'm done with this profession, to then reading something that reminded me what I loved about the profession.

It's so simple, yet so complicated. It kind of sneaks up on you, this one. Really simple conversations—"Am I pretty?" from Emily, her mum not really wanting to talk about it and these two women completely missing each other in that moment; the Gibbs trying to talk about their relationship, trying to talk about getting some rest, stopping and seeing each other and they just completely miss each other.

I think it made me stop in my life and make sure I wasn't missing anything. It's almost like a meditation. It made you be so present, which I think is the key to a lot of happiness.

Sarah Frankcom The thing that I really remember about reading it the first time was actually that the lens is really wide in the beginning of play. I'm thinking, 'What has this got to do with me?' Then forgetting about myself as I got drawn into the characters. The blow of the play comes like life. It completely blindsides you. Experiencing that sensation in a play, I can only say that it helped me understand a bit about what had happened to me, because it felt like life. Some of the most remarkable and unexpected difficult things happen in life. You do not expect Emily to die.

Youssef Kerkour My immediate read of it was that there must be something else going on here than what I'm just reading, because it can't just all be this mundane. You're trying to read between the lines at all times and see what it is you're actually playing. But it's really well hidden with *Our Town*.

Norah Lopez Holden My initial reaction was, 'Oh, is this a little bit twee? Is this a little bit overemotional?' Just kind of cheesy, I guess. Then I reread it again, and looked at it through Emily's perspective, and her character, and how I related to that character as a young woman growing up in this world, trying to work out who she is in relation to her family, in relation to the rest of the world, and then the importance of time and chronology.

Sarah Frankcom Because it is the Stage Manager's story, I thought about it being a woman. I think that's definitely a way of doing it, but it felt to me that the thing to do was to locate the energy of the Stage Manager as someone who is subtly on the outside, the person that facilitates, the person that you could miss, who as the play goes on becomes more and more remarkable and particular as you get to know them. Youssef's just been in a big comedy series playing a refugee. But he was brought up in Morocco, so English isn't his first language. He had a bit of his education in America. He's Muslim. He's big. He's a big guy with a very gentle presence. He feels so, so far away from Emily Webb. There was something about the juxtaposition of those two that felt really important.

Youssef Kerkour She very much felt not only that this is something she had to do, but it was the perfect time to do it. Because I'm Muslim, she felt that that was poignant, to have a Muslim actor playing the Stage Manager, which I totally agreed with.

Sarah Frankcom The starting point for me was how the play needed to come out to the audience. So, when the audience came into the theatre, there were nine or ten big trestle tables. We reseated people so that some were sat on stage and the actors were sat at the tables, but the actors were just in normally what they would wear, so you wouldn't know they were actors.

Kelly Hotten I moved here about five years ago from London and, at first, I was really shocked by how chatty people were, because, in London, if someone starts talking to you and you don't know them, you're like, 'Okay, they're a nutter.' But in Manchester, people are just up for chatting more and so it was pretty easy.

Patric Elue I remember feeling like I'm some sort of undercover agent. 'I can't let them know that I'm an actor, I have to keep my cover.' Once your name was called, George or Emily or whoever, we'd stand up and you could see their reactions, looking at us like, 'Oh, yeah, I knew it, I knew you were an actor,' and some of them being absolutely blown away and thinking 'What?!'

Sarah Frankcom The play started with the Stage Manager walking in and just starting to talk. There was no blackout. There was no sense that the play had started. It just started as a conversation with an audience. Then as he started to explain the town, different people that were playing different parts stood up.

Kelly Hotten I think people in the audience really enjoyed that because they weren't being tricked into anything, they were absolutely part of it. We were like, 'Oh, here we are telling you a story. We're just like you and this is about you.'

Youssef Kerkour The Stage Manager comes wrapped in temptation when you play the part. Temptation to make it interesting in some way. Actors don't get into this business to be a conduit for the writer. We get into it because we need to ride a wave of feeling and create a character and create something that we can feel ourselves surfing emotionally and mentally and physically. If you try and do that with the Stage Manager you torpedo the play.

Carla Henry At the beginning of the play, you were an actor standing up ready to take on the role. Any sense of knowledge of where you were going as an actor or as a character happened in that moment, you had a knowledge of the fact that you were going to die. You were standing as an actor listening to what was being said about the character you were playing. It meant that you could have that moment at the beginning, have the knowledge, but you could shut it down and then meet it at the end of the play.

Sarah Frankcom Within a family, there was someone from London, someone from Yorkshire, someone from Lancashire, someone from Newcastle. I think that place celebrates the imagination of an audience. That seems to me that's what Thornton Wilder was totally ahead of the curve on, how much of the act of imagination an audience makes collectively when they see a play. I cast people for the quality that I associated with the character, but I felt like if the play was going to have a resonance, it was quite important that we reflected the here and now of some of the voices that you would hear on the streets.

Youssef Kerkour I still maintain that you can use any old accent on stage in a play like that. It doesn't really matter. You could watch it Punjabi if you understand Punjabi, and go from thinking you're watching a play about somebody else's universe to realizing that it's about your own.

Nicholas Khan I remember Sarah talking to us about going to these Quaker meetings. I don't know if it's to do with her life and what she'd been doing, or maybe it was just something that she sought solace for. She would sit down, and she would not believe how extraordinary, how quiet they were.

Sarah Frankcom The thing for me was whether the American was really deeply in it. I don't think it was. I mean, some purists were very upset with me about it. But it felt like it worked. I felt like Thornton Wilder would've approved.

Youssef Kerkour I think we had license. I don't think people came to *Our Town* knowing much about it. So, you can change the format without people going, 'Oh, they changed the format of *Our Town*,' which a friend of mine from the States had noticed. That being said, it means you need to try and investigate the scenes, try and figure out how you can present them.

Nicholas Khan I thought it was so revolutionary for its time, the way that the Stage Manager works his way through the play. It had the philosophy of the play in essence. It was like a precursor to all that Deepak Chopra, Anthony Robbins, and *The Secret*. That sort of new linguistic programming, that recontextualizing your life.

Youssef Kerkour We discovered very early on that I had to very much set up that something was going to happen. I had to deliver it in a way that said, 'Now listen very carefully, because something's about to happen here, and it's important that you understand.' The daily life starts to seep into everybody's bones. They can feel that they're tapping into something quite universal, but they don't quite know what it is. It all leads up to the memory moment. That's the one-two punch that nobody expects.

Sarah Frankcom Audiences genuinely felt like it had been created specifically for them. Because of the marketing and the way that we talked about it, a lot of people came thinking that it was a new play.

Nicholas Khan I always kept thinking, every time I listened to Youssef's speeches, it wasn't written then. It could not have been, because it was just so modern. It spoke in so many different perspectives.

Youssef Kerkour Who is the Stage Manager? That's the $1,000,000 question. I ran the gamut. I ran the gamut from it's God to it's Thornton Wilder himself, which is kind of where I settled—the undying spirit of the creator of this piece who is meant to represent that same spirit in everybody else, the thing in all of us that has always been there since the dawn of time and creation that we all share within us. If you gave voice to that thing, what would it be?

I ran the gamut from thinking the Stage Manager really exists to the Stage Manager does not exist, he's a ghost. At some point, we had to try to get really specific. It's like *The Winter's Tale* where you're pulling your hair out trying to figure out why Leontes is doing what he's doing. The minute you say, 'Once up a time, there was a jealous king,' everything opens up. Once upon a time, a Stage Manager walks onstage and shows you something.

Patrick Elue In rehearsals, one particular day, Sarah went round and asked us, "Have you been in love before?" Or, "When was the first time you've been in love?" One by one, we answered it, and when it got to me, it was probably a bit of bravado or being a bit shy, but I was putting on the whole, "Oh, no, I've never been in love." It wasn't until getting it up on its feet and doing certain exercises—then I started to grasp how George was feeling.

Norah Lopez Holden I thought how strong and smart and intelligent, how much agency Emily had within that narrative. The first part of the process was discovering that and giving her agency and intelligence, which young women coming to watch it would identify with, as opposed to seeing this old-fashioned American Dream, small town young girl with a soda shake in her hands, which closes a lot of young women off.

Patrick Elue I think the way me and Norah played it is that we both knew, our characters both knew, what was happening without us having to actually say directly. It was almost like a telepathic understanding between the characters. We know that we both feel strongly for each other, but neither of us have got the bravery to come out and say it.

Norah Lopez Holden Imaginatively and emotionally, that third act is quite a leap. It felt difficult. It's very complex writing. As an actor, when you get complex writing, it's a blessing and a curse, because you never feel like your work's quite done, or you've not quite fulfilled it, but at the same time, it's really exciting to keep digging.

Youssef Kerkour Sarah gets every actor to write a letter to someone, to the most important person in their life, as the character, to reveal a really inner part of themselves. She folds them up and she keeps them and she reads them. I had to write two letters. I wrote one as Youssef, and I wrote one as the Stage Manager, because it was impossible to just focus on a character. As the actor playing the Stage Manager, it was full of, 'I don't know what I'm doing. I think you've made a mistake. I'm so scared.' The Stage Manager was saying, 'I know you've hired an actor to play me, and I think that's great.'

Sarah Frankcom Often directing a play is a bit like archeology. If you're painstaking in how you take it to pieces and then put it back, you can find some things that you really weren't expecting to find. This play is that. Millions of moments. I think the complexity in the relationship between the two sets of parents was a really brilliant sense of two different marriages, one of which feels more sustaining and more positive than the other.

Carla Henry There were moments in the early stages of developing Mrs. Gibbs where I looked at her and made assumptions about who she was from my life as a mother and as a wife. I made assumptions about how happy she was or how contented she was and then very quickly, there was a very clear choice that I made. I felt she was really content with being a mum that was just there for the children. I made absolute black-and-white decisions. For her to serve her family was the most important thing for her. At times, when she was peeling peas and stuff, she was thinking about the possibility of traveling, having experiences outside of the norm, but she put them to bed because she loved just loved her children dearly and deeply and she was happy to live in the dream of what her life could be like, as opposed to the reality of doing anything different.

Nicholas Khan We spent a lot of time in the first few weeks trying to find out, 'Why Doc? Why is he tired? Why does he go to Civil War? Why doesn't he acknowledge that his wife needs a trip? Why doesn't he expend that money to go?' Then, after two weeks of his doing all of that, doing brilliant work, discovering who we were as mothers and fathers, all of that pain, Sarah said, one afternoon, "You know all that work we've been doing? Put that inside you now and then let's just play it normally as we do." That's what do we do in life. We don't walk around with the pain, with the death—we do the front.

Sarah Frankcom I think with the Webbs, and certainly in what we discovered in rehearsal, it felt like there is a lot of regret in that marriage. There's also something about what the wedding is for the parents and what the wedding reveals about the parents. The wedding feels like it's a moment of crisis for Mrs. Webb. For Mrs. Gibbs, it's a moment where she has to look after her child. She has to hold George as he has his, 'I can't do it. I can't do it.'

Kelly Hotten I think her sadness and her frustration resonated with me. I'm not saying that I feel those things as strongly as she did, but I understood her anger at the way the world is towards women sometimes. My interpretation of her is that she as a young woman was often told that being nice and being pretty, being a good, sweet girl, was what she should be doing, and then to be a good mother and a good wife. Of course, we want to be a good mother and good wife, but I think she was pushed into a marriage quite young, before she really knew herself. I think she felt she never really fulfilled a lot of her potential, which is why Emily was pushed so much.

I felt there was some other darker feelings there that she didn't like. She was feeling jealous of Emily because Emily has this brilliant relationship with her dad. I think Emily has probably outgrown her mother. She's probably smarter than her mum, she's probably had a better education than her mum ever had. So, Emily can talk to her dad in a way that she isn't interested in talking to Myrtle. Myrtle wants to keep up, but in some ways can't.

Nicholas Khan I wanted more about Doc Gibbs, more scenes with him, that it erred more on his responsibility about being a doctor in a very small town. I remember wondering at one point what that must be like, being the doctor and having the responsibility of keeping Simon Stimson in tow, keeping all the people's secrets. I imagined what Simon Stimson must say to me when he comes to me. Do we open up? Is it as much therapy as being a doctor? Am I having those conversations with him?

Patrick Elue There was one exercise where you just speak aloud your subtext or what you're thinking. I remember that as being interesting and quite funny, because you didn't expect to hear some of the things you did from other people and their subtext. Also, the fact that, after the exercise is finished, I still continued and I think someone had to stop me and go, "Patrick, it's over." I remember there was one where we had to hug people, and then eventually everyone else left the circle and it was just me and Norah, and then we embraced and hugged. That, for some reason, became quite emotional. I think it was probably the fact that we didn't hug each other throughout that exercise.

Nicholas Khan Sarah asked us to write a letter to one of the other characters. I wrote one to Patrick, who was my son, saying it will be all right when he's older, I hope you're all right, something like that. My other one was simply saying to Simon Stimson, I'm available to you to talk, because of him hanging himself and him being the being the alter ego of Thornton. You had that idea of homosexuality in that sort of community being so taboo. I remember Doc Gibbs saying to his wife that we offer a hand to him, but even he couldn't help him that much.

Youssef Kerkour A lot of the movement rehearsals were separate to my rehearsals. We tried to incorporate the Stage Manager at one point, into the movement pieces, into explorations of relationships between people. I think we did that for about a week before realizing that it doesn't work. You can't have a Stage Manager that is part of the company. It has to be a consciousness that is removed from the show.

Norah Lopez Holden What really works is that he is an absolute outsider. I found that really useful in the third act when Emily directly talks to the narrator, this omnipotent presence who isn't connected, isn't in the town, but knows everything about it, which feels quite haunting. With the accent difference, that happened immediately. Also, there was a wisdom. The difference in me and Youssef's size and voice and accents was really helpful for that—to remind the audience that they're watching a play. It's a nice, cheeky little reminder, this huge narrator.

Youssef Kerkour It's wrapped in temptation, this part. The temptation there is to feel along with Emily. I must admit, I hold my hand up to say there are some performances when I just had to go there, because as an actor that's what you want. We want to feel those great big waves of varying emotion and ride them. To keep an arm's distance from that, to let Emily do all that feeling and to just be there as this voice, is very, very hard. You have to just keep doing the same thing you were doing all along and somehow find a way of giving the Stage Manager a bit of an arc. But the power is there being no obvious change.

Carla Henry I think that is the only play where I've died and then experienced living after death. I think what was really beautiful about *Our Town* was that you got to create what that could potentially be like, that it was just a continuing to exist and it wasn't a massive great big deal. I loved playing her dead, welcoming somebody into another world. I think that that's what I take away from *Our Town*, the idea that we can welcome people into something that is very unfamiliar to them. We have the ability to make them settle in. They belong even after something that's been a traumatic transition. Just by trying to make them feel comfortable, you can help them exist.

*   *   *

Sarah Frankcom There was an amazing thing with the hymn, "The Ties that Bind," which made me go, "Oh, my god." I did research where that had come from. It was written by a minister for his church in the North Country of England. He had been the minister for a community in the north of England, quite a rural community, and he'd been approached to have a much bigger ministerial job in London. So, his family packed up and they were about to go and he was saying goodbye to all his parishioners on the steps of his chapel. And his wife knelt down and said, "We can't go. Our ministry's here. This is the place. This is where we're supposed to be. This is where God wants you to be." They didn't go and he wrote the hymn for that town. I thought, 'Where the bloody hell was this Wainsgate Baptist Church?'

Out of my kitchen window, I could see a chapel. It's about two, three minutes down the hill. I live in a small Yorkshire town called Hebden Bridge—and it's where the hymn was written, at the end of my road. The event happened on the steps of the chapel that I walk past almost every day. That hymn went from there all the way to America to become a massively popular hymn. It felt like it was all coming back to where it had started. That's a very Thornton Wilder thing.

I felt a really big thing about the hymn, but I also felt how we sing and collective singing. With the aftermath of the arena, there'd been this real need for people to sing. In the square outside, there'd been an amazing thing, where everybody had sung the song by Oasis called, "Don't Look Back in Anger." Someone just started to sing it and it infected the whole of the square, about 10,000 people were singing it by the end. It was amazing. That sense that sometimes you can tell the story of a community through singing the same song but in different places, at different events. I felt that hymn, and the relationship of the choirmaster to that hymn and what the choirmaster is putting into that hymn that he can't express, is in everything.

*   *   *

Sarah Frankcom It's the only show that I've made where genuinely I think there was a real synergy between the professional actors and the young people and with the Elders, in that they came to pretty much all of the rehearsals. We didn't slot them in, we created a process. The really lovely thing was that they all warmed up together. The Young Company and the Elders are quite used to making work with each other, but this was the first time that they'd worked together on something in the main house. Normally, they share their intergenerational work in the studio. There were some really, really brilliant friendships from a 16- or 17-year-old to someone that's 88.

Norah Lopez Holden It's very evocative in the room, imaginatively and emotionally, when you've got such an age gap. Very often as an actor, you have to endow an actor as being older or younger, so it's quite nice to have that actual lived experience. It changed the atmosphere in the room a lot to have the Elders Company in, because not only in number, but in approach, it meant that it was more communal. As an actor, you can get so inward-facing of your own process. Having to expand that to accommodate everyone is kind of what the play's about.

Carla Henry I remember in the rehearsal room crying my eyes out, just watching this woman walk across the space. I think of the impact of having the Elders Company, having the weight of the Elders Company, the actors from the Elders Company's age. Having not just one person, but many of them in that space. It just added a wealth of education, a kind of life, literally years. Presenting the years that they'd lived and the life that they carried with them in their bodies. It makes such a massive impact for me because it was a very real thing.

Sarah Frankcom We had chairs and tables for the first act. The second act, we went on to a traverse and just used the chairs. Then the third act, those chairs went into a circle. And then as the audience came in, you were aware that this thing was happening, where [the company, including the Elders] would arrive at the entrance to the circle of chairs, with just one place to come into it. They would arrive holding their shoes. They would come in and then choose to sit somewhere. I just wanted them to be themselves. The great thing was that they very simply just watched what happened. And then, they went to sleep. There's a really, really amazing thing of watching an older person, someone in their seventies, get down and lie on the floor and go to sleep. They laid their shoes by their side, they took their jewelry off, they undid their belts and then just went to sleep.

Carla Henry I loved playing Mrs. Gibbs in the afterlife. I remember Sarah giving me a note that I told her off about, which was, "Carla Henry, you're being too ghostly in the graveyard scene." And I said, "Well I am a ghost, what do you want me to do?" I remember making a choice about Mrs. Gibbs trying to cause Emily to rest and breathe out, to believe that this is a time that the quicker that she just rests and settles, it would be the easier, the transition from death to life, trying to get her to understand that she can't run away from it. Getting her to take her place in that circle. That was a physical thing within the production, to take her shoes off and getting her to be rooted.

Sarah Frankcom The play elicits massive conversations about life. Having both ends of the spectrum so intrinsically part of what we were doing every day meant that actually that the older people were really up for talking about death. We created a long improvisation where they passed through, they passed over. They actually enacted their own moment of death. It was done very simply, but that's a big thing to do with older people. They still talk about it as being the best thing that they've done. Lying down and just going to sleep and feeling the ground was what a lot of them felt they'd like their last moment to be. I had to put it in the show.

Youssef Kerkour All of a sudden, I grabbed Emily, and I moved her out of the way. I told her to look up, and we both looked up, which makes the audience look up. The platform from the ceiling that had been there the whole time starts descending with this beautiful music, and a top light that shone down, and then the snow starting all around it. It was this beautiful, perfect birthday breakfast scene on this huge platform big enough for five actors that had been suspended from the air, the only light being a top light, and snow falling through the light. These gasps were going up all over the place. It's what Emily was experiencing. Everybody had that moment. It was so out of place in the best way possible. I stood on the outside holding Emily, then I let her go, and she went into it.

Patrick Elue After the funeral, George came back, and instead of lying down, he just went to his knees. When I think about men or when I think about guys crying, it tends to be a quiet grief. That's not to say, obviously, men don't cry out loud and sob loudly. For the character of George, because of how expressive he is and gregarious and open, I felt like for Emily, it was more of an internal grief.

Norah Lopez Holden In the preset at the beginning, we used to talk to audience members. I remember having a couple at our table. We had a chance to speak to each other and get to know each other, and I was asking them about who they were, why they were here, did they come to the Royal Exchange often. I remember the husband saying, "Well, actually we're from Leeds, and we've come here because my wife is getting treatment. She's got terminal cancer, and one of the hospitals nearby is offering some kind of treatment to her, and we saw this programmed, and while we're here, we wanted to come and watch it." My heart fell, because I knew what they were about to sit through. I remember feeling really anxious. Then the play started, so I got distracted and couldn't really think about it. But then I clocked the same couple at the end. I just saw him seize her hand, and they were both crying.

Carla Henry What's wonderful and what was brilliant about having *Our Town* in that space, in the round, is obviously the audience can see each other. It's our town, it's our space, you can't hide in that space. Every part of you can be seen in that space. You've got people looking at you, you've got energies coming from the back, you know you're being watched, but equally the audience can watch each other, so the experience is overwhelming. You can see the audience watching each other reacting. You sat next to audience members and they might be crying, or they might be physically closed because they don't want to feel anything. It kept everything really fresh and alive and very, very real.

Sarah Frankcom When people come on and are themselves, and they stand and accept the audience's thanks, that's really powerful. If you've had the beginning of the play that we'd had, that was such a powerful moment because it's going, okay, we've done that, and you've identified it and it's triggered things for you. But actually, we're back in the moment—I'm here and you're there, and we've got a world that we're going out into. Wilder knows that moment, he knows what that moment at the end of the play means when actors from that play stand in front of an audience and people clap.

Nicholas Khan Sarah always had the strength of this story that you could say it in a McDonald's, you could say it on the train, you could tell that story in the train. If you had a big cupboard, you could tell that story in a cupboard and everyone would listen.

Youssef Kerkour I had the beard at the time. I looked like the stereotype of a terrorist. I think that's what we were hoping. That's certainly what I was hoping for, that there would be an unconscious recognition when I walked onstage that this is what the stereotype looks like. I felt, as I always feel, if they open up the program and they see, "Youssef Kerkour," and a big, bearded dude walks out, that there is an immediate subconscious hit that you can then subvert and play against.

I think if you're going to respond to a tragedy like what happened in Manchester, the best way of doing it is to get people to just think about their life in a new way, and that's what the play does anyway. Tragedy or no tragedy, people would have responded emotionally to it, because it makes you just see your life. I think with the bombing in the background, in the periphery, the result was magnified a little bit.

Sarah Frankcom There was a good period of time where people were more connected, the gap between people had lessened. So, I think the sense of the care that we take with each other, and the way that we need to meet each other felt like it was in a place that was very receptive. The audience wanting to process and experience with each other, because something had happened which was hard to understand.

Norah Lopez Holden From Day One it was always very practical, to try and get the best possible production out of it. We didn't want to gratuitously use it as a way of being like, 'Oh, and it's like the bombing,' because that's not what it felt like at all. If anything, it's only hearing audience reactions that made me realize that, and brought back home the personal bit.

Sarah Frankcom It's opened the door wider for what's possible in our theatre— what is a piece of theatre, how a piece of theatre can reach out, and how a piece of theatre can hold.

Kelly Hotten I found out I was pregnant three days into rehearsals. Nobody knew that. Sarah knew it and the actress playing Mrs. Gibbs knew it and eventually the actress playing Mrs. Soames knew it. I think the fact that I was pregnant, I couldn't deny doing a play like this whilst there was life growing inside me, everything just resonated enormously with me.

Sarah Frankcom It set a bar for how bold you can be with plays that you think have to be done in a certain way. And actually, I don't think we did anything that Thornton Wilder would've been disproving of. But we certainly just made a production that was absolutely for this theatre at the time that we did it with the people that we had. The sign for me of a great play is when the play feels like it was absolutely written for us. That's what it felt like. It felt like he'd written it for us. In fact, we have people in the young company who didn't realize and someone said, "When's Thornton Wilder coming?"

Montgomery County Emergency Services, 2014

Mental health workers think that we must have all the answers all the time. We have to look strong, self-assured, and competent in the face of diseases that can confound us. I had to convince these people that it was okay to be intimidated by the process of putting on a play, and that being vulnerable, or innocent, or earnest was what would make this venture succeed.[1]

from an essay by Gabriel Nathan

The Norristown State Hospital in Pennsylvania opened in 1880, some 20 miles northeast of Philadelphia, dedicated to the treatment of mental health patients. Designed in a campus style, its grounds covered 225 rural acres. At peak capacity in the 1930s, it housed slightly more than 3,000 patients. However, as mental health treatment evolved and public health policies changed, the patient population of the hospital decreased. The facility began leasing buildings to various independent organizations.

One such tenant is Montgomery County Emergency Services (MCES), a not-for-profit emergency mental health care facility founded in 1974, which serves patients facing immediate crises, functioning as both a triage center and inpatient hospital. It also provides support and guidance to criminal justice organizations in matters of mental health.

In December 2014, members of the staff of MCES mounted a two-night production of *Our Town*, emerging out of morale-boosting initiatives spearheaded by the organization's leadership at that time. While some might leap to the assumption that the production cast MCES patients or was performed for them, that was not the case. The production's cast and crew were drawn from the facility's professional staff of some 250 and the performances were offered to the general public. Proceeds from ticket sales were designated for the Patient Fund, which provided clothes and basic necessitates for the often indigent individuals that MCES serves.

Chris Mamrol and Erin Keeley in the 2014 Montgomery County Emergency Services production of *Our Town*, directed by Gabriel Nathan. Photo by Julie Peticca.

The staff impresario was Gabriel Nathan, a theatre major who worked at the facility and drew upon his theatre training to act as producer, director, and lead actor for the production. While a handful of cast members had some minimal background in school and community theatre, the company was comprised largely of complete novices, hand-picked by Nathan for qualities he saw in them as their colleague, rather than by audition. The production was sufficiently novel that it yielded a feature story in *The Philadelphia Inquirer*.

The hospital campus offered one unexpected asset to the production: a full-scale auditorium with a stage, constructed at a time when the campus was more fully occupied. While little used and slightly antiquated, the auditorium was not derelict, having been used occasionally over the years for meetings and conferences. It was located only a few hundred yards from the building in which MCES operated and offered an unexpectedly well-appointed home to the production.

Our Town was the first play staged by the staff of MCES and there has not been any production since.

In this chapter:
John Fulford, Howie Newsome
Christa Godillot, Mrs. Gibbs
Michael Hagerty, Dr. Gibbs

Erin Keeley, Emily Webb
Dr. Anthony Mateo, staff psychologist
Gabriel Nathan, Stage Manager, also producer and director
Steve Roddy, Simon Stimson
Cindy Syfert, Mrs. Soames

Gabriel Nathan MCES was founded in 1974 after two suicides at the county correctional facility. It was decided we needed a facility where people experiencing an acute psychiatric emergency can either go themselves or be involuntarily sent so that they can be evaluated, stabilized and discharged. It's a short-stay facility. The average length of stay is five to nine days.

This is a locked inpatient crisis psychiatric hospital. We've dealt with some very seriously mentally ill people. There were acts of violence on the unit, pretty much daily. As a consequence, the bonds that formed with the staff were very strong because we had to be together to be able to do what we had to do every day and go home safe. That didn't work all the time. But that's the nature of the work: individuals who were struggling with suicidality, had an inability to care for themselves due to their mental illness, people with co-occurring substance abuse disorders.

Anthony Mateo I think as a hospital we were really in a stuck place, not really feeling a lot of camaraderie. There was an element of us versus them, administration versus the staff that were providing care for our patients, and I think a lot of mistrust among departments. This was a presentation, or an experience, that brought many departments together that at times frankly were at odds—not through any fault of their own, but really an environment that was created by our leaders.

Erin Keeley It's a stressful environment, and we deal with people at their worst. It's a difficult job sometimes and we need to be able to decompress and bring us all together, where it's not like the psych techs against the nurses against the social workers time.

Gabriel Nathan I had been asked by our medical director at the time, Dr. Rocio Nell, to run a board and staff retreat. I think that the theme was team building. I did a variety of different activities. We had 60 or 70 staff members and board members up in the boardroom. I wrapped up different people in Saran Wrap and we had a contest to see who could get to the other end of the room without speaking, and different groups of people assembling small Lego projects together while only one person could leave the room and look at the instructions. Stuff like that.

Anthony Mateo It was something that I know a lot of us talked about. I think the hospital really tried. On some level, there seemed to be a recognition of people are really unhappy and mistrusting. I don't know that the big players knew the full extent of what was happening at the hospital.

Gabriel Nathan It was getting towards the end of the night. I was looking out at all of these people, nurses, psych techs, therapists, social workers, board members, psychiatrists. Some people had worked there for over 30 years, really in the trenches of mental health. Some were on their third month, very new hires. I was somewhere kind of in the middle—I had four years in at that time. I was really struck by how we go through our day. MCES is 24/7, 365. There's three shifts of people. It's a machine that has to keep going. In order for it to do that, while we are working with some of the most seriously mentally ill people in the county, we don't have time to look at one another.

In that boardroom, I told the story of Act III. I told the story of Emily going back to her birthday as a young girl, and her plea to her mother, "Mama, just look at me for one minute as though you really saw me." I asked the staff to stand and look at each other. A couple people kind of joked around like, 'Ah, is this our kumbaya moment?' I said, "Just shut up and do it."

They rose and it was quiet in a place that is rarely quiet. People looked at each other, people who have gone through tremendously difficult things in their personal lives and in their professional lives. The tears started rolling out of people's eyes. Staff members gripped onto each other's hands. You saw lips curling down. It just took my breath away. I said, "Okay, you can sit down now. So, all that was going on and we never noticed."

That was the genesis of *Our Town* beginning at MCES. I didn't realize that night that that's what was going to happen. But the next day, Dr. Nell called me into her office. I thought I was in trouble. I sat down and she said, "Last night was so beautiful. What are you going to do as a follow-up?" I had not planned a follow-up. I just looked at her and said, "I would like to do *Our Town* with the staff." And she said, "Wonderful. Go and do that."

The dreaming started. I would sit at home and read the play. I heard voices. I heard Steve Roddy, who is a nurse at the hospital, he worked night shift, I heard him when I would read Simon Stimson's lines. I heard Naomi Finkle who was the nurse manager as Mrs. Webb, a thin, crisp, serious woman. People started coming into my brain.

Mike Hagerty I thought it was pretty neat. I didn't like all the sadness in it, but it really hit home. I was thinking that the most important thing are other people in our lives, and it blew my mind. It drove it home to me right when I finished reading the script.

Anthony Mateo Initially, my thought was, this is not going to happen. At that point, as a guy who was working full-time at the hospital, part-time in an outpatient practice, having two kids—I couldn't wrap my head around, 'How are they doing this?' I think my initial reaction and how I went about it with Gabe was, I just don't have the time. I'm someone that typically overspends myself, so I was not wanting to put myself in that position.

Christa Godillot I said yes thinking it would never happen. I just didn't foresee that it was possible, especially the cast of characters he had assembled. That's how it started.

Cindy Syfert In December of 2011, I had lost my partner to cancer. It was a horrible thing for me. I was sort of frozen for a long time. I got up, went to work, came home, and sat in my chair trying to figure out what I should do. Was there more for me in this life? Is it worth living? Not really actively thinking about killing myself, but what am I doing here? When this came along, it was a good two years that I was like that. I'd work, I'd put on my mask. I'm fine, I'm getting through my day, and come home and just stare at the walls. By the time this play came around I thought, 'This is something I need to do. I need to get involved with people again.'

Gabriel Nathan I was very ruthless in terms of how I approached people. I knew there were certain approaches that would work better with some staff members than others. I really tried to work my angles to get people to say yes. It's so funny. These people did dangerous and kind of unthinkable things every day, and yet the idea of this play was maybe the most dangerous thing they had been asked to do since they started working there, because it was new. I think there were only three people in the show who had ever been on stage before. So, the first step was approaching people and sometimes gently twisting some arms.

Erin Keeley I got the email from Gabe and I immediately knew that I wanted to do it because I've always had an interest in theatre. I was in a play in high school, and I really enjoyed it. I jumped right in. It sounded like a fun idea.

Cindy Syfert Gabe didn't drag me. In fact, I approached him. He sent out some email asking if people were interested, and I went, "Yeah, me, me, me." Not that I was ever any good, but I had a history of really enjoying being on stage in college.

Steve Roddy Gabe approached me: "Would you be interested in being in the play?" I let him know that this was actually a bucket list event for me. I had always wanted to act in live theatre. Gabe told me that he somehow saw me being Simon Stimson. I was fascinated with that. To me, he's the pariah. The play, when it starts out, it's like a Norman Rockwell painting and Stimson doesn't fit in there.

Cindy Syfert The kind of job that I have at work, I'm in charge of security at the window and making sure that patients don't get stuff that's contraband or something that they can use to hurt somebody else. I'm constantly saying no to people, and consequently people seem to always get pissed off at me.

John Fulford I didn't read the play. I only read my lines. I have a learning disability. I probably read three books in my entire life. I learn everything through consistent pattern. I begin to recognize things within things.

Mike Hagerty It really hit home because I was thinking, 'You know what? We live amongst all these people that matter to us and you're going to wake up one day and they're going to be gone. You're going to wonder how you spent that time and why you didn't spend more time concentrating on the people and less time concentrating on just getting through life, just making a living.'

Gabriel Nathan Our first rehearsal was August 25, 2014. It was sweltering and there was no air conditioning in the theatre. I was watching these poor people, who had agreed to do this crazy thing, and sweat was just dripping off them onto the scripts. I felt so terrible.

Cindy Syfert I hadn't really made friends at work. I've been there for 25 years now. I knew all these people, and we were friendly at work and always having each other's back, of course, if there was a dangerous situation, but I was very uncomfortable around this group because I didn't feel like I knew anybody.

Erin Keeley I remember it was August, and it was stifling hot. We're all sweating, fanning ourselves with our scripts and Gabe's explaining what the play is about. He was just so thankful that we all wanted to be there. You could tell everybody was excited about it. I guess I felt a sense of community. I felt closer to my co-workers even on that first day.

Christa Godillot I was a foster child and my foster mother worked at MCES as a nurse. I've known most of those people since I was 14 years old. I went back to work as a tech from age 19 to 24, then I raised children, and then I went back as a nurse. They're like my family. I had grown up in that community. I was a child in the '70s when the state hospital changed, when the mental health laws changed and people were released from the state hospitals, and they literally took up rooms in the boarding homes that were across the street from my apartment. A lot of those people raised me in some sense. They made sure I had food, or they took me to the Woolworth's to buy me a hot dog when they got their check. They're my people. Not just the staff members, but the patients.

Erin Keeley At the time that I worked there, when the play was going on, I think I had been there for six years. I knew everybody in the play, but a lot of them I didn't work with directly. Naomi, who played Mrs. Webb, was my supervisor. It was nice to be outside of work with people who had authority over you who were just as clueless about what they were doing as the rest us.

Gabriel Nathan Our original Joe Stoddard after a couple rehearsals was like, "I can't do this. I'm doing too many things. I'm sorry." So he had to be replaced. Our original Constable Warren hit a deer on his motorcycle and had to be helicoptered to the hospital in October. I visited him at the hospital, and he kept saying, "I'm coming back, I'm coming back." By November, it was clear that he was not and I had run out of time to replace him, so I just ended up doing Constable Warren's stuff.

Christa Godillot I was working Saturday, Sunday, and Monday 12-hour shifts. If I remember correctly our rehearsals were Monday night and Wednesday night. Most of the time I would be running from the most acute unit there. I would've been working for 12 hours three days in a row, running late to rehearsal, which was on the same grounds, but I was either finishing up documentation or medicating someone's emergency. It was, pardon the expression, a shit show. So, you're going from that to, 'Okay, now I need to decompress in less than five minutes, and reroute all of this anxiety and adrenaline.' Just bottle it up until I'm done with two and a half hours or however long that rehearsal was. Most of the time in the back of my mind: I'm a mother of three, I had laundry, I probably had shit that they hadn't done for three days piled up waiting for me. It was really the last place I wanted to be initially.

Gabriel Nathan I was in the little room next to the chart room looking at the chart of a patient who had been admitted overnight, and in the actual chart room, I could hear two staff members going over their lines. I heard, "Potato weather, for sure," and it made me so happy. I was almost giggling in the next room.

Mike Hagerty I thought Dr. Gibbs was a little bit of a jerk. His wife's one desire is to go to Europe. He's taking the reins and deciding that a Gettysburg trip is good enough. A simple guy that didn't want too much complication or fanciness in his life. He's pursuing his dreams, not letting his wife pursue hers, but loved her all the same.

Gabriel Nathan Someone would say something in group and it would be either a close approximation to a line from the show or they would quote the show. The staff members in the room who were in the play would just light up. Or walking down the hallway whistling, "Blessed Be the Ties that Bind," and passing a staff member who would smile. It was like being in a little club.

Steve Roddy There's these long corridors to the building and on the second floor, it's where all the offices are. I would often take my breaks up there, a lot of people do, but I would pace the hallways to get my exercise. I'd be repeating my lines. I'm coming round the corner and I'm doing my ranting, when the on-call doctor, who was up there, gave me a look. I said, "I'm practicing for a play." I remember him looking shocked, like whether I was psychotic and talking to myself. But I was getting into character.

Erin Keeley We all needed something to focus on. There'd be times where people that work together would be outside of work, and we would complain about work the whole time. When we were working on *Our Town*, we didn't do that as much. We were focused and it was a way to decompress and come together. It was a relief to be able to be there in that capacity and not so serious. What we do was hard and it was better to work as a team, as a community, together, on something that wasn't as hard. It was hard, but it wasn't as hard.

Steve Roddy I remember Gabe wanted me to construct a history of Simon Stimson, a history that I could try to live. The biography that I created for him was that his dream was to be a concert pianist and that he ended up, while he was at the conservatory, whether Boston or New York, he met a girl that was from Grover's Corners, impregnated her and ended up back there. Ended up being the choirmaster. I guess he felt a failure, in his ambitions to be something more than he was, something that I think was the source of his drinking. Often, addiction can fuel one's failure to manifest or to realize your potential.

Erin Keeley It was an emotional time in my life at that point, where I felt like I wasn't where I was supposed to be and I missed out on things. I was going through a tough personal situation and it was easy for me to get there emotionally.

Cindy Syfert I thought Mrs. Soames had a lot more character than evidently some other people thought she had. I liked her. Now, this was totally my interpretation of her few little soliloquies during the wedding. In my opinion, she was a kick-ass little lady who said what she wanted to say and didn't really worry about this small-town business of who was going to say what about who.

Christa Godillot Mrs. Gibbs—she just held the fort down. She knew her role in life as a woman, as a mother, as a wife, as a neighbor. She did it well.

Erin Keeley I do remember thinking, 'Emily is not like me,' because she did have that 'I'm so good at school,' and 'I'm so good at everything and I can remember everything.' Though she always needed reassurance. 'Don't you think I'm smart?' or 'Don't you think I'm pretty?' So, there was a similarity. Emily, when she was alive, was like everybody else in the play, just completely oblivious. Then when she was dead, that was where I really liked her, because she gained an appreciation for all the things that she had and had lost.

John Fulford I had a job to do. That's how I approached it. [Howie] reminded me of this man I used to know as a kid in Oklahoma, a farmer who used to deliver milk to my house. I visualized him. This very quiet man. I recall him being my size, which is about six foot three, 250 pounds.

Mike Hagerty Having to hug people at the funeral—and my boss—was very uncomfortable. My director's supervisor was there and she was playing the editor's wife, and it was not the easiest thing to do. It felt like you were crossing boundaries. She felt the same way, you could tell. Gabe was saying, "Do what you have to do, because it's not real. You're presenting what these other people are living." I don't recall emotionally how we got through it or how we got beyond it, but it came off without a hitch.

Erin Keeley I guess I could tell that a lot of people felt the same way that I did. That insecurity. 'Am I actually doing this? Do I look like I'm acting or am I playing this part well?' I can't remember anybody voicing their struggles, because it was such a relaxed atmosphere the whole time we were rehearsing.

Steve Roddy My character commits suicide and of course I deal frequently with suicidal patients. He's an alcoholic and many of them often have addiction histories as well, so many a time I'll be working with these patients and trying to be empathetic and trying to understand them. Having been exposed to it enough, it was a chance to maybe try to act out the role that so many of the people I work with actually live, their realities.

Gabriel Nathan Because some of the staff members were really very anxious about doing a play, some of them used alcohol to cope with the fact that they were going to a rehearsal and doing this uncomfortable thing, after working at a very stressful job for eight or twelve hours. That really pissed me off. I was not happy to know that that was going on. Staff members knew that I disapproved and they made attempts to hide it.

Christa Godillot We got in trouble for bringing wine. We're like irreverent children. Just mocking one another, good natured. When you take the situation where literally someone's throwing feces on you five minutes ago, and then you walk in, and you're getting chastised for being late. 'Well, I needed to wipe the shit off of myself. I'm so sorry.' It usually takes the full ride home with very loud music and sometimes screaming to decompress.

Gabriel Nathan It being a state hospital campus, there's no alcohol allowed anywhere on the campus anyway. We were breaking a Pennsylvania state rule or law. I had addressed it and it was happening anyway. I was upset about that. But I had decided to let it go, because if that's what people felt they needed to do, I knew I couldn't stop it.

Christa Godillot I remember I had dropped a couple lines, probably more than a couple, and I remember Gabe saying my line for me, and Cate who was working with him saying a couple of my lines, and I felt shame, like I had let everyone down, including myself. I was embarrassed. I was really humiliated, and I couldn't get my thoughts together, because then my thoughts were racing. I was anxious, my face turned red, and then I started crying. I couldn't stop crying, and I felt like I couldn't breathe. It was a full-on panic attack.

It was either the next day, or later that week, Gabe called me and he's like, "Whoa, we can't ever have that happen again. You can just have your script with you. We'll work it in somehow. I don't ever want to see that again." Which was even more embarrassing because I pride myself on being a smart girl. I'm a resilient girl. That forced me out of half-assing it. It forced me to really invest something of myself.

Erin Keeley Gabe had a lot of moments of evident stress. I think he got frustrated sometimes when the group of us would be too chatty with each other and too jokey. He wanted a little bit more focus and who could blame him because he was taking it very seriously, as I think we all were.

Gabriel Nathan I remember one rehearsal in particular where we were getting pretty close to the production day, and it was the scene actually where George goes to visit with Emily on the wedding day, and they won't let him see her. People were fucking lines up just left and right. The scene could not proceed more than 20 or 30 seconds before someone was calling line or flubbing something. I remember saying, "Guys, what the fuck? Get your shit together. We're getting right down to it." The guy playing George Gibbs looked at me and he said, "Who do you think you are? You can't talk to us like that."

Steve Roddy I think nerves were a little frayed at that point. We had just been doing this over and over. The tediousness of the repetition. I think it was our nerves too. We wanted to do well. We were making similar errors and thinking, 'Are we ever going to get this right?' But Gabe did sort of a heart to heart, half-time talk. 'Come on, folks, let's try to regroup.' You really had to dig deep and say, 'All right, we can do this, we just have to recommit and it's going to happen and it'll be over soon enough.'

Gabriel Nathan It was a really interesting moment, because I stopped short. 'Who *do* I think I am talking to them like that?' I'm the director, however I'm also their co-worker. It really stopped me right in my tracks. I was struggling with conveying my disappointment and frustration in a political way. I guess I had let my political mask fall.

Steve Roddy My background was athletic. I understood the concept of repetition and practice makes perfect. I know when a team's working hard. Not wanting to be weak link, I don't want to be the guy to cause the team to lose or the play to be a failure. It was like getting ready for the big game. But it wasn't competition and we weren't trying to beat somebody. We're trying to put a play on and do it to the best of our ability. I had been there before. Working very hard in with a common goal with a lot of individuals.

Cindy Syfert I was not able to go through that graveyard scene once without crying. I was thinking about my partner. He was a guy who had some real desires in his life and never was able to meet any of them because he was so busy trying to meet his desires, if that makes any sense, and who didn't see what was around him. He was unaware of how people really felt about him and how much he was loved, and always trying desperately to be loved, not realizing that there was somebody right there that desperately loved him. It brought all of that back to me.

Mike Hagerty My mother was going through a tough time, she was going into assisted living, and my brother and I were pretty much sole caregivers at that point. Just about everybody—friends, family, anybody—you normally connect with in life, you appreciate them, you're there with them doing what you have to do, but you just don't have the time to really appreciate who they are and what they've contributed to your life. The play itself just opened my eyes a little bit about that, because before long it's gone, and it's over, and what have you got? If it's just a bunch of stuff, you've wasted your life.

Anthony Mateo I was noticing a lot of anxiety around the performance. Last minute jitters, which was also a component of why I didn't participate. There was definitely a part of me that was envious of the folks that were part of the production. 'God, I wish I could be a part of that.' But knowing myself, and knowing the anxiety that I bring to the table about performing, about needing to excel, I thought that the anxiety would outweigh any of the positives that I would experience.

John Fulford I had a bit of a panic attack. At intermission, I needed somebody to yell at me, somebody to slap my face. I needed somebody to get me past it. I've never had a level of anxiety like that before. I have been in very, very bad situations, but I had no anxiety, no issues, no fear to any great extent. I understood at that time what it meant to be slapped in the face and somebody could have done that for me. You see it in shows, somebody's slapped in the face when they get hysterical and they calm down immediately. I see how that worked. Or could work. At that time. Because I was losing it. Steve Roddy helped me with that.

Steve Roddy I can only compare it to the athletic experiences when I played the different sports that I have, football, baseball, basketball. When the action is happening, you don't notice the crowd. You don't. You can almost tune it out. It's almost as if they're not there. You're doing something that you've been practicing and practicing and practicing and I remember thinking how with the lighting, it's hard to see out into the audience. I remember being comforted by that.

Gabriel Nathan I think that one of the discoveries, and I know this because of things that staff members have told me afterward, was that people understood that they could create art. I think that that's not something that a lot of the people who were in this production knew about themselves and that's a pretty significant discovery. That was very validating. Day in and day out, the staff of MCES was consumed with working with a unit full of Simon Stimsons. That's hard. I think what this play exposed them to is that there is so much more than that.

Cindy Syfert For us who work at least in the crisis department, it's easy for us to be less than therapeutic to people who have drug problems and alcohol problems and forget that there may also be something else going on. People who have drug problems and alcohol problems maybe don't have a mental illness, but damn it, they do still end up killing themselves out of desperation. That was a heavy-duty reminder for me when I found out Simon killed himself.

Gabriel Nathan It said twice in the play in regard to Simon Stimson: "I don't know how that's goin' to end." There's not a day on the unit where you don't see a name on the census in the morning, or walk up to a patient, or walk past a patient in the hallway, or look at someone in group or in the cafeteria eating their lunch with a plastic fork and a spoon because of course they can't have a plastic knife, and think to yourself, 'I don't know how that's going to end.'

Anthony Mateo When I saw the play, I immediately saw how everyone was active and invested and vulnerable. I was really moved. Even talking about it now, it brings back that sensation of just awe.

Gabriel Nathan Sadly, when you look at some staff members, we are totally not okay. That constant exposure to trauma and stress – people not making the money that they should. They're working two jobs and double shifts. That adds up and sometimes that doesn't end well. "Well, the best we can do is leave it alone" flies in the face of everything that we know about suicide prevention. Thornton Wilder understood this, because to me that's the commentary that he's making, it's the biggest wrong you can commit against your fellow man, to turn away and just go, 'No, that'll be whatever it is. Not my problem.' It's all of our problem.

Erin Keeley It made me try, in my counseling style, to give patients that moment of thinking of the bigger picture, not just this moment that they're in distress, or this moment that they're in court, or having a hard time, or not having a place to live.

Gabriel Nathan I think that it was incredibly cathartic. I feel that there is so much that these people hold inside that they don't get to let out. To be able to do that through characters was very therapeutic. To know that they could rely on each other in this totally unique and different way than they do at work was also healing.

Mike Hagerty It totally changed my thinking on how I approached people in general, including patients, including other staff members, family. It really had an impact. Its timeliness with my mom's going downhill and everything. I think it sort of drove a message home, pretty quick. It felt like it was a point where I recognized afterwards that there was more to this than just getting through.

Anthony Mateo Just talking about the pain of living, and comparing that to the potential nothing of no longer existing. I'd rather experience this pain, because it's a reminder of, 'I'm alive.' It really reinforced this idea of living, and acknowledging that pain is a really big piece of living, a really big piece of evolving and transforming into something bigger and better. Then again, it was nice to see my friends. I instantly saw everyone that participated in the production in a very different way, in a much more dynamic way. I walked away with a really deep understanding of, 'God, it's so important to be in the moment.'

There were two moments that after the performance I can recall as if they happened yesterday. One was seeing Gabe and telling him, "I have such love in my heart for you." Just feeling gratitude. Then another: one of our nurses, John, someone that I never imagined would participate in something like this. Kind of sarcastic. Someone that I didn't know very well, and didn't see completely. Seeing him afterwards and saying, "You were amazing."

Gabriel Nathan Dr. Mateo, who saw the show with another psychologist, hugged me and he said, "I am just so filled with love for you right now." It's that feeling of love and of elevating us as a hospital community that felt so low all the time and felt disliked by mental health advocates and disliked by the county at times. That constant state of being disliked was elevated in an evening of theatre to this feeling of love for the play, for Thornton Wilder, for allowing us to be something other.

Cindy Syfert None of us are professional actors or actresses, and I don't feel like any of us worked through our acting skills to do it. The work we had was just getting our butts over there so many nights a week. Looking back on it, I can only attribute it to how we worked together on a day to day basis and how close we are on a day to day basis without seeing each other that once we started seeing each other, it became like an explosion.

Anthony Mateo I think this is an opportunity to feel, and to express and experience really deep emotion. Grief, regret, excitement, anticipation, and everything that was lacking in the retreats that the hospital would provide for us for team building exercises, the experience and the expression of emotion was always lacking. I felt like this was such a cathartic experience, on many levels. Just personally coming to grips with my own personal sadness about things that were happening in my life, the sadness over where we had gotten as a hospital, the anticipation of, 'Hey, things are really possibly going to change.'

John Fulford They were just moved, they were touched. They were able to go someplace that they probably wanted to go, as far as acting, or putting themselves on stage. It did have an impact on some of the folks. I was just listening to what they were expressing. I don't think it really brought anything out of me, either purposefully or indirectly. I didn't have any connection that would make me respond like they did. MCES was a job, then they go home. Maybe they go home alone. Or maybe they go home to something that is very routine. That time of going and doing what they're doing at rehearsal, changed all that up. I think that it gave them that ability to do something different, and live through somebody else differently. I think it was therapeutic in that respect.

Erin Keeley It was extremely cathartic and it actually made me feel braver, because I was in a difficult time in my life. It was kind of like a turning point, and being able to get that emotion out gave me more confidence. It made me able to not, in a sense, yell what I needed out of my life and I made it happen. I feel like the play played a part in that.

Christa Godillot My biological mother passed in September of 2013. Everybody who worked with me knew. I really kind of died myself. I started drinking a lot. I really just did not cope well, because I did not want to feel that grief. I didn't anticipate grief. It dredged up a lot of painful things for me that I was not comfortable dealing with. It was very painful on many levels. I was working myself into the ground. I was 45 years old. Life in general, trying to manage everything, the timing of the play, couldn't have been worse I felt at the time, but at the same time, when I got through it, I was reminded, as I always am, of my resilience.

Steve Roddy Our lives—the drama is there, it's there for us to experience and embrace, or we can miss it. Coming away from that play, I think, it's time to live. Life is short. What is it—*memento mori* as the Romans used to say?

Anthony Mateo From my experience, as a therapist, as a person, it's through the expression of emotion that we heal. There's real curative power in emotion, and I think this is exactly what we needed at the hospital. I think it had a real curative effect.

Christa Godillot It was definitely something special about *Our Town*. I mean, the whole premise is you're not just here to exist. The most important thing that you're doing is seeing other people and their experiences, and living with them, and enriching those experiences, and while doing that you're enriching your experience. That sense of being present is really something, especially in mental health, we teach, like mindfulness, and presence, and living in the moment.

It forced me to be real. It forced me to experience painful things that I really was trying to hide from, and it was really at the end of my grieving process, like I had finally come up for air. My biological father died by suicide, his father died by suicide. I never would've actively done anything to harm myself, but it was the first time in my life that I could see the beauty of death. It was welcome, because I was in a lot of pain, and I had kind of just let go of that at the moment that we started rehearsing. It was kind of like taking something that's healing and ripping it back open. I wanted to be dead emotionally and I wasn't allowed to do that, so it was probably better from a mental health standpoint.

Cindy Syfert I think I began to become willing again, like I was when I first started there, to listen more to what these people were saying to me, try to understand more what they were experiencing, and to let them know that I did. I'm way past burnout. I'm confident that I wasn't giving my best before this. I feel like this play brought me back to why I work there in the first place, reminded me, 'This is what you're here for. These people don't have anybody else in their lives that understand, so be that.'

Mike Hagerty I really do think it was something we needed. For instance, I connected with Cindy. I saw her as just frazzled and hectic, and usually our words together were pretty curt.

Cindy Syfert For me, the whole thing was pleasurable. Remember the background I'm coming from. The whole thing of just being with other people, and I even at some point said to some of them, "I feel really silly. I know you guys don't like me. I really want to thank you for letting me in." Being very self-conscious—and feeling like I really was being accepted.

Mike Hagerty After the play, I had a total change of heart with her. I saw her in a different light. We just seemed a little closer, a little bit closer than had we would have been had we just worked together.

Cindy Syfert It's often the simple things that help bring people back. Let's take, for example, the guy that started doing drugs and has lost his job. His wife left him. He tried to commit suicide. His kids won't have anything to do with him. Now he's going to lose his house, and he doesn't know where he's going to go. That's a guy who doesn't have anybody, whose friends probably don't want to have anything to do with him. Sometimes the very simple thing of saying, "You must really be in pain right now" helps people tremendously, just to know that there's another human being alive that knows you're going through some shit. That's what I can do.

John Fulford People were surprised that we pulled this off. That we were capable of acting. That we put something together that it went from first words to last words. And it kept the audience's attention. I think that there were some folks that just didn't think ... they thought they were probably coming to a twelfth-grade play. Or to a sixth-grade play. But then I think they were amazed, and they were actually surprised that they didn't have a sixth-grade entertainment.

Mike Hagerty After we were finished, people were just more open with each other in general. Even the people that weren't involved in the play, the doctors, had a new look at things. This might just be my perception. Dr. Nell kept walking down the hall addressing me as Doctor every time she saw me, and I said, "Wait a minute. Isn't that going to confuse the patients?" She laughed and said, "They'll figure it out."

8

Louisiana State University and
Theatre Baton Rouge, 2019

Because amateur productions can't block others nearby from licensing the same title, when academic theatre programs find that there's another production of the same show in or near their community within weeks of their own, it is often a source of frustration. That was, however, not the case in the winter of 2019, when the community-based Theatre Baton Rouge's Young Actors Program and Louisiana State University's School of Theatre in Baton Rouge both staged *Our Town* within a four-week period.

While Theatre Baton Rouge (TBR) had announced their season, including *Our Town*, before the Louisiana State (LSU) theatre program conceived of doing a production, instead of conflict, the confluence resulted in a partnership between the two entities. They would each mount their own production, but the two casts would meet at designated intervals to share their journeys to Grover's Corners together, in a connection that was to be something more than a buddy system but not necessarily a mentor–mentee relationship. Because the partnership wasn't planned from the start, the production schedules didn't align perfectly. The LSU production was mounted first, with the TBR production following four weeks later. But the result was that the staggered productions allowed each cast to attend the other's show, which they did, enthusiastically.

The Young Actors Program at TBR serves youths from ages 8 to 18, many of whom also participate in theatre programs at their schools; 32 young people appeared in *Our Town*. The undergraduate School of Theatre at LSU enrolls students primarily ages 18 to 22; however, one student in his mid-30s was in the cast of *Our Town*.

Geographically, the two theatre groups were fairly far apart, while still within Baton Rouge, the state's capital city. The school is situated due south of the State House, which is perched on a hill overlooking the Mississippi River. LSU's theatre program is housed in the College of Music and Dramatic Arts building, renovated a decade ago but dating back some 90 years. The theatre where *Our Town* played was a small art deco-inflected proscenium house, located directly inside the main doors of the building.

Makaylee Secrest and David Culotta in the 2019 Theatre Baton Rouge production of *Our Town*, directed by Jack Lampert. Photo by Howard Sherman.

Marielle Lambert-Scott, Angelle M. Thomas, Fa'amaepaepa Laupola, and Sydney Prochaska in the 2019 Louisiana State University production of *Our Town*, directed by Shannon Walsh. Photo by Howard Sherman.

In contrast, Theatre Baton Rouge is located east of the State House, farther away from the river, in the back of the sprawling, only partially occupied Bon Marche shopping center, near a highway. It has been the company's home since 1962. Without its lighted sign on Florida Boulevard, the main thoroughfare on which the center lies, TBR would be completely invisible to passers-by. Within its somewhat unprepossessing, yellow-painted cinderblock exterior, the company has a comfortably appointed mainstage as well as a studio black box, where *Our Town* was produced.

Both Baton Rouge *Our Town* productions were as spare as Wilder directed. At TBR, beyond the standard tables, chairs, and ladders, white tape along the black floor delineated the locations of the Gibbs and Webb homes, with tape also outlining roofs on the bare black back wall. Two square, thin wooden frames were suspended from the ceiling, which would be used as George and Emily's bedroom windows. At LSU, a light scrim covered the back wall, and the ladders, instead of the usual A-frames, were rolling metal stepladders that inclined to a single top step, without steps for any manner of balance or descent on the opposite side.

Trios of Stage Managers shared the role in each: one actor for each act at TBR, and a shared ensemble of three at LSU. The costumes were predominantly traditional, save for the trio of Stage Managers at LSU, who were costumed according to the elements of the text they sought to emphasize.

In this chapter:
Jenny Ballard, managing artistic director, TBR
Willis Brei, Howie Newsome, LSU
Juliette Gregoire, Mrs. Soames, TBR
Nicholas Herring, Simon Stimson, TBR
Marielle "Théo" Lambert-Scott, Stage Manager, LSU
Jack Lampert, director and director of the Young Actors Program, TBR
Fa'amaepaepa "Lilo" Laupola, Stage Manager, LSU
Braedon M'Bala, Howie Newsome, TBR
Phillip Moran, George Gibbs, LSU
Sydney Prochaska, Stage Manager, LSU
Thomas Prochaska, George Gibbs, TBR
Samantha Schilling, Samantha Craig, TBR
Rain Scott-Catoire, Simon Stimson, LSU
Makaylee Secrest, Emily Webb, TBR
Angelle M. Thomas, Emily Webb, LSU
Shannon Walsh, director, LSU
Ke'Shone White, Sam Craig, LSU
Streisand Nicole Zeno, Mrs. Soames, LSU

Jenny Ballard It seems more and more that *Our Town* being taught in schools is going by the wayside—at least I don't hear about it a lot here—and so we thought it was very important to be educating these kids with classics of this nature.

Shannon Walsh We had just done *Love and Information*. Kristin Sosnowsky [Theatre Department Chair at LSU] didn't want to do another Caryl Churchill, so she said, "What about *Our Town*?" But because Jenny and I are friends, I was like, "You know that we can't do it. They just announced that they are doing it, so I guess this is off the table." Kristin said, "Well, I'll call Jenny," and I said, "Okay, good luck with that."

Jenny Ballard I think we've always tried to, as theatre organizations throughout town, respect what everybody is doing and try to complement each other's seasons rather than compete with each other's seasons. Kristin was coming at it from a place of, "I don't want to be stepping on feet. We really want to be doing this production. How can we figure out a way that we can both do this production and it be meaningful for both companies?"

Shannon Walsh Whether or not my school would claim it as such, a huge reason why I wanted to direct this show is because LSU is a predominantly white institution and has been one for so long, it does not have the best relationship with the Baton Rouge community other than football. The leaders of each of the theaters in town made a really specific choice that we just are too small of a market to continue to compete with one another. There had to be some kind of dialogue.

Part of that is about not only reaching out to the Baton Rouge community but making it so the Baton Rouge community, the LSU community, sees themselves on our stages. Institutions are slow to take that up, because they've been here so long, even though the rhetoric and the discourse is there. That's where something like *Our Town* and casting it the way that I cast it goes five times further than trying to push some policy through that's going get hung up in a thousand places and not happen until five years down the road.

Jenny Ballard Theatre Baton Rouge is in a terrible part of town. We're located off of Florida Boulevard, which is a rundown area that historically has a lot of crime. A substation of the Baton Rouge police department has moved in a couple of doors down from the theatre which has helped a lot, but my board members are constantly saying, "Should we move to a different location?" I keep saying, "No, we should not. We need to stay right here and we need to grow the community around us. There's too much history in this area." I think it's impossible not to think about things like economic disparity when you look at LSU versus the area that Theatre Baton Rouge is in.

Shannon Walsh I wanted this show to confront the feeling of alienation that I felt our students were really struggling with. That they were struggling with in the world. I wanted to cast people who were not being regularly cast. I also wanted to cast as many people as possible, in part to create a sense of belonging among our undergraduates that sometimes gets fractured.

Jack Lampert I think working on *Our Town* gave them a sense of belonging. Shannon and I both created "our town." That was something we talked about at every rehearsal. I know she did, because I heard it and I was doing it too. We're not doing a play, we are in our town. This is *our* town. It belongs to you. This is where we live right now. Through my warm-ups every night, that's part of the conversation. "Where are we?" "Our town," they all say.

Jenny Ballard Jack is an openly gay man and he talks about his partner Jim on a regular basis with the kids. I think that that makes them feel free to be who they are, it makes them feel free to explore who they are, and I think that's something special that Jack allows them to do, honestly. I think that's a really good thing.

Shannon Walsh There are so many queer and gender non-binary kids that do shows at TBR. For my money, with where my daughter is at, TBR is where she feels like family. Where she feels that she is understood, that everybody has a different thing that makes them unique and beautiful and she loves that. The gender line in the South is mind-boggling to me.

Streisand Nicole Zeno The first show [LSU] announced was *Anne Frank*. You could hear a pin drop, and everyone who was a person of color—we were so disappointed in the choice. I heard *Our Town* and was like, 'I don't even know what that show is, but it doesn't sound like it has Black people in it.' I grew up with people speaking Creole, Cajun French, and stuff. But I read it and I was like, 'Okay,' because I knew Dr. Walsh was going to cast it in a certain way, and so I had confidence in that.

Angelle M. Thomas I think we made it our own which made it even more special to me. Just being on stage with other people of color is always so comforting, for me, as a person of color. But seeing the way that everyone interprets the characters, you do get the sense these are white people in white neighborhoods in this time period. Seeing Lance and Dalacia and Jeremiah, who are all Black, come in with these different accents and do these scenes, it changed the way that I think about some of them.

Even my mother made a comment, kind of like a joke but kind of not, about how it was funny that Emily dies during childbirth and that I'm a woman of color, because women of color in America are statistically at much higher risk when giving birth to pass away. I feel like we got to tell so much more through our own lens, and through our own experiences of people of color. Then some of us having queer identities, it also opened up an entire world that from reading the script you really don't get, just because of who the script was written by and who it was written for.

Rain Scott-Catoire We cast it so diversely, that's why I think it didn't matter that I was a woman. Knowing that, going into it knowing that from the neck up we were just going to be us, ourselves, I'm not bothered in any way by the idea of playing a man. I never tried to make myself look manly, and that was because of Dr. Walsh's reassurance at the very beginning that we're just us.

Makaylee Secrest The script has a lot of small-town conventions in it, so it makes sense for it to be an all-white town. But we are living in a different world and it's still a story that is so important—queer identities, racial identities, all of that. I think it's great that we're diversifying it because it's not a story for one type of person. It's a story for every person on this planet.

*   *   *

Shannon Walsh We knew part of that collaboration was going to be some kind of mentorship. We came to decisions about over multiple lunches over the summer and into the fall between Jack and I. Spitballing ideas like, "Hey, wouldn't it be cool if they shadowed each other?" We set up a loose schedule. Initially we were going to try and pair up or have rehearsals at the same time every other week. Then we had to sort of tweak that and it ended up being almost every week.

Jenny Ballard There was talk early on when we were trying to figure out how to best make this a partnership about trying to do a combination production. We realized that would be way, too, complicated with the little amount of time that we had trying to work out the logistics.

Jack Lampert They started three weeks before we did. When we were just starting our read-throughs and starting to think about blocking, they were already in the process. So, the first meeting that we had, the LSU students came over to us and we played a lot of theatre games and let them all get comfortable together and learn about each other without really talking about the show.

Shannon Walsh A lot of my college students, when we said we were doing this, were like, "Okay, that's cool. I don't know how I feel about a kid following me around rehearsal." Because their expectations were so low, it just exploded.

Angelle M. Thomas In the past four or five years, I have experienced great, really heavy losses in my life from some of the most creative and influential people in my life. Reading about Emily on the most normal day that she had in her life and her experiencing all of that—I can just go back and think about things that I would want to share with these people that are exciting. But I'm also remembering I had those days with those people and I don't have them anymore. That was when I knew, 'Okay, I want to audition for Emily. I need to be a part of this process.' Even if I'm not Emily.

Lilo Laupola 'How's this going to work? Why would young actors ranging from like eight to 18 be doing *Our Town*? Is it going to be the same?' The rehearsal I went to over there … Okay, I cry sometimes in our productions. A little tear here and there. I wasn't expecting it there. 'Oh, these are just kids, telling the story of their mothers. Whatever.' I did not expect those tears I had. They get it. I think that's what got me the most. These young kids. Like little Ethan who plays Wally— I talked to him one time, and his perception of *Our Town*, and his takeaway? Oh, my gosh.

Shannon Walsh We did a lot of work to make them own those characters in multiple ways. I told them that they shouldn't be trying to imagine some historical place in New Hampshire at the beginning of the 20th century. I wanted them to imagine these characters as if they were their ancestors. Their own ancestors from Louisiana. Who is your grandmother? Who is your great-grandmother and how would they be moving through the world? But then I also encouraged them to try and really find the resonances with their lives today. That this was not some dusty historical or even dusty classic piece, that this was a piece that really was about the cosmos.

Jack Lampert We spent the two hours that day really playing games with each other and it was wonderful. It got all of them really comfortable. Then the second meeting we came to shadow them because they were already in the process of running the show. What I think it taught my kids was that they could be as comfortable as they wanted to be to create their own character.

Shannon Walsh My actors had to commit to coming on their day off to go to TBR. I had to be flexible about that and say it wasn't mandatory. I think not making it mandatory is part of what has allowed it to be so generative, because to a certain extent, unless they're called to be there, they only are there if they wanted to be.

Jack Lampert Those characters could become individuals. That's what my kids got out of that first shadow experience. Because the LSU kids were all individual in what they were building.

Shannon Walsh The third time, where we ran concurrent rehearsals, came about because of an issue of space. They didn't have a space to rehearse on that night. So, I said, "Do you know what? If you come here, let's put you in the acting studio and you can have a full rehearsal and we'll have a rehearsal next door." Because we were working Act II, the majority of my cast could go and watch them work Act III, and all of my actors came back weeping. Just weeping.

The LSU Stage Managers

Shannon Walsh Early on, when I talked to Jack about splitting up the Stage Managers, he said, "That's such a great solution." So, he decided to split the Stage Managers, with one that leads each act. They don't work as a unit like mine. I gave my actors the script and said, "Choose your lines and how you want to do it," and that's what they did. Those were all their own choices—where they said lines after one another and where they said them in unison.

Jack Lampert With the two gentlemen in the first and second acts, I wanted them to be basically constituents of Grover's Corners. Then I wanted Ellen, who was the Stage Manager in the third act, to feel like she was from somewhere else. Not necessarily a body from the cemetery, but possibly a being from somewhere else who observed everything that happened and controls the third act.

Lilo Laupola For me, it was that idea of the hearth, the home, and a familial presence. We were going through the script, saying, "These are the lines that I want" and "I think this would be good for you." It was about finding which lines resonated with our character.

Sydney Prochaska We met about a week after [Shannon] came with up with the idea. We'd all gone through the script, and kept in mind that Théo is the hearth. I was harmony and relationships and love, and Lilo was death and the afterlife. We had this very open conversation about where we saw ourselves, that each of us had a specific act that we were beginning and ending, that resonated with our character.

Théo Lambert-Scott The way that we divided it up to me felt so natural. It was almost as if Thornton Wilder had written it that way.

Sydney Prochaska Each of us had an idea, had the vision that Shannon gave to us, and we all, based on our previous experience with acting or directing, used that to build a character off of—almost an allegory. We were given this phrase, this word, this idea, and we found the character within that.

Lilo Laupola The way she described it was that almost every mythology has that three-part goddess. It's birth, love, and death. That's what I carried with me.

Sydney Prochaska Three parts of one whole. She used *A Wrinkle in Time* often, the idea of time lords that manipulate situations, and manipulate characters, not in the show, but within each other, in order to show one unity.

Lilo Laupola Breaking up that single male character into three people, with differing races, and gender presentations—I think that is a representation of that move towards inclusivity, and more . . . I don't want to say welcoming, I'm not here to say that the traditional image of the Stage Manager isn't welcoming. But in a world where we want a more diverse crowd, diversifying that Stage Manager in a literal way is representative of that.

Théo Lambert-Scott We just had such a deep connection with each other. It really did feel like we were so in sync. There were times where we wouldn't even talk about what we were going to do on stage, and we would just do it.

Sydney Prochaska The Stage Managers split into three, but played by three women in college, it felt natural, and it felt as if we were up there to welcome the audience in a different way. It was to show that everyone on stage is representative of everyone in the audience.

The Emilys

Makaylee Secrest When I was first reading the script, I didn't quite understand why Emily is in her grave and she's talking about the patent device on the drinking fountain. It seems so random. But through our collaboration and talking about it, Angelle helped me realize that it's like a level of discomfort being in that state, but also Thornton Wilder knows what he's doing because it alludes to advanced technology.

Angelle M. Thomas Emily reminds me a lot of my great grandmother, of being just matter of fact. She knows who she is, she knows what she wants, and she knows how to get what she wants. Then it comes down to George, and she just loses all of it.

Makaylee Secrest My Emily Webb, she reminds me a lot of me in a lot of ways, but also not like me in a lot of ways. Definitely that stubbornness and her self-secureness. She knows what she wants. I'm really glad Thornton Wilder decided to go that way with it because I don't know if that's how women would stereotypically be portrayed in 1905. Emily does represent every girl—there's so many things that you can relate to with her. Her dilemma is wanting George, but also what else she wants.

Angelle M. Thomas I wish it hadn't have been written that way—that she had to make a choice between the two of them. But I do understand that that is a reality that is present in our world.

Makaylee Secrest It bothers me every night. Every time they say on stage, George is our president, Emily vice president, I look at Thomas and I'm like, 'God!' Even the fact that Emily doesn't actually get to voice the words I do. He orders for her, instead of letting her get what she wants. I know that's supposed to be a nice gesture, but it's still just silencing her another way.

The Mrs. Soameses

Streisand Nicole Zeno We did our read through right before Thanksgiving break. When they were coming home from church, talking about Simon Stimson, that's when I was like, 'Oh, I like this play, because it's so relatable right now.' The talk coming home from church choir practice, that's literally my life with my mom and my grandma, and all my aunts.

Juliette Gregoire My mom and I were in the car and she was reading it with me. When they were coming back from church and they were talking about Simon Stimson, I was like, 'I think I can relate to this character,' not because she sits and she talks to people after church, but because she has this gossipy tint to her. It's not necessarily in a harmful way, but she cares about people, to let them know. Which is definitely my personality type. I don't talk about people for ill intent. I genuinely want to know what's going on and has anybody noticed it. My dad has a drinking problem, and everyone in my town has a drinking problem. Hearing that was like, 'Oh, I know what play this is.'

Streisand Nicole Zeno I decided a lot of things about Mrs. Soames. I decided that she had no children of her own for reasons which may be tragic or just unfortunate. Her husband probably is a factory worker and that's why in every scene, she's with a group aside from him. She's concerned with everybody else's life. She doesn't have a good, stable home life that she wishes she had, so she latches on to people in Grover's Corners.

Juliette Gregoire Mrs. Soames for me was more she and her husband didn't always get along, so she wasn't really at home much. She would find groups of friends and she would invest more of her time into her friends, into her social life, more than trying to be at home or somewhere she doesn't really want to be part of.

I was excited when they told us that we were going to be combining casts. 'I can learn something from these people. They're older than me, some of them might have more experience.'

Streisand Nicole Zeno For me it was, 'Okay. Hopefully my person has struggles with the same things.' Not, 'hopefully they struggle,' but we can relate with similar struggles. I can let them know that, 'Hey, even if you struggle from feeling like you're not where you need to be in acting or you don't look a certain way, how you think an actor should look, or you just don't fit in, I can help you with that.' I'm in college and I still struggle from those feelings. But you can overcome too.

Juliette Gregoire Hearing that from her, I appreciated that so much because I have struggled with that before, thinking that I wasn't the right look or the right type or shape for a certain role.

The Simon Stimsons

Nicholas Herring I come from a small town on the other side of the river. When I first read it, I was like, 'Wow, I can really relate to Simon,' because I'm not a small-town person. I'm moving to Baton Rouge. I saw the similarities between us. When I was playing the role, I'm lost, I just wanted to be understood.

Rain Scott-Catoire I did not see a relation at first. I was excited for the challenge, but I was like, 'How am I, a 19-year-old woman, going to relate in any way to a drunken old man, somebody who's bitter and angry, and not usually what I'm like at all?' Simon's bitterness and his anger, it only stemmed from his ambition, and his love of music, and the world, and wanting more, but then not getting it. I completely relate to that, because I too am from a very small town. Growing up, all I've ever wanted to do was to get out, and to move away, and not be stuck there. That's one of my biggest fears, is getting stuck. And he got stuck.

Nicholas Herring I chose to play him gay. It was very easy for me to find that in him.

Rain Scott-Catoire The first day that we met, Dr. Walsh had asked me, "Everybody in the town talks about what happened to Simon Stimson, but Thornton Wilder does not tell you what happened to Simon Stimson. I want you to figure out what happened to Simon Stimson."

Nicholas Herring For me, Simon grows up in a small town. His parents want him to play sports and do all this stuff, but he has this love for music. So, he starts singing in the choir at the church, and that really becomes his home. He has these big dreams and aspirations. Once he graduates high school, he moves to Europe or some big place with a lot of arts. I definitely played him gay, so I think he realizes in that that's what's different about him. He goes to Europe and he starts playing music, but then he learns his dad is dying. Even though his dad was not always there for him, he felt like he had to come back. I think he found someone in Europe, but it was in secret because of the time. I think he had to leave all of that wonderful life he had behind, and go back to Grover's Corners to take care of his family because he's the only son. He can never go back to Europe and build off from where he was, because he stopped. That's what's eating him away.

Rain Scott-Catoire For my story of Simon Stimson, he grew up in Grover's Corners with a mother and a father. His father was an alcoholic, too. He had anger issues, and he took it out on Simon and his mother. His mother was the opposite. She was very soft spoken and kind. She was probably the one person that encouraged Simon in his music. I think music was the one thing he loved more than life itself. It gave him purpose. It gave him reason. He wanted to go far with that. I think he wanted to be a concert pianist or a composer of sorts. I think in that small town, especially being a man in that town, I don't think anybody really encouraged him in that way, especially not his father. I think he never felt believed in or encouraged, except by his mother. So, in my story of, 'Oh, so tragic,' I think his mother eventually dies of an illness and he's left with only his father. So, he has no encouragement whatsoever. He didn't have the encouragement that I do in my life. I think that's when he starts to fall into that slump, and gives in to his worst fears.

The Georges

Phillip Moran There's been this huge uptick in research about mindfulness and meditation and being in the moment. *Our Town* really speaks to that, especially in Act III when it just hammers you with it. I think that it could have been a little bit different when it premiered and even 20 years back, because the way we view mindfulness has shifted a lot recently.

Thomas Prochaska Having a computer in your pocket was unheard of 30 years ago. It was certainly unheard of 80 years ago. They didn't even know what a computer was. We have connection to everybody through that. We can talk to anyone in the world just by typing in a name, just by texting them. It's simple. There's a connection between people. There's also a disconnection. Not being able to see them face to face, have a conversation.

Phillip Moran I think that resonates with George, asking Emily to write to him. It's something that wouldn't really be an issue in today's world. I'm doing a long-distance relationship and you write the letters every once in a while for special occasions.

Thomas Prochaska Playing devil's advocate, there's a connection and there's a disconnection, obviously. You have people that are still friends from high school that live around the corner from each other. Then you have people like my parents who went to school 2,000 miles from where we live currently. Being able to connect with them through social media is a wonderful thing but it also makes you miss what you had a little bit more.

Phillip Moran The future is so scary. If you think about it too much, it can consume everything that you're doing. There's also just getting in our head too much and being so far in there that we can't see what's happening around us. You spend so much time thinking about what's going to happen.

* * *

Jenny Ballard At a talkback, there were a few comments from both the LSU students and the young actors about wishing that they could have all been on the stage together. So the goal is to continue partnerships of this kind and eventually see if we could do some kind of combination production.

Shannon Walsh We were listening to the youth actors and the student actors talk, the way in which they've been informed by each other's performances and then been prompted, especially the young actors, to say, 'I see that choice and I'm gonna make a different one,' or 'I see that choice and I'm gonna blow some different air into it.'

Jenny Ballard The young man playing Howie in the LSU production said that one of the benefits for him of working with the young actors was that it was amazing to watch them work using their imaginations so fully. He said that he felt like in the past few years, he had forgotten how to do that, that he had gotten so consumed by work and school work and everything else that he stopped to take time to really use his imagination when he was on stage. He said seeing the work through their eyes reminded him of what that was like.

Rain Scott-Catoire I'm guessing a lot of older people can relate to the, 'Oh, we took all of that for granted.' I think that's something if you think about that when you're young, you can perhaps prevent. Maybe what you can kind of avoid when you get old is regret, and thinking, 'Oh, I didn't live every day to its fullest.' Maybe it's not a reflection back on your own losses, but a prevention of future ones.

Jenny Ballard They take it so seriously. It's really, really impressive to look at this group of kids and see them treat this like a professional theatre experience. Rain, who played Simon at LSU, was saying that she was in a production of *Our Town* when she was in high school and that everybody was always crying when they got to Act III and that she never really understood. She said they started rehearsal here and she had the same feeling, but she said they came over to the theatre one day and that they watched the young actors going through all of that and that she left the theatre and immediately started crying. She said that the experience of watching young children tell this story about the cycle of life and connecting as a human being was incredibly powerful to her.

Shannon Walsh Part of what happened for both sets of actors is that both groups came in thinking that this script was not about them. Through rehearsal they actually found out that it was very much about them. Their sense of ownership of the piece deepened in lots of really complex ways. To a certain extent I think they all also understood and felt keenly how this play is about their futures in a way that made them think more deeply about what growing up means.

Makaylee Secrest If I'm honest, I think some of my cast haven't looked too deep into it yet. I mean, they're kids. They don't really understand loss. They don't understand how important that is.

Angelle M. Thomas I wouldn't say that that was necessarily a bad thing for the fact that they are kids, that they don't really connect with that loss like that. It may be selfish for me to say this, but I would prefer that they wouldn't be able to have that strong connection that we may have with that loss because that they are so very young.

Braedon M'Bala I lost one of my friends due to suicide. Wednesday made it a year. It was very tough for me. I cried for like three months straight. This play really reminds me of that. Not in a bad way. It doesn't remind me to the point where I'm sad. It just opened my eyes more. You could be with someone, but the next minute, they could be gone.

Makaylee Secrest Throughout the process for a lot of the older kids, I'm watching them like not only grow as actors but also grow as people through this show. This show really opened these little kids up to being emotionally vulnerable with each other. I'm only a 16-year-old, I haven't that much loss in my life quite yet, but I'm surrounded by people that always have been and are.

Shannon Walsh This generation of kids has such an intimate knowledge of death being so close to them. The first conversation I had with my daughter about a school shooting was about Newtown and she was four, and then the regularity with which I have to have conversations with her, the regularity with which I have to sort of sit there and talk her through after Marjory Stoneman Douglas—and their school went on lockdown twice after that. They're constantly having to imagine that at any point somebody's going to walk into their classroom and spray them with bullets, and so I think that they have an ability to wrap their heads around death, even if they haven't experienced that kind of loss yet.

Jenny Mayfield Jack and our stage manager, Carol, did talk to the parents about the fact that the third act specifically dealt a lot with death, that there were some adult themes, that there was nothing offensive, but it very frankly dealt with death and the cycle of life, and some disturbing topics that eight, nine, and ten-year-olds shouldn't necessarily be exposed to. I know that Jack spent a lot of time speaking with them, especially about the third act, about what it means, talking about what that process is. I think that in the same way that books like *Charlotte's Web* introduce people to death in a very gentle way, *Our Town* does that, too. I think a difference with *Our Town*, though, is that step beyond, of actually making you think about the complete lack of existence once death happens.

Shannon Walsh We had a cast member who attempted to take their life during our show. Unsuccessfully, but as we came to the end, right before tech week, he was out for four days recovering. I told him, "I have a replacement for you. You do not need to come back. We love you." This cast member chose that in order to stabilize and feel welcome and feel like he belonged, he had to come back. He wasn't going to classes but was coming to rehearsals. Some of the cast knew what was going on, but a large majority did not. My students can tell you of people that they know that have attempted to take their life or successfully taken their life all over the place.

Willis Brei I had someone in my fraternity commit suicide earlier this year. The fact that you can see and talk to someone one day, and the next day, you can't, is hard to wrap your mind around. To know that you are mortal and that one day this is going to happen to you, I think as long as you take it the right way, it is a good thing. 'Hey, I don't have a million years. As a matter of fact, I don't have a lot of time at all. Maybe I should start doing what I want to do, because if I don't now, maybe I'll never get the chance to.'

Shannon Walsh *Our Town* actually gives them language to work through that. It's not therapy, but a grounding of what life is because of what death might be.

Nicholas Herring At my school, there are jokes and memes about school shootings, and disease, and death. We joke about it, and I think it's because we are so numb to it now. I think that's why kids our age are able to perform it, because it's something we're exposed to at a very young age.

LOUISIANA STATE UNIVERSITY AND THEATRE BATON ROUGE   125

Samantha Schilling It shows that everyone ages 100 to a seven-year-old should know that life is beautiful, and children and adults and elderly—everyone—shouldn't take it for granted. The school shooting—they didn't know. You just have to live everyday like it's your last.

Ke'Shone White Growing up in New Orleans was very bittersweet because I've had to deal with the loss of loved ones my age due to gun violence, so I feel as though I've realized how short we have to live.

Braedon M'Bala Just the other day, I was thinking of how life is so short and that I want to be able to achieve all of my goals in life in this short period of time that we have so that I won't pass away not achieving what I wanted to do in life.

Théo Lambert-Scott The whole process, I was thinking of my mom. She lost her mother when I was a year old and there's so many things in the show reminded me of her. I've seen my mom cry a handful of times. One of them was after we lost our home in Katrina. That's what makes my mom cry.

I've never seen her cry at a movie, or a book, or a TV show or anything like that. She came the opening weekend and she was in the second row. I saw her. As soon as Emily slams her hands down on the table and she goes, 'Look at me, can't we just look at one another?' my mom was crying, and that's when I broke. Because I was watching my mom think about what she would say to her mom. Watching my mom feel those things, and knowing that that's what she was feeling, it was a lot. I call my mom every day now.

Lilo Laupola My relationship with my sister has been actually a lot better since the production of *Our Town*. I think that goes back to me waking up to things I take for granted. I think watching TBR go through it, and us, it made me call home a lot.

Sydney Prochaska If the play was old fashioned, they would die and there wouldn't be anything after. There wouldn't be an Act III. There would be some sort of epilogue where they talked about how Emily passed away. I think that's what makes this play stand out. Thornton Wilder wants us to remember that there is something after this. How could there not be?

Théo Lambert-Scott It's not as though all of us are completely unaccustomed with death. We've had family members who have died. We hear about it constantly on the news. The idea of death isn't necessarily foreign. But the idea of our own mortality of making our life worthwhile—I don't think that that's as familiar a concept.

Angelle M. Thomas My dad passed away when I was 17. He had Lou Gehrig's disease, so it was ongoing and it's a feeling of relief that I have when I do think about his passing, because he's not in pain anymore. But I wanted to share this experience so bad with him. It really hit me on our last dress rehearsal, and just my mom encouraging me. She and my whole family sat in the front row for opening night and after the show I remember l held on to my mom for so long and she said, "Whether you know it or not, he's here with you, in that experience."

Shannon Walsh One of my stage crew who came up to me in the middle of doing tech and said, "I just need you to know. I sat backstage last night and wept and went home at 11 o'clock at night and called my mom because I just had to tell her I love her."

Juliette Gregoire In my opinion, the takeaway is, even though things may happen, there's always some kind of good that comes with the bad. There's always a light at the end of the tunnel. There's always something that happens for a reason. Whether you notice it now, whether you notice it ten years from now, it happens for a reason. And it's essentially good.

Shannon Walsh *Our Town* models what we theatre people think our community is at its best. Full of joy, belonging, connection, a sort of refuge from the harshness, particularly for my cast. Having a place where I think my costume designer said, "We went about this as if this was a place where everyone could be free to express themselves. *Our Town* is a place where everyone is free to express themselves." Perfect.

Lilo Laupola Throughout the process, everyone was asked, "Why *Our Town*? Why now?" Because it still hits. It still does.

9

Lookingglass Theatre Company, 2009

Anna Our Town *for Jess and me is about the beauty of the day you're in and the triumph of that beauty's elusiveness. It is about the impossible "Why," the heartbreaking "Why not." There are days when these questions are not only impossible to answer, they are terrible to even ask. Try to hold on to an answer for yourself and it slips through your fingers like mercury. Try to explain the answer to a child and it's like nuclear math. But there are some times, like when you look into the eyes of a beloved, that there it is, as simple as a recipe for chocolate chip cookies.*

Jessica *It is very, very moving, and important to us, that we are sharing this room with a group of people who have chosen to make their lives together. Not exclusively, not easily, not lightly. But every person in this room is a member of a small town that spends their moments together on earth asking the same questions, making and watching and sharing the magical little worlds that are that day's answer.*[1]

from introductory speech by Anna D. Shapiro and
Jessica Thebus, on the first day of rehearsal for *Our Town* at Lookingglass

Chicago's Lookingglass Theatre Company was founded in 1988 by a group of friends who had graduated from Northwestern University's theatre program. Designed as a true ensemble that would work together collaboratively, they quickly added other members, and gained attention for their visually inventive, highly physical form of theatre, which typically featured new works and original adaptations of classic pieces of literature, with company members variously and often simultaneously taking on tasks as actors, writers, directors, and administrators. The artistic directorship of the company is rotated among company members, and seasons are chosen collaboratively by members of the ensemble.

Lookingglass's 1999 production of *Metamorphoses*, adapted and directed by Mary Zimmerman, played a six-month run in Chicago. It was subsequently mounted on Broadway, running for 400 performances in 2002 and early 2003,

Laura Eason in the 2009 Lookingglass Theatre production of *Our Town*, directed by Anna D. Shapiro and Jessica Thebus. Photo by Sean Williams.

garnering three Tony nominations and winning one for Zimmerman's direction. Similar to *Metamorphoses*, Lookingglass's adaptations included works by Lewis Carroll, Fyodor Dostoevsky, George Orwell, and Italo Calvino; *Our Town* marked the first time the company staged an existing script from the modern theatrical era.

Performed between February and April of 2009, the Lookingglass *Our Town* was the second major noteworthy staging of the Wilder play in Chicago in less than a year, following both the May debut and October remount of David Cromer's 2008 production for The Hypocrites. Both were preceded in the Chicago area by a production at Writers Theater in Glencoe in 2003. Lookingglass's *Our Town*, pitched to the ensemble by co-directors Anna D. Shapiro and Jessica Thebus as a 20th-anniversary commemoration, was predicated on uniting as many founding and early ensemble members on stage as possible for the first time in a number of years.

To emphasize *Our Town*'s connection to the company's history, set designer John Musial kept the stage floor spare in accordance with Wilder's wishes, but he filled the ceiling with set pieces, props, and costumes from the company's prior productions, forging a connection between past and present that echoed the play's own multiple time periods, but without offering any literal comment on the text.

Except for the Stage Manager, who wore a brown three-piece suit, Janice Pytel's costumes were uniform in color, in the light-beige-to-white range, nodding in shape to the original period silhouettes, particularly with skirts for the women, but not slavishly beholden to what would have been seen in New Hampshire 100 years earlier.

Given the quasi-reunion nature of the casting, there was no attempt made to cast with age specificity. Indeed, because the majority of the cast members were drawn from the ensemble, most of whom connected back to a particular time in the Northwestern theatre department, almost all of the actors were within a few years on either side of 40.

In this chapter:
David Catlin, Dr. Gibbs, company co-founder
Kevin Douglas, Sam Craig, Si Crowell, Joe Crowell and others
Christine Mary Dunford, Mrs. Webb
Laura Eason, Emily Webb
David Kersnar, Simon Stimson, company co-founder
Anna D. Shapiro, co-director
Joey Slotnick, Stage Manager
Heidi Stillman, Mrs. Gibbs
Jessica Thebus, co-director

At the time of the production, David Kersnar was artistic director of Lookingglass Theatre Company. At the time of this writing, Heidi Stillman is the company's artistic director. The company members commonly refer to many of the founders by their last name because three of them are named David.

*   *   *

Jessica Thebus Anna and I have taught together at Northwestern for a very long time and we've had the unusual experience that directors don't have very often. Directors collaborate all the time with playwrights, with bunches of people from different positions, but directors rarely collaborate together. We've done it in the classroom and so we wanted to do something together. Anna suggested *Our Town*. We brought it to Lookingglass, being particularly interested in their identity as an ensemble company that had been together over years and changes and losses, and successes and failures. The passage of time within an intimate group of people seemed like an exciting place to begin with that play and with that artistic community, so we pitched it to them with that in mind.

Laura Eason I remember doing a show at the McCarter in, gosh, 2004 maybe. We got to go to the main theatre. There was no set. They were in transition for shows. So, the bare back wall was there. I just went over and just put my face against the brick wall and thought, 'This is where the first production of *Our Town* was.'

Anna D. Shapiro It's the only play that I've ever experienced that it kind of doesn't matter who's doing it. The impact is undeniable. I've seen it done by kids and I've cried as hard as when I've seen professional productions. I've seen it done by people who didn't understand it in the way I understood it and cried as hard as I did with the people who understood exactly what my access point was.

Jessica Thebus I remember teaching it with undergraduate theatre students. They first don't think they're going to be interested. Then when they are actually embodying the text and watching it, they are very moved. I also encountered some students who felt like it was about a small town in the northeast and why should they be interested in that town? That took a little bit of work to get that out of their heads into what the play is actually about. But it was successful, watching all these young people who come in with pre-conceptions or who easily jump to assumptions, then watching them cross the bridge that Wilder built.

Christine Mary Dunford My question was always, "Whose town?" It didn't feel like any town I was familiar with. It felt very white. It felt very middle class. The issues that were being confronted in it were not the issues that were relevant to me or I thought relevant to our culture. Just even the idea of it was frustrating. Working on it, I got closer. I'm closer to the ideas of community and the inevitability of passing in all its forms; passing time, passing life, life moving on. The idea of taking advantage of every moment just felt obvious and trite to me before.

Jessica Thebus It was a piece that was going to include everyone. The artists who were on the ground there every day, and the artists who don't get to be there very much. I think it spoke pretty directly to their needs at the time.

Anna D. Shapiro They spoke about that often through the process. Actually, being on stage with each other is something that hadn't happened in a long time with such a large group of people.

David Kersnar We had always thought of *Our Town* as an example of the kind of theatre that Lookingglass doesn't do. A play that's well known, that's already received its seminal productions. What more would Lookingglass have to offer as a company?

David Catlin When we started Lookingglass, I avowed that we as a company would never produce something like *Our Town*. We wanted to do shows that were original, that were challenging. So, when Anna and Jessica came to us, I said, "No." They said, "Well, could we just read it? Maybe let's just have a reading?" I begrudgingly agreed, we got the ensemble together, and we read it. It wasn't the way I remembered it. We got to Act III and we were destroyed by it, all of us just weeping at this incredibly beautiful play. Just astonishing. At that time, being 40, we were all in the zone of our 40s. That was a time where many of us had started having kids and there was this kind of community of the next generation of Lookingglass being born.

Heidi Stillman There was something really appealing about the idea of being in the show together, that it was based on this idea of ensemble. *Our Town* felt like Thornton Wilder is the ancestor, or grandfather, of our own aesthetic, because it's so open handed and theatrical.

Kevin Douglas No matter what walk of life you are, no matter what race, no matter what gender, there is something you can take from it. You can't find that in every play, especially of that time period. If no one knew who Thornton Wilder was, if you just crossed off the name and you read the play, nothing in there would make me say, 'Oh, you can't do this because of your race, you won't like this because of your political beliefs.'

David Catlin It was a period where our parents were getting to an age where they were dealing with issues of mortality. I think at age 22, I had this sense of not really immortality, but the sense of not caring a jot about it. It wasn't in my worldview. But at age 40-something with kids who I was worried about, with parents who I was worried about, suddenly that play just walloped me, along with my colleagues. Anna and Jessica were just kind of smirking at how right they were. They didn't say, "See, I told you so," but it was in that smirk that they had, as we're all just soggy with tears and trying to catch our breath.

Jessica Thebus There's a sense of having so many ensemble members in the play, that if it had just been one person from outside, it certainly could have worked, but there was something really fun about two of us doing this experiment together. It was kind of meta in a way, that was part of the project, that they were doing it together. They're obviously almost exactly the same age as each other, so the ages weren't significant. It was really about being who we all were within that text.

David Catlin It is, for so many reasons, precisely the kind of theatre that we want to do in terms of its high level of theatricality. What Thornton Wilder does in terms of saying we don't use props, it's just the simplest staging, is exactly the kind of work that we seek to do: a relationship with the audience in terms of needing them to actively engage their imaginations in the writing and creation of this world and this story that's unfolding in front of them. Before 2009, it was secretly influencing us.

Heidi Stillman He was just so avant-garde, so outside the bounds of really tight storytelling. I think we are known a lot for our physical work, and our visual work, but I really think that, at heart, we're a very theatrical theatre company. You'd think that all theatre companies would be theatrical, but I think there's so many shows right now that you could see on TV. We're always interested in stuff that really only works on stage.

Laura Eason I think the notion of "our town" means Lookingglass. That was just part and parcel of the whole thing. That the whole endeavor was *Our Town* is the company. That's why this makes sense for us to basically be all generally same age. I think the conversation between the play and the company was happening at every moment of the production. I think people that didn't know anything about Lookingglass or had no relationship to the company could still come and have a good experience. But it was really built on that concept of the company and our relationship in conversation with the play.

Anna D. Shapiro We joke often with our students, that together we make one really good director. We have very, very different skill sets, and very different interests. Yet, both of those sets of interests and skill sets seem to be necessary to be successful directing a play.

Jessica Thebus Anna's wonderful with actors and the community she creates and the specificity with which she can examine psychological motivation. It's really unique and that's fabulous. I tend to be visual, emotional, content with image is my thing, as well as dynamic of story. With *Our Town*, it's a great playground for both of those things.

David Catlin They're so damn intelligent, so they're able to give really astute observations that are not just intellectually astute but emotionally astute about who we are. We sometimes, as kind of a family, an ensemble, couldn't always talk to each other in a way without feeling like we were hurting each other. They were able to give feedback at times that was really right on the mark, that wasn't burdened with emotional history and baggage.

Jessica Thebus The whole thing is metaphorical, like a dream. Not in a sort of the dreamy way, but that this place is every place. This relationship is every relationship. This death is every death. You have to do a lot with a little. Yet it has to be very beautiful, it has to change and the story dynamic has to build suspense and all of that stuff. And it has to be real.

Anna D. Shapiro I think what it plays with is what we intellectually know, which is that we're all born and we all die. There's no plot to that, right? What *Our Town* does is it helps us by moving through it in such a simple, basic, kind of errorless, real way that's not actually real.

Heidi Stillman Our theatre is really small, we have maybe 190 seats. We can set it up however we want it. We had it in an alley setup. So, you're watching the show, but you're also in community with the people across the way. The whole thing feels like a town. I think that set up was really dynamic, and because it was almost a circle, and so intimate.

Anna D. Shapiro There were tables and chairs, there was a ladder for Emily's window. And that was it. The costumes were very simple. There was not a lot of differentiation from one character to another. It would be what actors would be wearing if you were in rehearsal clothes, but with this constancy of cream color to get it as simple as possible. What was hanging from the ceiling was everything we could possibly fit up there, from a previous Lookingglass production.

Christine Mary Dunford It was like a palimpsest for audience members who were familiar with our work over the years, so that must've been an extremely rich experience for those people. It was for me.

David Kersnar There was one night that I'm just staring up at this stuff and I was so overcome by the history that I went up on my line. I didn't hear it. I was distracted. I was horribly embarrassed. I'm just so overcome with the enormity of that we pulled off all these productions and our history together. But also, these are just little blips. All this stuff means something to me but it means nothing to anyone else other than it's a signifier of history. Productions are just sandcastles that we put out and wait for the tide to come in and take away. That's really what the message of the piece was, that we're all here, audience or performers, here in this moment together.

David Catlin Lookingglass had a really strong pervasive sense of community running through it, that's a part of our fabric. We often vacation together, we do things together outside of the rehearsal room and the administrative offices. It's been a valuable part of who we are and our identity. The production felt like that. There was history on stage, and history of relationships. Laura and [David] Schwimmer played Emily and George. They were at the time in their 40s and here they are at the soda fountain scene. George and Emily are not in their 40s. But Laura and David first met each other as cherubs at Northwestern at a time when they were 17 and 18 years old. So, when they looked into each other's eyes with the little crow's feet on the corners that start to creep in at age 40, they could see the eyes of that 17- and 18-year-old when they first met each other. That was present in the room and it lifted this notion of mortality, of aging, of ghosts, the kind of ghost of who they were crept into the room in a really palpable way. I got to play Doc Gibbs and Heidi Stillman played Mrs. Gibbs. We both have our own families, but in college, twenty-some years ago, I had a crush on Heidi.

Laura Eason There was a sense that this was a very rare situation and that who knows when or if it would ever happen again, that this many of us would be able to be in a play together. I think a lot of the old frustrations or hurts, a lot of the drama, is inherent to a group of people trying to embark on a creative endeavor for the first time in a long time. There's always bumps along the road and regrets and grudges. That's just always in the mix along with everything that's wonderful. But I think because everyone knew it was such a rare experience, and we were older at this point, we all, for the most part, were able to really enjoy each other and love the experience. I think because Anna and Jessica were our dear friends who we deeply respected, and we wanted to have them have a good experience, too.

David Kersnar Yes, there were the jokes and the hijinks that we play on each other. But I think that there was just this feeling of all for each other.

Kevin Douglas It seemed to me that everyone just fell back in place as if they had just started the company. They told stories, they would make jokes—and then, of course, let us in on the jokes that they would tell. I felt included.

Jessica Thebus I don't know that I feel that *Our Town* has a relationship to realism, which is very important. I feel it's crucial that the play feel true—and the play is true—but it's not crucial that it feel real. First of all, the Stage Manager tells us everything we need to know, introduces everybody. There's something about the science of, 'Here's this local tree, and here's the history.' That's all so open handed and yet, you know you're not looking at that, you're not even looking at something that's pretending to be that.

Anna D. Shapiro I like to see a range of different people, sometimes unexpected people, truthfully embody a story. I think that part of the magic of *Our Town* too is that you believe in the collective unconscious that carries the play anyway.

Heidi Stillman I think we were nervous and excited, to reach beyond, or under, our age. I never really got to play people my age when I was younger, and I hadn't acted in a really long time, too. I don't think I've acted since. I'm very tiny, have a high voice, and I played kids forever, well into my 30s. So, that actually was a really fun challenge for me, to play a grownup.

Joey Slotnick I don't think anyone auditioned. At some point they said, 'You have to audition for each other?' They found that odd. You know, I find it odd. I don't think we do it as much now, but we did. I said to Anna, "I would love to throw my hat in for the

Stage Manager." I think that was one of her ideas. I think Schwimmer probably said, "I would like to play George." I'm sure there are people for whom it was, 'Really, this is the part that I'm playing?' But I think everyone eventually everyone dug the process.

Laura Eason Pretty early, Jessica mentioned to me that they had the hope that it would be me playing Emily which was just the greatest compliment and sort of unfulfilled dream. I thought that ship had long sailed.

David Kersnar I played Simon Stimson in the production and I got my first legs in the theatre in San Francisco Opera. I was a little boy first soprano, San Francisco Boys Chorus. It was interesting playing this role connected to music. Going back to my childhood origins in performance and my own family's struggle with alcoholism. To play this role and to have my own personal connection to the struggles of the character.

Laura Eason I think there was a level of vulnerability for us. We really needed to lean on Jessica and Anna to get there and to believe that we actually could do it. Not that we don't have faith in our ability, but the play thematically is about relationships and the need for vulnerability in many ways in those relationships. That's what the process required in a way that I think we didn't quite anticipate.

Kevin Douglas What I've seen consistently with many actors when they're 20, is there's this quick pace, and you miss moments, you miss beats. Everything's quick. That was another lesson. They just took their time and in that they were able to find things that you can't find if you're a 20-year-old who's moving quickly and going to the next thing and hasn't lived life. Just from the stories I've heard, when you're building a company there's all this angst: 'We've got to do this this way, we've got to, it's got to get done.' Now it's, 'You know what? It doesn't have to get done in that way, there's a million ways we can do it. Let's figure it out together, let's take our time.'

* * *

Joey Slotnick As an actor you're not used to going out and speaking as yourself and really engaging with the audience. You're kind of behind this character. Jessica and Anna stripped everything away from me. They just wanted me to be Joey.

Jessica Thebus In the play, when the Stage Manager, right before the soda scene, invites the audience to remember—this is one of the most significant moments of direct address in Western theatre. I feel like the heart the play really is that invitation. 'Now you remember, now let's all remember together.' You know that you're remembering, the person across from you is remembering, the audience is remembering. We're unstuck in time a little bit together.

Anna D. Shapiro My memory is of being surprised at how romantic it was. Maybe in our production there was romance in it because of who the people were, because they were all of a certain generation and had gone through phases of loving each other when they were younger, had traded loves with one another. That sense of romance and watching a group of people in their 40s touch early romance. Historically, I have been more moved by the spiritual depth of the play, but I have images kind of burned in my brain of 40-year-old faces, looking like they were 18 again and in this particular case, these were people who remembered each other at that age. That was in their bodies. They were being looked by someone who was carrying that memory for real.

Laura Eason I never felt any pressure to be anything but authentic and as truthful as I could possibly be, able to lean into my deep friendship and love and admiration for Schwimmer and all that we've shared with the theatre company and his friends.

Joey Slotnick I loved it because I could watch. It just is me watching my friends play with each other on stage and playing these scenes. I really relished that, so I didn't feel alone. I felt like they needed me and I needed them.

Jessica Thebus Even when you're doing it, it's not unlike *The Glass Menagerie* where you think, 'This date looks like it's going to work out. This time, the Gentleman Caller's going to work out.' So, you all are just going along and then you get your heart ripped out over and over again.

Joey Slotnick Schwimmer and Laura are so good together, and have known each other for such a long time, since they went to college together. So, you don't have a history of people only knowing each other for a year a two. You have people knowing each other for 15 years, the trust that they have with each other. That never ever felt weird or different or odd. I just totally bought that they were those people.

Laura Eason I remember so many years ago, after maybe *Master and Margarita* or something in the early '90s, David just landed some gig—or maybe it was after the first season of *Friends*. He took us all out to a super fancy dinner, the whole ensemble. We were all making toasts. One of the toasts he made was, "I just want us to all be grateful that we're healthy. Our parents are healthy. We're all doing what we love." We were all in our 20s. In the moment, I was a little like, 'Yeah, yeah. I'm grateful for that. That's really nice that he mentioned it.' But in retrospect it has really stayed with me. It's just incredible that at that young age, he had the insight of, 'This isn't forever. Our parents are going to die. We're going to die. We need to be so grateful for what we have in the moments that we're in.'

Heidi Stillman I'm also looking across the table at David Kersnar, and having that scene, and just all those years of history. David and I use used to have a crush on each other, and we had a little tiny relationship for a moment, 25 years earlier.

With David Schwimmer, I'm both his mom, hugging him, as he's going off to get married, but it's also me hugging my dear friend, that I made this theatre company together with. It just has so many levels all the time.

Laura Eason I really pulled on a lot of that history in [Act III], in that pleading of, 'Just look at me. Let's just be here together in this moment.' Because in a lot of ways, I think that's what we as a company were trying to do so often, was create something that was a moment of total theatre, of mind, body and spirit coming together that would arrest you in a moment where you were nowhere else. You were only in that moment of theatre.

Jessica Thebus You teach that play and you end up kind of drowning in "Who is the Stage Manager?" The students always want to make one decision. I teach a course in direct address, which uses all kinds of different materials, but *Our Town* is one of them and I feel like it's the exception that proves the rule. I really do believe that you always have to know who you are and who you're talking to. Except in this play.

Anna D. Shapiro Part of what you have to present in the Stage Manager is essentially tabula rasa. You understand the mythic function that's actually not general, that's incredibly specific, but where that myth lives in me is very different than where it lives with anyone else.

Joey Slotnick I think my performance was not meant to be anything other than who I was. It was me. I wasn't making it schmaltzy or cheesy or making jokes. I was just being me, as close to me as the Stage Manager as possible. I don't think there's a whole lot of description about him. So, what those words meant to me, my take on it and our directors' too, but how they made me feel. How I can share those experiences?

Anna D. Shapiro There are essential truths, essential stories that are about the truth of human existence. If you have somebody, as Jessica so lovingly put it, a person who cares, a person who knows, a person who sees, a person you can trust, that is our dependable narrator. That's a mythic character in everyone's life, meaning that it is an essential truth that we all search for, we all need it, we all are lost without it.

Joey Slotnick He's someone to help put things in order, perhaps. I didn't see him as God, because it's hard to play that. For some people I'm sure it's very easy to play, but you just have to play the circumstances and almost to stay out of his way. To stay out of the way of audience members. To help you, but not to feel the things for you. That's what I found really was difficult, because emotion sometimes would take over and I wanted to back away from that. Because if you let that valve, that bell cap, off all the steam comes out. You want the audience to be able to do that for themselves and experience that. That was hard sometimes.

Christine Mary Dunford I remember one note from Anna that basically said: they're not all sugar and spice. They're not all sweet. They have difficult lives and they are fresh. When Mrs. Webb is shouting up to her kids to get downstairs, they should be, so it's a very realistic window into a family scenario. She wanted it to be a little bit more realistic than idealized.

Kevin Douglas The way I played him, Wally was very energetic, he loved adventure, he loved risk. It makes sense that something would happen on a Boy Scout trip. It makes sense that he would die in that way. Die doing something he enjoyed, but yet was dangerous.

Laura Eason Jessica and I used to make jokes during rehearsal that if Wilder had had a dramaturg, there were all these moments that would be out. This wouldn't be happening. There are all the kinds of moments where the rules slightly change the way he moves through time. I think it's really inspirational that he stayed true to these idiosyncratic moments and to his own voice.

It's funny to me that it has been relegated as this high school show because it is one of the most profound, powerful, true pieces of work ever written. I think that's why it endures. How did he have such insight into the human condition? How did he understand how quickly life goes and time goes? How did he know and was able to express it so beautifully? I remain, as a writer, really in awe of it. I also hold it as an example of being careful when people want to straighten out the parts that are a little twisty or unexpected, because sometimes that's where the best things lay, that's where the magic can be.

David Catlin I played Schwimmer's father. David as a person has a very strong paternal energy, which is maybe not something that would be expected. As we were founding the company, he was always the person who was the grownup in the room, even when not all of us were ready to be grownups. That was a fun role reversal, getting to lecture George about helping his mom out with the firewood. Schwimmer would be the first to jump up and help his mom out with the firewood. I got to be the dad that I had become, and I got to take care of him a little bit in the way that he's often always taking care of other people.

David Kersnar I was for a few years disconnected from the company and I was able to pull from that to help create the character as somewhat disconnected. I think Simon Stimson is not fully admitting the disconnection that he feels. He probably thinks that he's a functioning alcoholic, that people are not seeing the pain he's going through, and that the self-medicating he's doing is somehow working.

David Catlin Andy White and Christine Mary Dunford played the Webbs. They used to work together on staff at Lookingglass in the Development department and had a history of her checking up on making sure he had done all the deadlines and him wanting to do them on his own. They could draw from this long history of having worked together and spend a lot of time on a task that was not just making art.

David Kersnar A social psychologist that I follow once talked about how there's two kinds of people in the world. There's people that give oxygen and there's people that take oxygen. I think that's meant metaphorically. I think Simon Stimson is someone that went from blindly taking oxygen and then realizing in Act III that that pain was causing him not to contribute to the world in a way that I think that he was hoping that he was.

David Catlin In a fun way, we used to tease Joey because he was the first Lookingglass ensemble member who didn't go to Northwestern. But it was fitting in a way that he was the Stage Manager who was a little outside the action, guiding the action, not getting to play directly with everybody in scene. I think that was a functional dynamic for us.

Joey Slotnick As the Stage Manager, you're not sure who the guy is, what his background is. You know you can do all the prep work and all of the emotional work but performing it you have to be very present in the moment As the Stage Manager there has to be some distance or else you wouldn't be able to tell it. Maybe that's one of the beautiful things about that character: that you need someone in a story with some distance to it. Because if it was told from Mrs. Webb's point of view or from the doctor's point of view, it would be a very different play. Because there's someone who can step back and give you the lay of the land, you enter it the way you want to enter it.

Jessica Thebus For the people sitting in that room, there is an incantatory quality about it. There is a recognizing the situation. Going through the steps seeing it. Feeling your own grief, whether that's far in the past or fresh or in the future. It holds a presence like that, that I think our culture is lacking. I think that's why we are so deeply moved by it.

Joey Slotnick When it comes down to it, the problems that we have are always the same. Our children grow up, they leave, they have their own lives and then they die. We all die. We all die. What do we want to leave behind, what's important to us?

What do we obsess over? Who do we love, who do we choose to love? Who do we choose to connect with? I think that's always, always the same, whether we're holding a cell phone in our hand or we have a newspaper or we're riding a horse and buggy, I think that everyone has those same concerns.

Christine Mary Dunford The questions it proposes transcend the period in which it was written and set. Questions of what is of value? Questions of how do we appreciate the life we have while we have it, and how do we truly see and appreciate and support the people we're with in the moment? I think those questions transcend specific time periods, and to some extent, cultures. I think it leans toward a universality that makes it feel accessible to many people in many places in many times. It's kind of a once upon a time, where you get to make up what the time was, and that inherently begs comparison to the present moment.

Jessica Thebus Everyone's going to die. Even people that were on *Friends*, they are also going to die.

David Catlin In the first moments of the show, Joey comes out as the Stage Manager and he introduced all of us. We were in whatever clothes we wore to the theatre that day. We just nodded and waved to the audience. Then half of us went to the lobby and half of us went to backstage. We had these massive quick-change stations set up and we had to do full costume changes out of our street clothes into the costumes within 45 seconds or 60 seconds. We're all literally stripping down, not completely naked but pretty darn close, and then quickly pulling our costumes on. There was something so beautiful and fast about that, to be vulnerable and exposed in front of each other. We were in the task of making a piece of art. You allow yourself to be incredibly vulnerable and exposed. There's a certain level of trust that is absolutely necessary in order to do that.

David Kersnar We would warm up in our green room and stand in a circle and look at each other and play silly games that we hadn't played for a long time. That we hadn't played since we were just starting the company. So, it was this simultaneous reminder of our youth, and the youth of our company and our community and ourselves, and how important that was.

Laura Eason Before Act III, I'd need to step out of the dressing room because all the women shared a dressing room. I would really need to get into my head space to be able to walk out and be in the cemetery. I needed to sit quietly. I needed to hear Joey's voice. You don't have the opportunity in the show. You just arrive fully in that moment. I was really trying to think about what that loss would be like. She's in a liminal space of trying to figure it out. She's not full of sadness. For me, it was important to really be connecting to a true sense of loss and to be in a place of disorientation. I would just sit. My father, who has since passed away, and I were very close. I used to call him a lot. I would just think about the day when I wouldn't be able to call my father and that would emotionally get me where I needed to be.

Heidi Stillman That was really intense, that act. Luckily, we still haven't crossed that spot in life yet with our ensemble, but I have no doubt that that is going to be part of our experience, as this community of artists. It's very profoundly moving, affecting, in a lot of ways. That act, in some ways, as an actor felt a little easier than some of the others, strangely. I think I just felt more comfortable in that realm, because it's more abstracted, and less real. It's less about behavior, and more about big ideas and the eternal.

Kevin Douglas There were moments, especially in the death scene, while on stage, where I would have to remember I'm in the play. I would just be, 'Oh, she did that differently.' Or really listening to the words: 'I didn't catch that before.' Then realizing, 'Jeez, I've got to focus. I've got to be back in the play. I've got to stay in the play.' I had to figure out what is death and what does that mean to me sitting in this chair. Otherwise, I was thrown off. Even as a ghost or a spirit, even in death on stage, you have to have a motivation, you can't just be there, you've got to find a reason to be. Otherwise, why is your body there? Why don't we just have empty chairs?

David Catlin Emily has died in childbirth and though it's not explicitly stated, who delivers the babies in that area? It's Doc Gibbs. He's there when it happens, probably. That's all in between acts, but he comes on stage with that, that he wasn't able to save her life. Probably had to clean up after it, and how awful that would be. That's a part of who he is. In this instance he failed or maybe feels like he failed or couldn't help enough.

Heidi Stillman The other moment that was always just killing to me, was the marriage, and the sending him off into the world, and into the grown-up life. That always felt really potent, in a friend way, too. All being there, gathering, witnessing together. We'd all been to each other's weddings, and been to the hospital on the day our babies were born. We've all had so many experiences like that together, as an ensemble.

Kevin Douglas Laura's urgency would change from night to night, the urgency to get back home, or back to that life. Her desperation. The more desperate she would be to go back, the more painful it would be when she realized that she has to return to her grave. The more she wanted it, and the more she was let down, the more painful it would be for her and the audience, and all of us.

Christine Mary Dunford I think if I were teaching it from an adaptation point of view I would instruct the students to research, to read the play again and again and again, and to come up with a proposal about what his big ideas are, why it needed to be written in the world, what he was trying to ask us to consider. Then I would ask them how that's relevant to them in their lives, and how they make this play, maintaining the truthfulness of its core agenda, its core truth, in their adaptation.

If I were teaching it in terms of acting, I would probably use it to have actors invest and develop strength in their imaginations. I might talk to them about archetypes, and I would certainly talk to them about race and cultural norms, assumptions, and whose town is it? Whose town isn't it? When you think about that, who does it speak and who doesn't it speak to? Who does it include, who does it exclude? Does it exclude anybody? Does it include everybody?

David Kersnar It proved to us that good stories win. That's something that we ask ourselves at every production retreat: why must this story be told now? I think that in asking that question of this play that's done so much, we were able to really get down to why Lookingglass had to tell this story now. I think largely that was because Anna and Jessica pushed us to really take it to the next level and to really deepen our choices and in that way that production pinpointed a transition with a company that we were going from in terms of the life of a company.

Laura Eason My parents came and saw everything. They had their own relationship to the theatre company and to all my pals and to all the shows we'd done together. When they looked up at the ceiling, they were having their own memories of Lookingglass and being a part of it for all these years that I've been involved with the company. It was nostalgic for them, too, in a really beautiful way as it was, I think, for all the people that have been following the company for a long time, that had watched us grow up and build this thing that was bigger than us.

David Kersnar We may never come back together in that way again and that's okay. Because, if a company doesn't constantly change and grow and transform, it dies. So, we have to be at the forefront of that. That means as individual artists, letting go of control of this company.

Heidi Stillman Any time when we are all together, it's good for our theatre company. It's good for our ensemble, because we enjoy each other so much, and we get so much energy from each other. We've done this crazy thing together that's so important to all of us.

Christine Mary Dunford I think in a sense that we were looking at ourselves getting older and we were looking at our company changing, us changing, and moving on. I think there was a direct parallel experienced in Act III. I don't think it made me think any more about life or the company passing, because our company, we've been thinking about that from the first moment. That's built into our DNA. My experience with the company has been a series of celebrating and mourning. Celebrating what we're becoming, but mourning what we didn't become, but also celebrating what we've become that I didn't imagine.

Joey Slotnick I want to reread the play now. I want to do it again now because it will feel, I'm sure, different. It's a play that spans time. You can read it now and it can mean something totally different and then you can think back and think, 'Wow, that's where I was in my head.' I think I would bring more experience, more life experience. And trust that that is in my soul.

10

Intermission: The Church of Grover's Corners

The liturgy of The Church of Grover's Corners, isn't the Old Testament, the New Testament, the Koran, or the Book of Mormon. The Church of Grover's Corners isn't Protestant, Presbyterian, Methodist, Unitarian, Baptist, or Catholic. Nor is it Jewish, Muslim, Buddhist, or the Latter-Day Saints. It's not any denomination you might know of or be part of. It doesn't have its own building, be it church, synagogue, temple, mosque, or ashram. People don't feel compelled to dress up in their Sunday best, their churchgoing clothes, in order to attend, and don't even want to, because weekend casual is the prevailing style.

But for all the things that have been ruled out, seemingly leaving very little, have no doubt that there is a Church of Grover's Corners. By the end of 2019, the Church had offered up its voice twelve times since its inception.

The Church of Grover's Corners isn't any kind of theological institution. Taking part in its rituals in no way contravenes any religious traditions you may or may not follow. Atheists are welcome, too, after all. You see, the Church of Grover's Corners is really an informal gathering of members of the Louisville creative community, who began coming together in 2018, roughly every other month, to read *Our Town* aloud. That is its only text and its sole reason for existing.

The meetings echo some time-honored American traditions. They take place in various homes, where friends, neighbors, and even strangers are welcomed. As it is a potluck, with all in attendance bringing some manner of entrée, side dish or dessert, it could be a summer picnic, or for that matter a barn raising. As a reading of a play in a home by a largely amateur company, it is a reminder of the days before regional theatres, when small communities, in particular, might have groups that met, not unlike a book club, to read a play aloud. Though there isn't much drinking in Grover's Corners, there is an open bar at The Church.

Unlike genuine religious orders, whose origins may be rooted in the distant past, with relics and apocrypha, the Church of Grover's Corners is sufficiently new that its origins aren't shrouded. It's a fairly egalitarian group, so there isn't any hierarchy, though the founders are Gregory Maupin, an actor and musician, and Tara Anderson, a producer of live events and public radio programming. They're right there at meetings, appreciated, but not necessarily revered. You can receive The Word right from those who initiated the Louisville community, although the words of communion were written by Thornton Wilder more than three-quarters of a century ago.

The very first Church meeting took place on February 11, birthdate of the play's Emily Webb—an accident, so Maupin claims. In written remarks that day, Maupin talked about his experience of playing the alcoholic choirmaster Simon Stimson in a production of *Our Town* at Actor's Theatre of Louisville (ATL), the city's largest professional producing theatre, in 2014. He described how the company remained on stage even when they weren't in particular scenes.

"I never once got tired of hearing this play," Maupin said. "These words, these generous thoughts about humans and how they work, and kindness and appreciation, and how all these particular-though-fictional details of a specific day in a specific place in a specific era told many truths that feel universal. I can't say whether they really are. I'm not universal myself. But they sure feel universal."

By the time of the eighth meeting in March 2019, at Anderson's home in Prospect, Kentucky, Maupin was no longer relying on notes. His somewhat looser narrative about the origins of the Church continued, "We had a bunch of sort of godless theatre heathens backstage, who had a conversation. 'You know, this is the church that I would go to. We've been doing this every morning [student performances] except Mondays and pondering the sort of things that this play makes you ponder. Let's just get together and do this once a month.'"

As Maupin explained, the ATL cast couldn't keep reconvening, as they had been drawn from around the country. But musing on the idea years later via Twitter, Maupin paraphrased Anderson's response to that story as, "Oh, god, let's do that now. The world is a mess."

After experiencing the first gathering, as Maupin told the two dozen or so March 2019 attendees, "The fun for me, the reason for doing this regularly, is that, when you're in the cast of a show—as anyone here who has been in the cast of a show knows—there is something about the repetition. There is something about the definition of ritual that is going with intention to do a thing again and again and again."

The assignment of roles for each meeting of the Church is handled by Maupin and Anderson; it varies from meeting to meeting. There is no effort to adhere to age, gender, ethnicity, race, disability, or sexuality as written; if someone wants to play a role, they ask for it, and especially if they've not read it before at a Church meeting, they're quite likely to get to do it. When I planned my visit for the eighth meeting, I was seized by hubris. I asked if I could read the Stage Manager.

While this all took place in the very early days of creating this book, I was certainly familiar with *Our Town*. It's highly unlikely that I would have undertaken this project if I wasn't. But being within it, even if only for one reading, in a charming suburban living room, among mostly strangers, was revelatory. It's not so much that I heard the play differently, but the moment I knew I would read this role, I flashed back to my high school theatre days, and to all I have learned over years of working at theatres, though never as an artist of any kind. I suddenly had what I'll call "actor brain."

For my purposes, actor brain is when you focus first and foremost on what you have to do. In most plays, one is considering how they might play scenes with others. In the case of *Our Town*, actor brain reveals something quickly if it wasn't obvious before. Save for a handful of lines in Act III—and when the Stage Manager steps into playing other characters—it is a role of monologues, of direct address. You play a scene for the audience, but not with the rest of the company for the majority of the evening. As lengthy as the Stage Manager's speeches may be, there are also pages at a stretch where the character doesn't function at all.

Do audiences ever realize this as they watch the play? Do they stop to think how unnatural this might be? After all, it's not a one-person play. It's not a case of a character stepping out of a scene on occasion to confide in the audience. It's a character predominantly talking to the audience, parceling out information.

Had the Church gathering been a cold read for me, a heretofore unknown text, it would surely have felt different. But Maupin's invocation of ritual certainly took hold, as I spoke aloud for the first time words of Wilder's which I have always found most beautiful and meaningful.

"This is the way we were," spaketh the Stage Manager, "in the provinces North of New York at the beginning of the twentieth century. This is the way we were: in our growing up and in our marrying and in our living and in our dying."[1]

In 2019, a time of ever-heightening political and social division, the Stage Manager, as he has for generations, issued a unifying reminder about those who went off to fight against slavery and inhumanity: "All they knew was the name, friends—the United States of America. The United States of America. And they went and died about it."[2]

Our Town has been playing on stages across the world since the end of the original Broadway run in 1938. It has become a ritual, a tradition, interpreted, reinterpreted, misinterpreted, over four-score years and counting. It may well be our secular liturgy, and only the folks in Louisville have recognized it as such, or at least done something about it.

The night I attended, this church of theatrical heathens had communed on, believe it or not, Angel Trumpet Drive. Only, in this case, the trumpet was the steam whistle of the 5:45 for Boston, echoing across a century.

11

Theatrical Outfit, 2019

We might see, even if only for the brief duration of our "insubstantial pageant," that what we hold in common is always and eternally more important than what divides us, and that the truth of these two stories, and all great stories that endure, is this: we belong to one another.

from program note by Tom Key, artistic director

In the script of *Our Town*, the second sentence of the stage directions at the start of Act III reads, "On the right-hand side, a little right of the center, ten or twelve ordinary chairs have been placed in three openly spaced rows facing the audience."[1] In the script of *The Laramie Project* by Moisés Kaufman and the members of the Tectonic Theater Project, the stage directions at the start of Act III read, "The stage is now empty except for several chairs stage right. They occupy that half of the stage. They are all facing the audience and arranged in rows as if to suggest a church or courthouse."[2]

This similarity is not a coincidence. The intent with *The Laramie Project*'s directions is to deliberately evoke *Our Town*. Kaufman and Barbara Pitts McAdams acknowledge this in the Tectonic company's book *Moment Work: Tectonic Theater Project's Process of Devising Theater*, as Kaufman had done in interviews prior to the book's 2018 publication. *The Laramie Project* itself is set in a small town in Wyoming, and is drawn from the Tectonic company's interviews with members of the community in the wake of the murder of Matthew Shepard in 1998.

In an email in late summer of 2019, Kaufman wrote that while he knew that a few companies had produced the two works in repertory, he was hard-pressed to name any. He was aware, in the weeks preceding the start of its performances, of the forthcoming production by Theatrical Outfit, a professional company in Atlanta, Georgia.

While the Act III settings may be similar, the original scale of the two shows diverge. The first production of *The Laramie Project* was performed by eight actors, while the original production of *Our Town* had a roster of 49. It is not uncommon to find productions of *The Laramie Project* with larger casts, given the significantly larger number of roles, all designed to be portrayed by a small and versatile company; it is frequently expanded for academic and community productions, where larger cast shows can accommodate more actors and include more of their given constituencies without adding significant expense, since the actors aren't compensated.

Conversely, *Our Town* is less commonly produced professionally with two-and-half-score actors filling out the streets of Grover's Corners, save for when the producing organization can deploy non-professionals. David Cromer's 2009 Off-Broadway production had a cast of 24, the 2002 Broadway revival had 23, the 2019 Open Air production in Regent's Park worked with 18. Aaron Posner's production of *Our Town*, seen in 2007 at Two River Theater in New Jersey and remounted in 2017 at the Olney Theatre Center, made do with a cast of seven, however in the doubling and tripling of roles, the staging used puppets to fill out the community.

The Theatrical Outfit's rep of *Our Town* and *The Laramie Project* had a shared cast of 10, a slight expansion of *Laramie* and a significant but not unprecedented compression of *Our Town*. The Atlanta production saw the actor playing the Stage Manager stepping into some smaller character roles in *Our Town*, adding to those scripted instances when the Stage Manager becomes the minister and Mr. Morgan; the Stage Manager even sat among the dead for a time. The actor playing the Stage

Shaun MacLean and Asia Howard in the 2019 Theatrical Outfit production of *Our Town*, directed by David Hyatt Crowe. Photo by Casey Gardner.

Manager, Mary Lynn Owen, played, among many other roles, Kaufman in *The Laramie Project*, suggesting a common spirit overseeing both accounts of small-town life, one telling a story, the other hearing and assembling facets of a story.

The two productions shared a design team and the setting, of a few wood-framed scrims which could be translucent or made opaque with the use of projections and lighting, was used by both shows. However, the Theatrical Outfit productions employed separate directors—David Hyatt Crowe for *Our Town* and Clifton Guterman for *The Laramie Project*. The casts rehearsed each show every day, four hours in the morning for one and four hours in the afternoon for the other, only spending full days on a single show for tech rehearsals. *Our Town* began performances first, with *Laramie* following; there were five days during the five-week run when both shows could be seen on a single day.

While the two directors collaborated in casting the productions and finding design elements which might be common to both shows, they were not in constant conversation about how to link the two productions conceptually or in staging. That left it to the actors—and the audiences—to discover the conversation between the two shows, particularly on the double-header days, when they could be seen just hours apart.

In this chapter:
Maggie Birgel, Emily Webb
David Hyatt Crowe, director of *Our Town*
Allan Edwards, Dr. Gibbs
Clifton Guterman, director of *The Laramie Project*
Michael Hanson, Simon Stimson
Asia Howard, Mrs. Soames/Rebecca Gibbs/Joe Crowell/Si Crowell
Moisés Kaufman, author with the members of the Tectonic Theatre Project of *The Laramie Project*
Tom Key, artistic director of Theatrical Outfit
Curtis Lipsey, Howie Newsome/Sam Craig
Shaun MacLean, George Gibbs
Stacy Melich, Mrs. Webb
Mary Lynn Owen, Stage Manager
Maria Rodriguez-Sager, Mrs. Gibbs
Jayson Warner Smith, Mr. Webb

Moisés Kaufman The first time I saw [*Our Town*] was with Spalding Gray on Broadway. It was one of the most cathartic experiences I've had in the theatre. I think that what Thornton Wilder managed do was astonishing. He elevated the mundane into the sacred. He taught us that the theatrical space is a space where we can have conversations about our most intimate fears, and our most intimate aspirations, and our most existential questions.

Tom Key I have to admit that just learning about what happened to Matthew Shepard was so brutal and tempting me toward despair and terror, that I was anxious about going to see a play about it. But when I read *The New York Times* review and it compared *The Laramie Project* to *Our Town*, that opened up a bridge within me to go to *Laramie*. There are probably maybe three to five plays that have rendered me speechless, and that was one of them. I really couldn't speak for a period of time. I was in such a state of not despair or terror or horror, yet I was in a state of gratitude and wonder for life itself. That is what *Our Town* does for me.

Moisés Kaufman This crime that occurred in a town of 27,000 people really forced that community to look at itself. When they were speaking of themselves to the community, they would often say, "I thought this was *Our Town*, and then something like this happens." Or they would say, "If we ever thought we were *Our Town*, we just got a rude awakening." I think that *Our Town* is an image that a lot of Americans use to describe their sense of community.

Tom Key I wasn't thinking about season planning, I wasn't looking at a script of *Laramie* or *Our Town*. Just out of the blue, I thought, 'Huh, I wonder if we could do those two plays in rep?' I had been thinking about wanting to do both plays, but putting them in the same season seemed really difficult. Then my inner Geiger counter about decisions went off. I got very, very, excited for a number of reasons. One was that I believed that there are probably a lot of people like me who would be very eager to get to a good production of *Our Town*, but who might not know about *The Laramie Project* or might be anxious about reliving the trauma of that event. I thought that by choosing to do the two together, we could draw attention to the public that there's meaning between these two plays. If you trust one, there's a better chance that you might trust the other.

Moisés Kaufman I think Wilder uses other story points to build his narrative upon. So, it is about children, and growing up, and getting married. He's trying to tell the whole scope of a lifetime, so death goes at the end of that narrative. I was interested in putting a town under a microscope as a result of an event. So, the event had to come first. If you see *The Laramie Project*, it's true that we enter after the murder is done. But in the narrative of the play, the violence doesn't occur until the end of Act I. The death is not until the end of Act II.

David Hyatt Crowe I was an actor in my 20s and my 30s and I performed in a production of *The Laramie Project* at the Alliance and Actor's Express. Then I was in a production of *Our Town* at a company called Georgia Ensemble Theatre. It was a very traditional approach to the story. It was a cast of about 28 or 30 and everybody played one person. It was done exactly as it was written. I remember being very moved by it, thinking it was a very good production. I played Howie Newsome. The thing that moved me the most was seeing the bodies, the number of people on stage.

I remember that the director went against type for Emily, and for George. They were two actors that I would have never dreamed would be cast in those roles and it really worked. Emily was a fuller-figured girl, and the young lady was very lovely, but she played her almost plain. She didn't doll herself up. She kept it very, very simple. The boy who played George was sweet, but he wasn't handsome, and he wasn't really charismatic. He was just goofy. There was something that just felt authentic about that.

Tom Key On a practical level, we could budget for ten actors and ten understudies. I put that as a creative question to David and Clifton. Clifton did this wonderful three-panel poster board chart with each character and the tracks that they would play. We saw that it could be done.

David Hyatt Crowe I looked at *Our Town* and said I can do it with as few as ten but not less than ten. Clifton was looking at between eight or ten for *Laramie*. We started figuring out, okay, we have ten people. We didn't want to have a young person playing Dr. Gibbs. We wanted to have that visual response from an audience of an older man and a younger man as George. We knew that you didn't want to mess with that too much.

Clifton Guterman Moisés says, 'ten of us total went to Laramie the first time', nine plus him, their leader. So, it was a nice coincidence when we figured out what David could manage and get it down to for *Our Town*. It was much more of a talent for David to figure out than it was for me, because I was getting two extra people.

Michael Hanson I know that David and Clifton were really trying to play Tetris with who could fit into both shows and in what capacity. My suspicion is that I was primarily cast to play Aaron McKinney in *The Laramie Project* and from there, they just tried to figure out how I could fit in *Our Town*.

Mary Lynn Owen I always thought that there were limited roles for women in the play. It never occurred to me that I could be the Stage Manager. I just thought that these women were my option. I wasn't in it, and just went on my way, never really thought about *Our Town*.

David Hyatt Crowe Some of the ideas and themes in the play, or at least what I thought they were at the time, were things that I was living through. My family's had a really rough year. We lost our father a few years back and my mother just passed away in March. A lot of the questions that I've been asking myself, and a lot of the grief . . . it becomes a necessity to quickly grasp and understand these really difficult human truths, if you want to keep going. As scared as I was of that, I also thought that *Our Town* would be a great way to process some things.

Mary Lynn Owen I think I had seen some productions that moved me in the third act, but I couldn't quite connect to the events. I didn't understand what *Our Town* was trying to do, and I think that maybe I hadn't really looked closely at it. I certainly hadn't studied it. I'd never done it, I'd never taught it, I'd never read it cover to cover.

David Hyatt Crowe *Laramie* and *Our Town*—they're both plays about the overwhelming importance of a single moment. That maybe the idea of getting up and making bacon for your son in the morning is not a cinematic moment of joy, or an expression of love—but it is, really. I was thinking about the last days with my mother especially, which were terrible. I remember one night waking up. It was three o'clock in the morning, and we had not gotten in front of the pain. I was awake with her, and she was doing her best, and I was doing my best, and it just went on and on and on. I can't think of the word, but there's some Buddhist word for the importance of staying present in a moment, even when the moment is a difficult one.

When my mother passed, I was really hurt, and unmoored for a while. But one of the things I was able to cling to is that for a good year to year and a half, through the last part, the worst part of her decline, I was present. I was able to accept this a little bit better because I understood that, in those moments, she and I were together and we made the best of it. Working on the play reinforces that about these moments lining up somehow. Somehow, they can just stand up and hold their own in the face of eternity, in the face of this overwhelming emptiness.

Maria Rodriguez-Sager David openly spoke about his loss. This was something that was very acute to him. He did bring that up, and it colored his approach to the play. Several of us in the cast, because of his openness with that experience, were, in that sense, given permission to be able to speak about our encounters with loss. It was never something that took over the play, but it was something that was given permission to live and to be present with us.

Mary Lynn Owen I began thinking about the particulars of what [Wilder] was saying. I began noticing the references to time, and to erosion. Just geographical erosion. How we're all aging. Emily and George began to have faces. These two couples, how they contrast so completely. How they spend their days.

Shaun MacLean The first reading [with the cast] definitely brought it to life. Even though I wasn't in the bowels of the play yet, it was my first hair on the back of my neck standing up. 'Wait a minute, there's a lot more going on here than I first realized.'

Maggie Birgel The only thing that caught me off guard at first or put up any kind of barrier was the conversation before they entered the soda shop and the lines about, "It's not as easy for a girl to be perfect as a man," and cooling down my modern-day feminism a little bit and instead connecting more to it. The way I was able eventually relate to that was connecting more to the insecurity of being 16 or 17 rather than making it much about gender, more about identity and professional prospects.

Asia Howard Yes, it was a white town and not very diverse, but the scenes of the play are what live on. Because of the universal nature of this story of a community, and it could be any community, it can live on and take new form with new faces.

Maggie Birgel I think the play can rise above the time in which it was written. Our cast was not all white. I really enjoyed the choice of having the narrator be played by a woman, just in terms of how that informed a lot of her lines. I think it's a fair criticism that yes, it was written in this time period with this group of people in mind, but I think the reason why *Our Town* is still being done is because it speaks to something a little bit more eternal, or that connects humanity on a deeper level beyond just this specific time period and this specific community of people.

Asia Howard David was telling us that we're going from this very minute scale of everyday life, and our perspective grows with each act. I loved that the beginning is so focused on routine and movement and these very small things that mean so much to us that we sometimes lose sight of the bigger picture. Then it grows into something larger than all of us. I really enjoyed when David was working with me on the Rebecca monologue at the end of Act I, because we talked about it being this microcosm of what everyone else is eventually discovering within *Our Town*, this discovery of something beyond the immediate.

Jayson Warner Smith It really made me think of my grandfathers a lot differently. I understood them even more. I was channeling a lot of the way they moved, the way they talked, the way they interacted, into Editor Webb, because even though I was born in the '60s, I'm a modern man, and have different points of view than people would have had at the turn of the last century. I needed to find a way to feel that, to justify that, and it really was nice to have that kind of conversation with two dead men in my life.

Curtis Lipsey Everyone always makes jokes about Howie Newsome. I wouldn't say it's the most appropriate joke, but people always make jokes about him being married to Bessie. And I'll leave it at that.

Shaun MacLean George became a deceptively difficult character for me to find, because we do see him at these different ages, and we do have that scene where

Emily is calling him out for being a jerk. David and I had some slightly different opinions on how much of a jerk George was, or was actually being. I think that George got wrapped up in what every high school boy gets wrapped up in who is popular and handsome and on the sports team. 'Okay, well, what are the important things in my life?'

Curtis Lipsey Howie's the friendly face that you see every day. He is that person that you pass in the grocery store, he is the mailman that comes by every single day of the week, and maybe you wave. Howie is the everyday routine that you look over, and you don't even think about. He represents this habitual nature of life that we overlook.

Michael Hanson I'm generally a very positive person, but I think a lot of people have that side that just feels completely other and drowning in the bleakness as Simon does. I was delighted to watch what everybody in the cast was doing but I tried to embrace feeling a bit other. I very much agree with the theory that he was gay at a time when he really wasn't permitted to be openly and I think that's Thornton Wilder airing that side of himself, the side of himself that he felt he had to keep locked up, in a community that certainly wouldn't have accepted him, and that from his perspective is completely closed-minded about art, culture—and just difference.

That's his private trouble. But the way that the text is written, to me implies that he also has plenty of problems that are known. Because when people talk about Simon's troubles, I don't think they're talking about him being gay. I don't think that would be something that could be really clearly spoken or articulated at the time.

Jayson Warner Smith I had an idea early on about the relationship between Editor Webb and Simon Stimson that helped me a lot, because there's this scene where Simon comes stumbling out drunk and Editor Webb is nice to him. I thought, well it just doesn't make a lot of sense as to why he is so nice to him. It just seems too treacly and too sweet. So, I made it a much more serious deal, that maybe at some point Simon and Mr. Webb had hung out in a barn one afternoon in their teenage years and fooled around a little bit. Editor Webb was able to pull out of that and conform to society and get married and have children and live a straight life, and Simon was not so much able to do that, and that's why he ended up on the path he was on.

Michael Hanson I had a list of other issues that would be a bit more publicly known. In my mind, his wife had a baby not too long ago, not too long before the main events of the play start, where the baby had died very shortly after being born. It was a baby that Simon didn't want initially, but once he met it, was very excited about his new little daughter, and then she slipped away.

One more little background character thing I had for Simon. If you look at the dates of the play, it makes sense that his father would have served in the Civil War. So, I imagined that Simon's father would have had some authority in the war, and then would have come back and had none, and probably would have taken out a lot of his aggression on his young, different, sensitive, musically-oriented son. As a consequence, Simon would have been used to being separated and belittled from a very young age and feeling resentful.

Mary Lynn Owen When I began working on it, because I am a woman, because I look at life through my own perspective, I began to secretly suspect that Thornton Wilder—I don't think he realized this at the time—I think he wrote a beautiful woman's role, maybe even more suited to a woman than a man. Women I believe are, from the get-go, very much in tune with the passing of time, of the seasons. Once a month, our bodies mark time. When we are pregnant, we mark time. When we raise children, we mark their time. When we take care of our elders, we mark time.

Also, the Stage Manager interrupts the action and a lot of the times the Stage Manager interrupts women. I think it's a very particular choice when a man interrupts women talking and when a woman interrupts women talking. When I, as a woman, say, "Thank you, ladies. Thank you very much," I mean it. It's not just so we can get on with the play because you said your thing. As a woman I feel like I'm saying, 'Thank god for that interlude, because you just showed us something that the rest of the play wasn't able to tell us.' The interruptions are more honest and integrated to the story, and respectful.

Maria Rodriguez-Sager Mrs. Gibbs spoke to me from the moment I laid eyes on her. I relate to her because she reminds me a lot of my mother in the sense that she has big dreams and has big hopes, but she's also a woman of her time where that woman wasn't allowed to pursue those dreams. She was essentially sequestered in this town, born there, raised there, never left there, until her daughter got married and moved away. All of a sudden, that provided her the opportunity to be able to travel outside of that little town.

There is this strength to these women that, even though from the outside appear to be trapped in this particular life, somehow in the midst of that they live in their strength, their courage. One of the things that was touching to me was, even though she has very few lines with Rebecca, in that one little breakfast scene, somehow, she reaches out to Rebecca and gives her permission to have her own money and to spend it in her own way. There's a difference how Mrs. Gibbs speaks to her daughter versus the way that Mrs. Webb speaks to her daughter. Rebecca never had to ask her mother, "Am I pretty?" Mrs. Gibbs, of her own volition, just would tell her, "You look real nice." I think in her own way, Mrs. Gibbs was trying to lay a foundation for her daughter that she can one day hopefully take flight further than she was able to go.

Maggie Birgel One of the early discoveries was the first scene between Mrs. Gibbs and Mrs. Webb when they're snapping beans, especially because of the physical routine, having a task to do with your hands, that you can really lose yourself in as a person, which we do so frequently in daily life. It was such a lovely world to explore that in, to really figure out a moment where these two women take a breath and a moment to really look at each other and see each other as people and as individual women that have a narrative that's more than just their husbands and their children and what their secret hopes and desires are, like when Mrs. Gibbs talks about wanting to go to Paris. How do these moments happen, and what do we do with them?

Asia Howard The majority of my characters were children, and I loved that, because it seems like in *Our Town* the children are the ones who have the freedom to really reflect on how the world is impacting them. I think at that point those characters haven't gotten into the societal expectations of how they should express what they're feeling, so it's unadulterated human expression.

Maggie Birgel I think the conversation that informed me the most was her conversation with her mother about school and asking if she's pretty. I think that Emily is confident in her intellect, is curious about the world, and is naïve enough to believe that that will be a part of her life forever. "I'm going to make speeches all my life." I think her vision for her life was probably something a little bit more than having a family. I do think it's part of the tragedy of the play and of Emily, that she doesn't have a chance to do that, mostly because of the time in which she was born, but also because she dies so young.

Stacy Melich Mrs. Webb is by herself. It hit me how lonely I think she was, but not in the sense of how we are now. In that time this is what you did, this is how life worked, and this is her job in life. She is doing a great job with her children. She runs a tight ship at home, she makes sure her husband has dinner and coffee and all those things. But the relationship is so different than the Gibbs. I find that dichotomy tells a lot about what she has had to accept.

Then, when Emily returns to her twelfth birthday, the communication that Mr. and Mrs. Webb have at that time is much richer, and it gives a lot more information as far as him wanting her opinion and trusting her opinion and it just seems to be more of a union—more conversation—and it made me wonder if their marriage was that strong in the beginning. It was a full, happy life and that as he got busier with the paper that they just grew apart. Here's this woman that really doesn't know anything else except that she loves her children and she wants her children to go off and lead good lives and have children of their own. Her only reason for living is for her children, which is sad because she loses both of them.

Curtis Lipsey Emily asks if she's beautiful, and if anyone would be interested in her. Every single show we'd be backstage and I'd just tell everyone, "She doesn't think her daughter is beautiful. She doesn't think she's pretty. She thinks she's fine looking, and that's about it, but she loves her too much to tell her to her face, 'You are not pretty.'"

Shaun MacLean These characters are, a lot of them, these archetypal characters. Emily's the dreamer. She wants to get out, she wants to break out, she wants to see life beyond Grover's Corners. That's juxtaposed with George, who's the devil you know. He's the one that she ends up settling with, because it's the familiarity. "Millions have folla'd it, George, and you don't want to be the first to fly in the face of custom." I think there's a tragedy in the fact that they both settle for each other. Then having the tragedy of her dying in childbirth, almost as a result of that. Who knows what would have happened if George had gone to college, and met some other girl and decided that life in Grover's Corners was not for him? It would have forced Emily to go a different way.

Mary Lynn Owen At the very end when Emily is dead, and she's asking me as a woman if she can go back—to me there's something so beautifully poetic about that, that I'm shadowing her, and looking at who she was, who I am in a sense, and who all of us are when we're younger. There's a particular moment right after that when she asks for advice, and except for Mr. Stimson, the only people who answer her are the women—Mrs. Gibbs and Mrs. Soames and me. We're all almost doulas. That's how I began to feel—a person who allows birth and change to happen.

Stacy Melich Having a woman play the Stage Manager, and tell our stories, I feel it changed or lifted up a lot of things that were being said. It's different for a woman to say, 'Do you see these two women? They have been doing this and this and this and this for 40 and 20 years and they haven't gone crazy. They haven't gone crazy.' It's funny if a guy says it, right? It's this little quip, this throwaway line. But with Mary Lynn saying it, it gives it weight.

Asia Howard The Stage Manager is of this world but not of it, an outsider looking in. She's omniscient, but then at the same time she can jump in and interact. The Stage Manager usually doesn't play the undertaker, but I thought that that was a really interesting choice because it made the Stage Manager even more a part of Grover's Corners. I felt like having a woman Stage Manager interacting with this world made it feel less like a puppet master, less godlike.

Stacy Melich In the third act, when Emily comes back to her twelfth birthday, just that whole idea of her not being seen, of Myrtle not looking at her daughter, not hearing her daughter, I was very surprised how painful it was as an actor to have to do that. To have to cut off all impulses that you have to comfort someone when they need something, to not give someone what they want and need.

Michael Hanson Playing some of the smaller characters, you really have to ramp up before the scene begins and just be living in the middle of the moment, as soon as you're on stage or soon as you start speaking. Simon Stimson, for instance, when we drop into choir practice, you really need to find out who he is very quickly. It really comes down to just being in the play before you even walk on stage.

Maggie Birgel Sometimes, offstage, when I had a moment to myself, I would close my eyes and I would go back to my childhood home and do a little mental tour of it. I started to remember all of these details in a sensory way that I hadn't thought about in years, little things about the way a certain room smelled or the texture of things or a memory of an experience, climbing a tree in the backyard and that kind of stuff. It was such a gift to me to live in that mental and emotional space.

Curtis Lipsey Sam Craig has been away so long, and has been so involved with the life that he has outside of Grover's Corners, that he has forgotten everything. He doesn't even remember how his cousin died. It's pretty fair to say when you find out that your cousin has died you would get the reason. He asks where his father's and mother's graves are. That's a pretty big thing. I would know where my parents are buried.

Asia Howard The way that people use memory to shape their perspective of their town, of their home, because with memory it can be as perfect as you would like it to be, but it's also manufactured in your mind. It's your creation of what was, and I think it's interesting to see the way that Emily delves into memory in a way that doesn't allow her to distance herself from it or make it more perfect. In *Laramie* people are coping through memory of a loved one that they've lost or using memory to justify their own actions. Memory and legacy, I think, were some things that were really strong between the two pieces.

Curtis Lipsey I was talking to my girlfriend, and we were dating long distance. She came to see the show, and she wrote down every single thing that we did that weekend, because of the play. I mean in detail. Day by day. I remember reading it, and I was like, 'Oh, my goodness, I actually forgot that we did half of these things.' I think that's just like what the play is saying to us.

Mary Lynn Owen There's a lot of denial in *Our Town* about what's really going on between people, and what the struggles are. The face you show people and the private face that you never show. I think that was very much a part of *Laramie*, even though people just kept saying, 'Live and let live. Live and let live.' What was so sad to me about *Laramie* is that there were a lot of desperate lost youth who were dying young. Just like in *Our Town*. We lose Emily at the prime of her life, and also in *Our Town* people keep making tragic mistakes, or they keep saying no instead of yes to certain things. Neither of those children, even though they're the descendants of brave pioneers who dug up stakes, crossed the ocean, and put up a new life. Their descendants can't seem to break out of their little boxes.

Shaun MacLean We have *Our Town*, this quintessential American town, the gilded memory of what small-town life was like in America at the turn of the century. Then *Laramie*, we have that quintessential American town, that small-town life, a hundred years later. Look at where that can go. Look at what can come out of an environment like that, for better and for worse. I think that they mirror each other nicely: 'Well, yes, here is the romanticized, gilded memory of small-town Americana. But then, what does that look like today? How could those things drive us apart? How can it lead to tragedy?'

Maggie Birgel What makes them so relatable is their examination and their movement between looking at the microscopic and then the macro, zooming in and out into one person's story, one particular person—a lot of times Emily, but some of the other characters in *Our Town*, and then obviously Matthew in *Laramie Project*—and starting with that one person's journey and stepping back, step after step after step, connection points of how people are affected by this one person's story, zooming out as the play goes on until we are all in this emotional and mental space of an awareness of the vastness of the world of humanity and a curiosity about what it all means and why, what our place is in it?

Jayson Warner Smith They talk about Simon Stimson, "Well, he's seen a peck of trouble." Then, "There's nothing we can do but just leave it alone." It stays the same.

Michael Hanson I think the one thing that Simon Stimson and Aaron McKinney, or at least the character of Aaron McKinney, have in common is serious mental troubles stemming from some sexual confusion. I don't want to call being gay sexual confusion, but I do think that the way he's been forced to relate to his sexual identity leads to a lot of confusion and anger and frustration. Aaron McKinney claims as part of the gay panic defense that he used in the trial that he was sexually violated by bullies when he was growing up. For the purposes of the play anyway, I chose to believe that that's at least partly true.

Asia Howard In *Laramie Project*, the people of Laramie are basically living Act III of *Our Town*. They are dealing with the death of a young person and reeling over the impact of that. Your everyday moments, your moments that comforted you because you were playing your role in this community, are now being shaken.

Allan Edwards Both plays are an attempt by a community to understand what they went through and that that's a mystery. There's really no way for a community or a member of a community or a pundit in a community to just state what happened. It's always reductionistic. The plays both acknowledge that the story of a community is kaleidoscopic and is multifaceted and layered with a lot of echoing and contrasting ideas and that no one, no one in any community, has a monopoly on the story. The story can only be told with all the voices speaking to each other, at each other, against each other, for each other. I deeply think that *Our Town* has that in common with *Laramie*, that the Stage Manager and his fellow performers telling that story don't know any more about what it means to be a Grover's Corners person than the people in *Laramie* know what it means to be a Laramie person.

Michael Hanson Elements of faith were at least indirectly responsible for what happened to Matthew Shepard to a degree. The rhetoric from the church fed into the mentality that led to the anger that eventually got Matthew Shepard killed. That side of religion gets explored in *Our Town*, if you want to say that somehow leads to the oppression of someone like Simon Stimson.

Stacy Melich Mr. Shepherd talks about, 'Maybe Matthew physically died in the hospital, but he really died on that fence with the Laramie lights.' This was his last view and so where is your spirit? How aware are you of your surroundings? When does that final moment happen? Religion, and just the philosophical idea of what happens to you when you die, both of them allude to the fact that it's not over after you're gone.

Allan Edwards I played the judge in *Laramie* who condemns Henderson. I had this long speech, 'You took him out there. You left him there. You could have saved him and you didn't.' Although the content of these two scenes seems so disparate, Shaun played Henderson and he also played George. I was the judge and I was also Doc Gibbs, so I had these parallel scolding scenes where I was scolding Shaun's character, a young man who was in trouble. I guess in both cases, I felt that paternal obligation to train young men up, to get them to be better men. It disconcerted me that I thought of Doc Gibbs talking to George at the same time I was being this judge scolding this young man who was involved in this terrible crime.

Maria Rodriguez-Sager [In *The Laramie Project*], Trish Steger is talking about jury selection. Henderson is sitting there in the courtroom and he's hearing these potential jurors being questioned. He's having to hear over and over again that they are willing to enact the death penalty on this young man. It helped that the young man playing Henderson was also playing George. During that scene, I would have a moment when I'm watching him and I see George—I don't see Henderson. All of a sudden, I'm experiencing the scene as Mother Gibbs. That, in a roundabout way, informed Trish and it informed those lines where she says, "Can you imagine hearing that? You know, juror after juror after juror?"

Shaun MacLean One life is taken by a murder, one is lost in childbirth. Both are tragic ways for a young person to die. This idea of life and death and something eternal, in all of us. For Matt, the eternal aspect that his life is carried on through this play, and the impact that it had on the world, on the greater realm of civil rights, and the work that his family has done. There's something eternal about that.

Mary Lynn Owen I think the Stage Manager's job is to keep revealing that truth, pulling back the veil, and pulling back the veil. In *Laramie Project*, we already know this thing has happened. The veil is right there. Are we willing to keep the curtain open? Or do we want to draw it shut again?

Michael Hanson I think finishing *Our Town* in the graveyard, especially as one of the dead, really causes the play to stop. It really settles and dissolves into darkness in a weird way. Whereas with *Laramie Project,* although we do end with that tribute to Matthew and we do end with the starry sky, I feel like *Laramie* ends with more energy and maybe a bit more optimism, a bit more of a thought towards tomorrow and what comes next. *Our Town* has always felt like a goodbye to me the way that it ends with just the night dying down and with most of the characters on stage dead and with the Stage Manager saying, 'Well, good night.'

I think the perfect experience of the life of an actor would be to have played the Stage Manager as the last play you'll ever do. And then the night before you pass away, you do a performance of *Our Town*. That would be the perfect way to go. Drift off later that night in your sleep.

12

Miami New Drama, 2017

To find *Our Town* in other languages is no surprise, since the play began receiving international productions within a year of its closing on Broadway. Call it *Unsere Kleine Stadt* (German), *Vår Stad* (Swedish), *Piccolo città* (Italian), *Nuestra ciudad* (Spanish), *Nasze miasto* (Poland), *Ons Dorp* (Afrikaans), or any other translation, it remains Grover's Corners. In most cases, however, a single language dominates. There may be times when a simultaneous translation via earpiece or supertitle is offered, but a single tongue usually holds sway.

At the very same time in 2017 that Deaf West was offering *Our Town* in both American Sign Language and English simultaneously, Miami New Drama in Florida offered its own unique spin on the language of Grover's Corners, presenting the play in English, Spanish, and Creole, the three dominant languages of the city. To clarify, only one language was spoken at a time, with the majority of Grover's Corners speaking English. However, at home, the Webb family spoke Spanish; across the way at the Gibbs house, Mrs. Gibbs spoke Creole, and while her children understood her when she used it, her husband had never really grasped it. English supertitles were provided when non-English languages were in use.

Our Town was not the first production of the recently formed company, but artistic director Michel Hausmann, a Venezuelan native, saw the trilingual *Our Town* as a major step in welcoming the diverse communities of Miami to join together in a single theatre. He cast the show with actors living in New York, Miami, the Midwest, the West Coast, and his native Venezuela, and enlisted playwrights Jeff Augustin and Nilo Cruz to provide the Creole and Spanish translations, respectively. Venezuelan actors Carlota Sosa, Rafael Romero, and Luigi Sciamanna traveled to Miami to appear in the production.

Designer Arnulfo Maldonado created a spare open space on the stage of the Colony Theatre, the 1935 art-deco venue where the company performs, with a wooden-planked floor and a concrete back wall. The one noteworthy digression from Wilder's directions was the creation of a flanking pair of short steps downstage, connecting the stage to the house. These nooks would substitute for the ladders at the end of Act I, and provided a spot for the Stage Manager to find repose in at times, when not participating in the action. The period costumes were

Chantal Jean-Pierre and Martin K. Lewis in the 2017 Miami New Drama production of *Our Town*, directed by Michel Hausmann. Photo by Stian Roenning.

brown, beige, and white, although the Stage Manager sported a traditional Cuban guayabera shirt. The show was lighted with a range of blues, purples, reds, pinks, and oranges, until the final minutes, when a soft white glow took over.

In this chapter:
Jeff Augustin, Creole translator
Michel Hausmann, director and artistic director
Chantal Jean-Pierre, Mrs. Gibbs
Martin K. Lewis, George Gibbs
Arnulfo Maldonado, set and costume designer
Rafael Romero, Howie Newsome
Thallis Santesteban, Emily Webb
Luigi Sciamanna, Mr. Webb
Keith Randolph Smith, Stage Manager
Carlota Sosa, Mrs. Webb

Michel Hausmann If I'm going to have the chutzpah of saying, 'I'm going to start a regional theatre in Miami in the 21st century,' then why? 'What are you going to do? How are you going to be different?' You really need to have a good reason. I think the reason was that Miami is the future of America. Miami is more multicultural, more multilingual, than America as a whole. But America is slowly going to Miami's direction. I think we can do theatre that is inclusive of different minorities that share the same space. How do we do that is going to be informative for America, where in the next 30 years we're going to be a country of minorities. Miami is America on steroids. We are the new Ellis Island.

Jeff Augustin If this had been somewhere else and someone asked me to do this, I'm not sure if I would've so quickly jumped at the chance. I did it because it was Miami and because of the racial politics and cultural politics in Miami. That's part of what this translation is giving some life to. Miami tends to be culturally self-segregated.

Michel Hausmann The Venezuelans live in Doral, Little Venezuela. All the Argentinians live in North Beach. The old Cubans live in Coral Gables and the new arrivals in Hialeah. The work we do is always an encounter of communities.

Jeff Augustin That this Cuban girl and this Haitian boy, in Miami, felt special and different and exciting and kind of explosive was doing something different to the play.

Michel Hausmann From the very beginning, I've been working with different languages at the same time and the layers that that creates on stage. It creates a nuance. That's something interesting to explore. It took me a few months of line by line imagining, 'What here? What not?' One family, the Webbs, are more like my type of family. I have my wife and three kids, who are all very small. We speak Spanish at home, 100 percent° Spanish. Whereas the Creole family was really much more mixed together—the English and the Creole. It's profoundly bilingual. There are many families like that. There's a few lines in Creole that we give to the father purposely, even poorly. The father is an American and the mother is Creole and the kids speak with their mother in Creole and with their father in English.

Chantal Jean-Pierre That's normally the case when you're in America and of a different background. That the children will understand it and the parent will speak it, but they often do not speak it back. I felt like I was forced to speak it myself because my grandmother didn't speak English.

Michel Hausmann I was also trying to fight the idea of the chestnut, of the Norman Rockwell *Our Town*. I'll be honest, I think that Trump's campaign, and eventually the beginning of his presidency, which was more or less at the time when we were starting to work on the show, inspired us to do this.

Arnulfo Maldonado For me it was mostly about trying to showcase these bodies in space and finding a way that the space could feel both expansive and claustrophobic and oppressive. I think there was something that David Lander, who did the lights, and I were playing with in the sense that we're playing with this openness with this very sort of open exposed space, but how do we create a sense of enclosure or tension in such a big open space.

Michel Hausmann The idea of "Make America Great Again" is calling to a time of turn-of-a-century small towns, all white, that nostalgia. I think Trump calls for this fake notion of nostalgia. *Our Town* is not about life in small town America in the same way *The Bridge of San Luis Rey* is not about a small town in colonial Peru. They're both about the frailty of being alive.

Arnulfo Maldonado We're taking a group of people that happen to be in Florida, but this play doesn't necessarily take place in Florida. It's about the community of people that make up that town. That felt more important than trying to be specific about any particular small town anywhere in America. The sense of community felt the most grounded in terms of this play, which is why we pushed the sparseness in its design, because it was ultimately about the people that make up this town and not the framework that makes up that title.

Rafael Romero In Venezuela now, we have no theatre productions really. Just very small ones. The theatre is very complicated to do because of costs and return. Theatre is now mostly based on stand-up comedy or something of the sort. Comedies that attract people and do not cost so much because they are two actors or three at most. A production like *Our Town* is nearly impossible to be done in this country [Venezuela] at all right now.

Thallis Santesteban We had very different cultures in the room. We had children. We had an older, blind actor. It was so many different factors, different kinds of people, and different cultures that work very differently. I think everybody that was Spanish-speaking except for me was from Venezuela. It's so many factors that we were trying to unite through this production.

Luigi Sciamanna It was my first time in Miami. It was a very intense voyage. I'm coming from a country that is living a very deep, tremendous, dramatic crisis. So, the first week I felt guilt in that city. Blessed to do a wonderful play with a beautiful part. Then, of course, I start working, rehearsals started and I forgot that.

Michel Hausmann Miami is 100 percent segregated, in terms of the theatre scene. You have theatre in Spanish and you have theatre in English, and they both thrive in their own way and they both have their own followers, their own stars. One has no idea that the other exists. It's extremely bizarre. This production brought together two acting communities into a room and there was definitely tension in the way. It was so strange, because theatre in Latin America has a different way of how we rehearse. It's a little bit more organic.

Thallis Santesteban It's culturally very different. I've worked in Mexico City, so it's a little bit similar, but the US is very rigid in a way. We have a break every 90 minutes, and you have to be on time, ready to go. I think Latin American cultures in general are a little bit more lax. You roll in, if you're five minutes late, it's not really late. We're definitely dealing with different cultures and different ways of taking direction. Working scenes in Spanish versus English, and going back and forth, with half of the cast not knowing both languages. It had an extra layer of challenge, while being what made it so rich.

Michel Hausmann In Latin America, things slowly build up. In the English language, because of Actors Equity, you pay your actors a living wage. They work eight hours a day for four weeks. In theatre in Spanish, a lot of the actors have telenovela jobs and then this is in the evening, so typically it's like a three-month period of rehearsals. This was eight hours for five weeks.

The last thing I do is blocking because that's so easy, but finding the truth is really hard. Sometimes by blocking, you are preventing things from happening. At the beginning of the rehearsals, the Spanish speakers were one way and the English speakers were the other way. You could see, slowly, a community forming.

Rafael Romero I felt they were very stiff. They wouldn't relax. But that's how they work, For me it was very, very interesting at first. They didn't understand us. They thought we were crazy maybe.

Carlota Sosa Clownish.

Rafael Romero And we were. Another thing, they didn't have that relationship we had with Michel. I met Michel when Michel was 20 years old or so. For me to talk to Michel is like talking to a younger brother or a son.

Carlota Sosa We Latins are very emotional mostly. That was the first thing where saw the difference in the first rehearsals. We are outspoken; not so much the others. I don't know what happened, but we prevailed.

Martin K. Lewis We didn't really focus on the differences. I don't think the differences were even really noticeable. I noticed it because this was my first time surrounded by so many different people with so many different backgrounds so relevant to the work that they were doing. Carlota and Rafael were constantly talking about the stuff that was happening at home, so that gave me an insight to what was happening in Venezuela. That gave me curiosity to start looking up

Maduro and looking up what was happening, what is happening, right now. Chantal teaching me about Creole made me want to look further into the history of Haiti and learn about the fact that they were one of the first people to have a slave revolt.

Michel Hausmann It was an experiment that could have gone very wrong. Absolutely. I was terrified to see if the concept would work or not, and it works not because I am a genius. It works because Thornton Wilder is a genius. It just shows the flexibility of his work.

Carlota Sosa You have to connect with public. You have to say something. To try this kind of approach, I think you get connected with the people of the town that you are in, that you are representing, and I think that's something that Michel is very keen about, to be connected with Miami and what Miami means in terms of the people that live there. I think that was very avant-garde. It was an approach that I think that made the play connect much more.

Jeff Augustin I think it's saying or asking, what is this idea of America? What is this idea of the great American play and what is the American story? I think of going back to my initial feeling of sitting in this room with a majority white audience and my first experience of *Our Town*, watching people cry and not finding my voice and my space. My space in those questions and as a special kind of human, larger questions that are beyond just the color of my skin. It felt like it was asking and including in creating a larger picture of what is possible in the kind of American story, who is possible in the American story?

Arnulfo Maldonado What I love about this play is that it's sort of like a glimpse into everyday life that doesn't try to powder it with too much conflict. You're seeing the sort of thing that you would see on any given day walking around.

Chantal Jean-Pierre All the productions I've ever seen of it were done by Caucasian Americans, so never in my wildest dream would I think that at some point in my lifetime, we would be crossing beyond that. But Wilder's nephew who's the head of his estate expressed that Thornton Wilder was always open to a wide diaspora. I was sold on the idea that Michel had of casting it half Spanish, half Caribbean or Haitian. That certainly spoke to me since I was raised in Miami and I'm of Haitian descent.

Michel Hausmann The thing about *Our Town* is the surprise. You don't understand that it's about death until you understand that it's about death. We started this with the whole company singing songs. Everybody feels and everybody starts singing, the audience starts to sing. That was a way for us to create communion. Immediately, there was this bond, because you were singing with them when you came in.

Then we gave you an opportunity to continue to sing with them after the wedding. The wedding comes in and everybody jumps onstage and we party and we have shots of alcohol and it's euphoria. We play Beatles songs and then we slowly kick you out of the stage and then everybody's sitting. That's when it hits you. That moment is there in the play. We sang songs in Creole, songs in Spanish, songs in English, so everybody felt, but then the whiplash comes.

The actor playing the undertaker, Joe Stoddard, is a blind actor. He was standing there and then immediately a young cousin, Sam Craig, comes in and approaches. There was something about this blind actor delivering those lines that felt not ghostly but very somber.

Arnulfo Maldonado The very first image of our particular production was the entire cast, in a line sitting up upstage center, and then bringing these same bodies that we first saw closer to the audience, but now the way that they're represented in these chairs is very different and we don't understand that difference until we're told. I think there was something about repeating that image, but having it feel like, oh, what was I seeing at the top? Was I seeing a collection of ghosts, is this something like looking into the past?

Michel Hausmann We did not try to do *Our Town* as an exploration of race and class. We wanted to just raise language and culture as an exploration.

Martin K. Lewis That sense of the other. I think there will always be the other. Thornton Wilder talks about the other, but so does Richard Wright in *Native Son*.

Carlota Sosa I'm going to say something that is very obvious. We were the Latins, and these other people were the Creoles. They get together because the daughter and the son fall in love. They are completely different cultures in the same town. They have to cope with that. In the beginning, they are maybe not so sure about it, in the version that Michel did. I'm not saying that it's the original play. They are neighbors, and they like each other, but it's very different when you have to become family.

Martin K. Lewis There will always be those that are disadvantaged and those that are advantaged. It has a lot to do with race and ethnicity. Other aspects, too. Economics, location, ableness. I don't think that other aspect will ever disappear just because you change who's telling the story.

Michel Hausmann We do a lot of multicultural work at Miami New Drama, but it's always empowering work. We have Black heroes all the time. Or Hispanic. I think that that, for us, is important. But we're much more interested in empowering minorities than telling the victim story.

Jeff Augustin I come from a very large Haitian family, youngest of seven. Five of my siblings were born in Haiti and two of us, the two youngest, were born here. My Creole is actually better in writing than it is in actual speaking, because my accent's godawful; my other siblings speak it so well. We wanted to play with this idea of what does it feel like to be in that kind of cultural in-between, of being a Haitian American first-generation kid.

One of the hardest challenges was trying to find certain ideas and colloquialisms that are just not Haitian. Trying to find the best, thinking of things my parents would say to me, thinking about trying to find pretty much the same feeling, the same attack, but trying to find the right language. Actual syntax structure wasn't as difficult, but it was how do I capture this exact same phrase in a culturally appropriate way for Haitians who would be watching the show?

Chantal Jean-Pierre You can never capture everything absolutely accurately because it's a different background and obviously he is writing it during a different time period. [Jeff] did his best to be as accurate as he could with what was written on the page in the American language. He tried without being too loose with it.

Jeff Augustin There were clear moments that Michel wanted certain sections very particularly done. I think there was one moment where I pushed and I said, "I think the father was owned in Creole in this moment," because it says something about their relationship. My partner is Jewish and so sometimes he'll just throw out Creole that he might've learned, in a certain specific, loving, sweet moment or in a funny moment. Making sure that those kind of things, those textures happened as well.

Luigi Sciamanna The challenge is not how to imitate the sound, but musically how everything must sound as a whole. Because we are playing English. If we were contrasting a man speaking in English and a man speaking in Spanish or being a Spanish character speaking in English, you are allowed, you are maybe freer to sound differently. But when you are Editor Webb, who is an American, who is an American character, playing with the other American characters, you must try to musically sound as a whole.

Carlota Sosa At first, it was like, 'Oh, my god, I don't know if I'm going to be able to do this task.' I've never done bilingual before, and it's not easy, because you tend to think in your own language. To express that in another one, and be credible, it's not that easy.

Luigi Sciamanna Of course, the play is offering the audience the chance to hear a non-American actor playing an American character. But I think you must believe the character is from the play. So that, I think, is a challenge. Keith Randolph Smith had the charm, that rhythm, that very New York-ian way of speaking and facing the audience. You have to be aware of that—I'm going to speak after this man. I have to be on his level of craft.

Keith Randolph Smith I've never been a part of something like that. At first, in rehearsal, I would read and know what they were saying, but then after that I *knew* what they were saying. Just to hear the intent and the musicality of the language was so beautiful for me because I always spoke in English. I became the audience guide for the people who didn't speak either or who spoke both.

Michel Hausmann He had everything, the empathy, the compassion, a little bit of an asshole. The Stage Manager needs, from time to time, to be a little bit of an asshole.

Keith Randolph Smith In my mind, I just made him an angel and I have no idea what an angel is. An angel to me is not human, but my form was human. I got to allow myself to be seen. I don't know where I came up with that. I didn't share that with other people, because I can only imagine if I'm like, 'I'm an angel,' they said, 'What's your real name then? Raphael?' 'No, I'm not one of the angels you know.' It's like there's many of us and I'm here to take this audience, to share a story with them and to help Emily—I mean, help all of them, because it broke my heart every time when George loses Emily and it's just like, 'Oh, to be human.' Then go through those losses that people go through. You miss the people you love and care about but you find a way to go on. A lot of us, most of us, do and it's difficult. I have no idea of where the angel came from. Maybe just a dream.

Michel Hausmann I knew that it was going to be a collaboration, because that role takes such a big part. It's like Hamlet. Whoever is your Hamlet is half of your directing.

Keith Randolph Smith I had seen Myra Lucretia Taylor do it at the Long Wharf, the Stage Manager, so I did call her and asked for tips, suggestions, advice, but I had no preconceived notion how I would play it or what would happen. She said the more the audience is your scene partner, the more you can connect with them as you talk with them.

In our production, I walked into the audience, I came from behind the audience, I sat on the steps sometimes and talked with them. It was very much not just me on stage speaking out, but being among them. That was challenging because the rest of the cast sat in straight-back chairs along the back wall. They would come up to do their scenes and then go back. I never sat back there. I would always be on the steps or I'd elbow [audience members] and go, "Look at that," and they were like, "Are you talking to me?" I'm like, "Yeah, yeah, I'm an audience member right now."

Michel Hausmann It was very important that the Stage Manager spoke English without an accent. We needed the standard English that very few characters spoke in the play.

Keith Randolph Smith I would sit there and watch when I didn't have lines. Watching them you go, 'Simon Stimson—why does he drink like that?' It's a sadness and people won't talk about it, even though they do gossip about it a little bit. I guess nowadays somebody would do an intervention and send in AA or something, but it's like, 'He's fine, just let him keep leading the choir.' It was a simpler time. They were more accepting of people's individual traits instead of always medicating them and sending them away. Something to be said for that.

Michel Hausmann People found it really funny. The first act is really funny because people see themself there. A mother screaming at a kid, "Stand up straight!" I would be approached by Creole families saying, "You got exactly how a Creole family is. You nailed it." Then a Hispanic family would say, "Oh, that's exactly a Latin family. They're all talking on top of one another!" That's Wilder.

A lot of the audience members, most of them, have no idea what *Our Town* was because 59 percent of Miami is foreign born. *Our Town* might not be something they grew up with. They took this at face value. They thought that this was a play about a Creole family and a Hispanic family. I was surprised that lot of people appreciated and understood it as that.

Jeff Augustin There was something about *Our Town* when he's talking about the moon and the universe that felt beyond us. Growing up in a Haitian culture, I felt that same feeling that somehow this doesn't matter, but the soul does. That the soul will continue. It's an Asian cultural attitude about ancestors and the spirits of your ancestors guiding you through life. But the soul, the universe, our place in this world . . . Your legacy is here. I'm a writer, I may get married, I may do these things, but at the end of the day, I am bone and this will be gone and my soul and my spirit will exist in this greater universe.

Chantal Jean-Pierre I felt that the culture of that play, what he painted of that time period, certainly overlapped with how we're raised in Haiti. The mother being at home. Her entire life, her entire concern, everything is about her family and supporting them and making sure that they have eaten and fattening them up. That's so my mother. The kids, they are her life. I guess it's similar to Americans, too. But in Haiti, in the Caribbean culture, that's it. That is all the mother has. They don't have a discipline, they don't have a career. This is the career.

Luigi Sciamanna Editor Webb speaks about *Robinson Crusoe*, and I read the novel, which I never read before. What was very interesting in the case of *Robinson*

Crusoe, which is a very problematic book nowadays and I understand that, is that when he gets to the island, he is alone. He understands that the only thing he needs to start a new life is a chair and a table. I was very amazed by that because it's what Thornton Wilder asked to be on stage, only chairs and tables. What a great link.

Chantal Jean-Pierre What's interesting about finding the middle ground between Dr. Gibbs and Mrs. Gibbs, is the fact that I was playing it from the perspective of a Haitian mother and the dynamics of relationship in the Haitian culture, as opposed to this American man who is adopting a particular way of life in terms of the period in this play. I didn't find it easy. I think we had to find that because Dr. Gibbs is very intellectually grounded and I find Mrs. Gibbs, from where I was playing her, emotionally grounded. When the two came together, when they had their brief moments in the play where you can see their relationship, there were some wonderful challenges in trying to find that middle ground. He's not quite giving in to my loving ways and my wanting to find the love in that moment, in the relationship.

Thallis Santesteban I think Emily's a very strong person. She's caregiving in a very strong way. I think how harshly she calls out George, and from then on, how much she cares for her parents, and her brother. She turns tragic because she dies, but she's innocent in a way. But it also seems like she's older than she is. She's one of those kids, and especially girls, that are just a little bit more grown up. It seems like she just knows more. People say, "old soul."

Luigi Sciamanna Robinson Crusoe thinks you have to hear the birds. You have to be in contact with nature to know who you are. That's very much like what I have to speak to the audience in describing Grover's Corners, how people are, in a way, so pure, because they are watching the mountains or they're watching the birds.

Thallis Santesteban Obviously she's very smart, very educated. She's good at school. She doesn't grow that much because she was young when she died, but it's always challenging to figure out a way to play age without playing age, to not pretend like I'm being a little girl in a mocking or fake way that's going to take the audience out of it.

Rafael Romero I'm 55 years old. I'm at a stage in my life where I'm starting to think about the day I am not going to be here anymore. The people I love are not going to be with me anymore. That's one thing I thought about a lot during performances of *Our Town*. When you become a father, and you have a brother, and you have a son, and you think about losing your parents, losing your spouse, god forbid a child, it's a thought that kills me. During performances, many times I thought about those things, about losing the people I know, the people I love.

Thallis Santesteban I think that's one of the challenges. The "Good-bye, world" speech and everything leading up to it. It's so heightened emotionally. The older I get, the more I work, the more I get to do these characters that get to such a heightened emotional state, the more comfortable I am in my ability to do that on stage. I remember playing it and knowing how important it was for the story, for me to be able to get there.

It's also just very exhausting, emotionally to do that every day, to die every day, and say goodbye. You want to, or at least I try to, hook it up in reality while not messing myself up psychologically by pretending that my parents died. There's a tight balance that for me as an actor I have to find between using experiences from real life, but mostly just imagination.

Carlota Sosa If you think about death all the time, you become like a zombie. As an actress, I play like I don't think about it. I think about the here and now. It sounds very cliché, but it's the way to do it, because you cannot play philosophy. You cannot play the thinking. You have to play people. In this play, remember that there is the character that tells the story, and we are just like playing the story that this character is telling. But we have to be alive. We cannot be, as actors, thinking about the theme, about the transcendence of this whole death thing, because then you can't play it.

Chantal Jean-Pierre The one line that I still remember today, that got me every time, was when Mrs. Webb says, "There's something downright cruel about sending our girls out into marriage this way." That got me every night. The fact that she's hoping the friends will tell her daughter how to be in a marriage and what to expect in a marriage, but not her. To me, it's quite resonant of the time period, about how much sex wasn't discussed and how you really were thrown to the wolves.

Jeff Augustin It's a family-rooted, community-rooted culture. You look out for the neighbors, you listen to your parents. Because at the end of the day all you have is that. I think part of that, too, is part of Haitian voodoo, which is widely misunderstood. A lot of times it's spirits that people are worshiping, a lot of times they are your ancestors. My brother passed away about 13 years ago and my brother, I think, talks—comes to me in my dreams and gives me advice.

Carlota Sosa These are universal issues, and won't change with time, because we live and we die. That's not going to change. Maybe we can live longer, and we are prolonging life, but that's going to happen anyway. Eighty years ago, that was so fantastic about it. I think that's why they do it all over and over and over again, because it's not stupid. It's simple, because it's important, the origin of it. We are so busy now, trying to live life and so we forget.

Luigi Sciamanna There was a very emotional day when we did the play for schoolboys and girls. Oh, my God, this is one of the greatest days in my life.

Thallis Santesteban We had one student performance where it was the only performance we had where the entire audience was people of color, and these were all kids. High school students. We started the play, and it started in English, and then the first line not in English was Chantal in Creole saying, "Children! Time to get up." As soon as she said that in Creole, half of the audience just started screaming and clapping and laughing, and they were just so excited to all of a sudden hear the language that they speak at home, that they've never heard on stage or on TV. It seemed like that was, 'Oh, my god. They're speaking Creole, my language.'

Luigi Sciamanna You have a young couple as main characters. That day, with a young audience, I think it was the greatest day because they catch everything. Mature audiences sometimes are too critical. They are thinking too much in the audience. 'Why this? I have to read. I have to read the subtext.'

Thallis Santesteban The reaction was unbelievable. Three minutes later, the first line in Spanish is said, along the same lines, it wasn't a laugh line or a joke or anything, it was just, "You'll be late for school!" And the other half of the audience exploded, because it was half kids that spoke Creole, and half Hispanic kids. This is electric and it's so important, and it seems so important for these kids to not only see people that look like them on stage, but also just hear that language, and hear these stories told how their lives are, which is going back and forth in English and Spanish and Creole.

Luigi Sciamanna The young people in the audience, everything was electrical. They laughed, they cried. They cheer about when George came out with his marriage outfit, it was hysterical in the audience. Because they saw themselves marrying some day. When she came out dressed in white as a bride, all the girls, I would never forget. Everyone was screaming. Everyone was crying. Everyone was expressing themselves, and I was crying. Everyone was crying. Even Keith was crying.

Thallis Santesteban That entire performance was unforgettable. I will never . . . it was insane and the reaction was insane, and so lively. The point where we ask people to come up on stage and dance with us. I was like, 'Oh, my god, Martin is going to get mauled by these kids.' They were so excited and they came up and danced. And I was like, 'How am I going to then come in with a third act, which is immediately very sad and serious? How am I going to get them to go with me on this, because they've been laughing so hard, and screaming?'

Luigi Sciamanna I remember walking through the aisle in the church, giving away my daughter in tears. It was because the exchange with the audience was unique. I'm not saying the mature audience didn't like the play. But their audience is mature. They hear, they clap at the end. They clap very enthusiastically. But that day it was in everything with laughter, with clapping, with cheering, with screaming, with crying.

Thallis Santesteban When we switched into the third act, it was silent for the rest of the play. We talk about representation matters, and it's in all different ways, and it's not just about telling current stories that are of different cultures. I think there's something about telling a story that has nothing to do with right now, but we're telling it in a way that a kid can see it. I feel like that makes it so much more relatable, if they're seeing and hearing themselves represented on stage.

* * *

Keith Randolph Smith I know we're social creatures, but are we meant to go through life two by two? It makes me ask myself the question—not the world. It's a thought-provoking play and it gets you caught up in your feelings even if you don't want to. I think it can soften the most cynical, stoic person, maybe to their chagrin. It has some magic fairy dust to it. I read it and I go, 'This is an old play and it can be sentimental, and it shouldn't work in this cynical age of the United States of 2019 with Venezuela going on, and Iran, and North Korea – and it just still works.'

Thallis Santesteban I remember doing the soda shop scene, and sometimes I would be able to pick out an older couple sitting in the front row, or close to the front row. That helped me get hooked up for the scene. I could see them having gone through this scene in the past. Especially with older couples. I could just see that reflection, and it's so moving, it's so innocent.

Martin K. Lewis That romance, though. I love that kind of romance. Not the romance that gets you hot and bothered, but that subtle kind of, 'I have this strong feeling for you and I want to explore it. I want to see what happens. I want to fall in love.' I think it's one of the reasons why I like playing the lovers in a lot of Shakespeare that I do because it's fun to feel love.

Thallis Santesteban It's also a challenging scene to play. It goes all over the place emotionally, and it jumps so fast. George and Emily communicate very differently, and the emotions are so different, but then they jump to the same place, and all of a sudden joy and love. It's just very complicated in the way that those teenage emotions can be. It's not as straightforward. The ending is very straightforward.

Martin K. Lewis That's essentially what I think the majority of George's and Emily's relationship was. It was always kind of like touching at what our future's going to be. That was my favorite part, essentially the first act, where they're just about to embark on this journey of being together.

Thallis Santesteban I remember I had a friend, we were so close growing up, and he was a couple years older than me, so he hit teenage years before me. All of a sudden, he got too cool for me. I remember that so vividly. For years, he stopped talking to me. Then, later in life, we connected, and now we're fine. But I remember so clearly that feeling like you lost a friend. And that was definitely one of the first crushes I had.

I think it's a very relatable story. That specific moment of having that friend where you were childhood friends, and then you start growing up and things start changing. Especially when it's, 'Are we friends or are we boyfriend/girlfriend?' When that even becomes a conversation all of a sudden everything changes, and there's something so tragic and also very exciting about it, of just what it is to grow up.

Martin K. Lewis You definitely have to find a way to communicate that tension without touch or without words like love. But I think that obstacle made the relationship clearer because Emily and George, you could see them going through how to communicate to each other how they felt without really saying it. And then them trying to deal with the anxiety of maybe misunderstanding what's being said. But I think that touch and go is what made the soda shop scene. This idea of two kids who don't really know what the future holds but they're trying to start a future together, without really saying, 'I want to marry you,' but essentially, 'I want to start my life with you.'

Keith Randolph Smith You could translate it, I believe, into Russian, or French, and I think it would have the same impact because you're talking about human beings, and living and dying, and the moments of our lives. You might be the most cynical son-of-a-gun in the world but when she says, 'We never really look at each other, we don't take time,' that's a universal human truth.

Martin K. Lewis You didn't think about the folks in New Hampshire when you looked at us. You thought about my dad. My dad came to the States on a boat.

There was a kid I was talking to after one of the shows. He was like, "You reminded me of my dad." He was another Black man. "You reminded me of my family and the lineage." That's what, I think, theatre and representation is supposed to do. Not necessarily supposed to tell you the same tale again, but bring you into the present. It's supposed to bring you to where we are now.

Keith Randoph Smith It's a timeless, timeless play and I would imagine he didn't sit down thinking, 'I'm going to write the most timeless play ever.' He just told the truth as he witnessed or experienced it and the reverberation, the echoes have been heard ever since and I think will be heard. I would put that in a time capsule and send it to Mars for when people eventually live on the red planet or the moon and somebody is going to say, "We should do this play." With spacesuits on. And it will still be the same thing.

13

Oregon Shakespeare Festival, 2008

Ashland, Oregon, is a company town, and that company is the Oregon Shakespeare Festival (OSF). Established in 1935, OSF has grown into a multi-stage complex, with both indoor and outdoor venues, performing from spring to fall and sustaining as one of America's few true repertory companies, with actors appearing in multiple shows and multiple roles each season, many spending years with the company and making their lives in Ashland.

As the festival has grown, it has expanded its repertoire far beyond Shakespeare to include not only other classic works, but new plays as well. Its American Revolutions series instituted by artistic director Bill Rauch has yielded a number of important new plays, including Paula Vogel's *Indecent* (co-commissioned with Yale Repertory Theatre) and Lynn Nottage's *Sweat* (co-commissioned with Arena Stage). While OSF has cast actors of color for decades, Rauch made diversity and inclusion both on stage and behind the scenes an essential part of his tenure.

OSF's *Our Town* was mounted on the theatre's Elizabethan Stage, an outdoor venue seating some 1,200 patrons, with a permanent stage setting resembling a theatre from the 1600s, complete with Tudor-style design framing the upstage areas and visible to the audience throughout, and a second level with archways and wooden beam columns. The thrust stage and the seating, however, save for the balconies, are open to the sky.

Performing *Our Town* at OSF without scenery as Wilder dictated did not yield a wholly blank space, but rather one evoking an English theatre of a bygone era, more than a century before America was a country.

In this chapter:
Todd Bjurstrom, George Gibbs
Anthony Heald, Stage Manager
Mahira Kakkar, Emily Webb
Kimberly Scott, Mrs. Webb
Chay Yew, director
Rex Young, Howie Newsome

Chay Yew I had seen *Our Town*, and I had walked out on quite a few of them, too. It wasn't my cup of tea. It was sentimental and everyone loved it, which meant I had to hate it. I didn't quite find meaning in it. I did the same thing with Chekhov. I think I was one of those weird students.

Todd Bjurstrom When I was in high school, my theatre department had gone to Ashland and we saw *The Skin of Our Teeth*. That was really the first time I had seen a Thornton Wilder play. When I saw that, I thought, 'This is the same guy who wrote *Our Town*? This is crazy', and I still hadn't taken it upon myself to actually seek out the play.

Chay Yew At some point in life, as we normally do, you grow into plays. I grew into Chekhov. I somehow came upon an opportunity when Bill Rauch said, "Hey, I'm starting my season at Oregon Shakes, there's a play I want you to look at, and it's *Our Town*." I said, "Oh, it's sentimental. Do I have to do this play?" And he said, "I want you to read it. Really read it." That had been probably 20 years since I had encountered it. I read it as a different person at a different age. I was quite blown away because I started to see nuances that I never had.

Mahira Kakkar When I was in college in India, I went to a really wonderful program at Jadavpur University. I had some incredible professors there. One directed *Our Town* and cast me as Emily. I think that was in '98. That was my first exposure to the play, and I was very drawn to it and very moved by it. I didn't quite understand it, and I don't think I was quite aware of what I was doing.

Anthony Heald I thought: what a wonderful play, wonderfully simple, wonderfully pared down so that the characters and the words paid off really well. I had never seen an actual production of it. I'm too old for George and there's a lot of nice roles in the play, but the Stage Manager is just an unbelievably wonderful opportunity. I was thirsty to play it for many years before the opportunity finally arose.

Todd Bjurstrom I'm not even sure if on my first reading of it, I felt the same way about the play as I do now. Some of the writing really does lend itself to some cheesiness. After having worked on it so deeply, it's one of my favorite plays, period. I reread it just this morning, and I found myself tearing up. I was getting emotional, honestly. I was like, 'This is crazy. How is this play that I haven't picked up for 11 years . . . these words are now touching me in a very different way.'

Kimberly Scott I did a production of *Our Town* at South Coast Rep with Mark Rucker directing and I played the Stage Manager. There weren't a lot of women running around playing the Stage Manager at that time [1998] that I knew of. I played it as a traditional stage manager with blacks on and keys around my neck. The actors got dressed, finished up makeup and stuff at positions you can see

Kimberly Scott and Mahira Kakkar in the 2009 Oregon Shakespeare Festival production of *Our Town*, directed by Chay Yew. Photo by T. Charles Erickson.

behind at the back of the stage, so it looked like the actors walked in as if we walked in off the street, just came straight to the stage.

Rex Young I had this feeling like, 'Oh, this old chestnut,' and it'd be dusty. 'Maybe Chay will make it exciting, make it more contemporary, or bring an approach to it that is enlightening in some way, that isn't just the traditional production of *Our Town*, which has been done a thousand times around the country.'

Anthony Heald Most plays, you sit in the audience and you watch it and you feel like this is happening. This is really a living room. This is really a dining table. They're really having dinner. You lose yourself in the play by being presented all the visual cues and having things happen in a linear fashion. But this play, dinner is not dinner. It's all about artifice. You're not meant to watch it and *think*, 'Oh, I'm in Grover's Corners,' but to *accept* that you're in Grover's Corners.

Kimberly Scott I don't think I understood anything about the Stage Manager because I don't think I really got the play until I was older. At that time, I was in my

30s, and I would definitely not play the Stage Manager the way that I played it then, now. For sure. I think that it's just one of those roles that you've got to have a little more life experience under your belt to get what Thornton Wilder's up to in that one. I think that the younger you are, you have a greater sense of immortality. It doesn't go on forever, for sure, the nature of life on Earth. You really hear it differently later in your life than you do earlier.

Chay Yew When I first got this play, I told Bill I wanted it to be cast with all white people and some Black, because I wanted to explore the race issue. He said, "No, it needs to be diverse and nontraditional." As a result, then we had to become nontraditional, but we had to make sure that everyone was represented.

Anthony Heald This was Bill Rauch's first full season as artistic director and his decision to have the quintessential American play directed by a Chinese American director, to embrace the multicultural, multiethnic cast, that became over the years his trademark here at the festival. The very first speech that the Stage Manager has is, 'Presented by the Oregon Shakespeare Festival. You will see so and so as such and such and so and so as such and such.' So right away, you're setting up the ground rules that this is a production being done today of a play and there are actors who are playing these parts.

Mahira Kakkar I think I remember him saying that it was a vision that he was extrapolating from the play's title, *Our Town*, and really taking it to embrace the world. That his vision was of *Our Town* being completely inclusive and reflective of the world that we live in today and that's how he cast it. He wanted to embrace the theatregoing community at OSF, that it comes from very diverse backgrounds in terms of everything—age, race, education, socioeconomic background.

Kimberly Scott If Thornton Wilder were alive today, I have no doubt that he would absolutely require that it'd be a multicultural or diverse company. Require. Because that's what he wrote. He wrote every corner of Grover's Corners even though that was only a small town.

We've moved through. We're moving. Now we've got to a point where diversity is accepted, understood. It's something that we still struggle with, of course, because we're human and I would daresay also because we're Americans, but it's definitely a part of what life is now for us.

Anthony Heald Sometimes today, when people are talking about things that they've enjoyed at the Festival that I was in, they talk about *Our Town*. Some of them will say, "But what really bothered me was—come on, in New England, in the early 1900s, to have a mixed-race couple and for Emily to be South Asian? It didn't ring true." My only response is: it's set up right at the beginning that this is a play.

This is a performance of a play with actors of the Oregon Shakespeare Festival playing the parts. I don't think Wilder's trying to create the impression that this is actually happening. That's why it's set on a minimal stage with no real scenery or no observable scenery. The essence of it is theatricality. The essence of it is the artists.

Kimberly Scott He would say, "Definitely. It has to be. Absolutely. Absolutely has to be diverse company." That's my belief. If it were at all possible, if he could contact us – we could get a Ouija board – I think he would absolutely say, "It must be a diverse company," because that's how the universality of the play is seen. The quaintness and the specificity of the time is more easily seen to by showing it with people that we recognize from our community.

Rex Young That became the radical statement, the modern statement. Just saying that this is a kaleidoscope experience and the fact that we have people from all different backgrounds examining this very specific, small background. I think that was his radical approach, if it's radical at all. People were upset by it sometimes. I think most of the time it just disappeared and people were lost in the story of the play, which is the best kind of subversion of ideas.

Mahira Kakkar I think there was pushback from the community because it's such a revered play and it's placed in New England. There were people who identified as being from there, who really felt like they didn't know if their culture was being entirely respected. Maybe they felt it wasn't authentic. I think some of the theatre-going community struggled with seeing such an inclusive cast; some of the theatre-going community loved it.

Chay Yew There were moments where I used people of color to make little points about the time. The professor was giving a presentation, and I had people of color holding up his things, his presentation. There was a moment that you actually saw, right, even though it is a nontraditional *Our Town*, that doesn't mean that racism did not occur.

Mahira Kakkar Chay said, "Look, we're making a statement with this. We're definitely saying that *Our Town* today looks very different from perhaps *Our Town* 20, 30 years ago. But this is what America looks like right now."

Chay Yew It was very complicated, too. There's a lot of context. It was Bill's first season. He had let go half of the company. When I came in, it was half hostility, half fear in the company because I was one of Bill's friends, Bill's chosen director, and everyone was very upset because some of their friends had been let go.

Anthony Heald Because there aren't those external cues, you focus entirely on the way the character expresses themselves physically and verbally. You zero in on the people in a way that's somehow easier than if you're being given all the trappings of most productions of most plays.

Chay Yew I remember very clearly one of the questions: "Do we need to have a New England accent?" And I said, "We can't." Then there was an uproar. "Why not?" "It should be!" I said, "Look, our cast is not all white. Because what Bill wanted, which I'm okay with, if we're going to go nontraditional, we cannot use the New England accent. For me, that would be colorblind casting. That means everyone's whitewashed. We can't because everyone's coming in with different identities, and because they are this thing called 'our town.' I'm really interested in this language that unifies them. Then by a unity, I can begin to see the differences." I think what is lovely and deceitful and scandalous about *Our Town* is it comes off as Americana. But then as you keep peeling off the layers, it's tragically human and individual and lonely.

Mahira Kakkar It's part of a larger conversation. Do you have to have a lived experience of something in order to be able to portray it? Is that always essential? How does culture move? How does art move? Who has the rights to tell whose stories? I mean, those are all things that also came up for me in the production, and those are still things that come up for me now. Learning how to be actually curious about those rather than shutting the conversation down was interesting to me.

Chay Yew What was interesting was reading between the lines of the play, what it was saying, what it wasn't saying, and all it was hinting toward. Even on the first page of the play, there was a notion of where people had lived. It describes the environment, and then very gently he would say things like, 'That's where the Canucks would live.' For the first time, it rang out—so there was segregation, there was race. It was almost trying to be Nancy Drew, uncovering this old masterpiece. I fell in love with it. I thought, as I'm excited, let's do some table work. And at Oregon Shakes, everyone knows the goddamn play. The first day, they were fucking off book, which made me insane. That means I have to do more work to get everyone on the same page.

Anthony Heald I told Chay when we started rehearsals, my method is to get the text entirely memorized before rehearsals begin. I would walk up in the mountains with the dogs reeling off the Stage Manager's speeches and then I went out on the Elizabethan stage in early March in the cold and did some of the speeches out there.

Todd Bjurstrom I think hearing it out loud for the first time was transformative. Hearing the voices come to life, getting it out of my own head and becoming more of an observer, at times, really made a big difference.

Anthony Heald I was determined to rehearse it the way I was going to be performing it. Chay was very accepting of that. I never looked at the director. The stage manager and all the assistants are sitting at a table directly down stage, but I never pitched anything to them.

Chay Yew I've never spent a week at the table excavating the play line by line, and the more we excavated, the more thrilled I became to understand where the role of women were. I felt desperate to find out more about the women. I felt the men would have their own lives. The interesting parts were the little struggles, the wars the women had to go through.

Rex Young I had not worked with Chay before, and so my assumption was that what this was about was that he was trying to understand a culture removed from his, and that was part of what the depth of his exploration was about. Since then I've seen his work, and I've known him, and we've worked together in readings, and not any special production, but I realized that that is also just part of his process. That he is very granular in terms of how he wants to understand the relationships in a play. The cultural signifiers of that play.

Anthony Heald Every time we approach a play that we've done many times before, we approach it in a totally new way. And so, with *Our Town*, the dictum was check your assumptions at the door, come in, and look at it for the first time. That's one of the burdens or opportunities for the Stage Manager—to surprise the audience, and not just slip into an easy repetition of a trope, but approach it with a fresh eye and encourage the audience to do the same.

Rex Young I remember the process of being around the table. It felt like an archeology project to Chay, like an anthropological project. He was very interested in the minute behaviors. I think it was two weeks before we even got up on our feet, just talking about relationships. What could be held within the vessels of these characters? Could domestic violence be a part of it, all of these possibilities? We looked at etiquette books on how to set up a dining table, and there was a lot of deep dive into the microscopic kind of behavior of this small town in New England. I just remember the doing of it, because that was unexpected, that we would spend this much time around the table on this old play when we spent half that time around the table on a Shakespeare play. But by the time we stood up, we did have an understanding of the role that we were going to now put together.

Anthony Heald [As the Stage Manager], your job is to make it clear. Your job is to welcome them in and make them feel comfortable, make them feel that they've got an ally on stage. That there's somebody who's going to take them by the hand and lead them through the story, with warmth and with humor but not in a showy way, not in a 'look at me' way.

Chay Yew I remember a conversation with Tony was I didn't want him to be too sweet. I think there is something wry about him. He's a little removed. And because he's never really described in the play in terms of his relationship to the town, but yet he knows it so well. Some people say he's God. I don't know, because if God is fucking with us, why does God need to tell us the story? What I do like about the godliness of it is, 'You want to go back? I'll take you back.' Which I always felt that conversation to be: they see God. I didn't want to be literal with it because then I think the whole performance would be something very different.

Kimberly Scott I saw David Cromer's Stage Manager and I thought they were going to have to carry me out of the theatre. It had to do with the fact that he just threw it away. Completely threw it away, which is what Thornton Wilder wrote.

Anthony Heald It's almost like doing a recorded book in that when you do a recorded book, you don't want to draw attention to your performance of the text. You want the connection to be between the listener and the text, between the listener and the author. And so, as a reader, you want to be as translucent as possible. I think the Stage Manager role is kind of like that, it's an emcee.

Chay Yew What I love about plays like these, actually they're not perfect, and as a result of it, we go back to them all the time. And the moment of dramaturgy I would say breaks, which I love and I basically forced it in a little bit more, is when Emily was dead. For the first time in any moment, the narrator's being interrupted. That was a moment where Tony completely would be taken aback. 'This is my story. Why is it hers?' And there was this fight. 'You want it? Here, have it.' And, of course, it's written that way, where it's infallible. She gets what she wants here, but to a tragic end. You can never go back. I think that play's exceptionally wise.

*   *   *

Chay Yew In the cemetery scene, Dr. Gibbs lingered. I wanted him to linger. He walked over to Mrs. Gibbs' grave, and she held in her palm of her hand the postcard from Paris. He picked it up, and he saw this for the first time, and he put it back down onto her lap. The little nuances of what people wanted was very fascinating to me. What I loved was the idea of longing. The longing, the idea of unrequited feelings in this play were very strong for me. It was specially my task to excavate those. And that became very thrilling for me. Another point of excavation was also

George's and Emily's relationship. I had deliberately made my Emily look bookish, wore glasses. I said, "I want you to be very smart because she's very smart. And all the boys, they'll look at you." George is the hot dude, but our George was a little beefier and was a doofus. He didn't know his homework. And every time when they both meet, he would diss her, and she felt ugly and not wanted. And when he finally asked her for a favor, we saw my Emily light up only to realize she's being used.

That's why I think when she dies, George is completely ... my George was unraveling. And when everyone had left, he just fell prostrate in front of her grave because I felt that was his love for her. That one beautiful scene about her, which I really love. I remember telling my actor Emily was born in the wrong place in time. If she was born a hundred years later, she would have been the CEO of some company. She's that smart. The only thing is that there's a huge fucking mountain in front of the village, the town, and she can never leave that place.

Anthony Heald There's a deep sense of melancholy in the play. So often, the sense of *Our Town* is that it's this feel-good play about small-town Americana. Chay, as I recall, he didn't overwork the sense of darkness, he was very happy to find the moments of humor and lightness and connection, but always in the background was this sense of missed connection and this sense of the fragility of the whole arrangement.

Mahira Kakkar For an actor to have an expectation on themselves to cry is a way to just kill it. It's like taking a butterfly and nailing it to the wall. It's also like as an actor, when I see that a playwright has written, 'Oh, then this person cries,' I'm like, 'Oh, great. Now, I have to try and block that out of my mind and try and find it.' It really was just like trying not to aim towards something, but trying to see how it would unfold every night. And some nights it was different and I don't think there was crying, but I have no idea how the audience responded to it.

There are times when I've been in the audience and definitely times I've been in an acting class when the actor's emotion or breakdown is not as important as the audience's. Sometimes it's more about what you keep under wraps. So, yeah, I don't know, it wasn't mapped out so much in that technical way, but it was more, and I think this is probably credit to Chay, who gave me the freedom to say, 'Find it anew each night.' He did emphasize in the first and second acts that he wanted a more reserved approach from Emily. But I think in the third act he gave me permission to do what I needed to do every night.

Todd Bjurstrom When we move into Act III, [Wilder] talks about all the other people who have died, and so I'm trying to imagine going to Wally's funeral and how hard that would be for Emily and trying to pull up a memory of grief—sitting back there trying to put myself in those shoes. I don't recall exactly when I hit the stage, but I'd come out, fill in the sound of some howling wind or something, and then I'd sit down. I'd be out on stage for a long time, I would sit there, and I would just start crying. Pretty much every night. I wasn't trying to cry. I didn't have a menthol stick or anything that I'd put under my eyes. I would be so engrossed in this play, and I would just be silently crying. It was very, very moving.

It was cathartic. I'm remembering that at the time, my grandfather, my mom's dad, was in the throes of Alzheimer's. It really highlighted the fact that everything that's happening to my own grandfather is perfectly natural – while it's horrible to witness – and that it's okay to die. Really, it's as natural as being born. This play, Act III, really is this examination of this progression of life and the progression into whatever comes next.

Rex Young I thought of Shakespeare as a writer, writing for a company like, "Hey, I'm going to throw a few reps a bone here in act five, give him this really hard speech." He paid attention to those characters. There's very few throwaway characters in Shakespeare and I felt that about the characters in *Our Town*. I also think it allows the universality of it, because within the characters of this small town in New England, you discover the whole world essentially in the smallest micro denomination. I think at best it opens up. It's like breaking open an atom or something, you know?

Chay Yew In a very Asian sort of way, we can talk about many layers of this play. So many goddamn layers, even the Chinese element to it, which I was actually very intrigued by, because Thornton Wilder had spent time in China. The idea of *Our Town* basically came out of Chinese opera, which I understood completely. It's almost Shakespearean. That's why he asked for no set, just very simply the things that you really need to propel the play.

* * *

Chay Yew The idea of the collective is the romance or the mythology we have of our communities. But how well do we know our neighbors? That's the beauty of this play. It ultimately shows us, as he would have said, like a star that ultimately runs its course, burns out. But how do we shine? Who do we shine with? And how do we live on this earth, this very short moment, and really use as much as we can? Emily's life was taken so quickly and the promise of her.

Rex Young Howie doesn't have a lot of lines. He relates to almost everybody in the play in some way. He's very connected, obviously, delivering the milk to the community. We had this imaginary cow, and I started to build it, and I was thinking, what kinds of people are more comfortable with animals than people? I started looking at the specifics of Howie. I was interested in trying to create a psychological picture for him.

We have a good friend who is a child and family therapist, and I was laying this out and she said, "Well, it sounds like Asperger's." I was intrigued by this idea and I started looking at the wide range of people on the spectrum, and how that manifests. That was a real inspiration. Chay and I spoke about that kind of purity and softness to him. So that's creating what made the smaller character much more interesting for me as an actor. I had no idea that anybody knew that I was playing with that, but it helped me make more specific, more informed choices at times.

Kimberly Scott Women in the early 20th century didn't work outside the home, they didn't do anything other than fulfill that homemaking, wifely, child-rearing thing. That's a choice I didn't make. To portray that and to give your heart fully to that during the two-hour traverse of that play—it's big, because that's so not my experience. It's so not anything I even considered as a young woman growing up in the 20th century.

I always knew I would leave my small town. Never considered staying there. I always knew that I would be a working woman more than anything else. I must have been eight years old when I told my mom, "I'm never going to have children." My mother was horrified. She's like, "What?" "I'm not going to have kids." I said it just like that. The fact that I knew that and I said it so off-the-cuff, casually, just discombobulated her to say the least. But to tell the story of a woman who is so completely away from my own experience, yet was absolutely a woman of the 20th century, it landed in a big way to give my heart a chance to go to those places.

Isn't theatre this chance to look at and examine and explore these other lives, these other opportunities that we may have passed or not had? And at the same time, more fully express exactly who we are?

Todd Bjurstrom George is this big, affable kid, and I think he's honest. I think that he's sensitive. I think he's smart. I think he's a lot smarter than certainly a lot of productions may portray him. I think he's really open-minded and curious about the world. He may not have all of the answers to all of life's questions, but he's certainly open to the possibilities of great things.

When George and Rebecca are at the window and they're looking at the moon, and she has that whole bit about the letter and the way it's addressed, I think that that moment really shines a light on how vast the universe is. I don't think that George had ever really considered his place in the universe. In some ways, he's got this perspective of you want to stay home, you want to stay close, you want to stay safe. But then there's this whole wide world out there that's just waiting to be explored, and I don't think that he even really realizes how vast it is until that moment.

Mahira Kakkar It was definitely formative in many ways. It helped shape me. It was a humbling experience each time. It helped me be more open, more curious. It helped me really appreciate the gifts I was being given, even if I didn't appreciate them at the time, I definitely appreciated them later. You know, sometimes you're climbing the mountain and you're just doing it a step at a time. You're not thinking about it, and then you look back and you go, 'Wow, I climbed that mountain and I did it with all these other people. That was quite something.' I'm so glad that I had the opportunity to do that. Not everybody gets that.

Kimberly Scott I love the play so much. It really makes me happy to even think of ever doing that play. I think that it's one of those plays that anyone asks me to do it, I say, "Yes," at the drop of a hat because it's so . . . I think that it's one of those plays that by doing it, you get to take a measure of where you are in life and how you feel about really big-picture life issues. I don't think acting is therapy, I don't think theatre is therapy, but I do think theatre is a gym for our emotions and our empathy and being human. I think that *Our Town* is one of those plays where you get the best workout and you're conscious of what it is that you're getting to examine and what you're getting to visit in your own life and look at things in your own life.

Chay Yew Any time when you add more to it, it always feels cloying to me. That's why I stripped it in the way that Chinese theatre would sometimes do. The whole thing is almost, in a way, Brechtian, again with Brecht being inspired by Chinese opera, too, because that's how he got distancing. In a weird way, Brecht and Thornton Wilder and I went back to Chinese opera to create this production.

Todd Bjurstrom If it was full of props and it was full of intricate sets, then I think that limits the audience and it puts a real timestamp on the production, whereas without the advantage of a prop, the audience can fill it all in for themselves and they can make it their own experience. It's like they're curating their own experience.

Rex Young The play can grow for you as you mature as a person, much like Shakespeare's canon does. You know, I was much more interested in the blood and guts of Shakespeare when I was younger and now I'm more interested in *Winter's Tale* and *King Lear*, but I think that there's young love, and there's romance in the play, there's tragedy, there's mature struggle with mature issues, relationship issues, dependent issues. I think that it's been surprising to people for this many years that they go back to it and they find something new in it. I don't know how he did that.

Mahira Kakkar Cheryl Strayed has a book called *Tiny Beautiful Things*, which is very well known now. And I think it's because of that. Small things—you don't realize how it's the small things that make up a life, that make a life beautiful. We're often running in pursuit of the big things that we think will make our life meaningful. But it's all the small stuff that adds up. I think that especially right now, when we're in a pandemic, and also in the 21st century, when I feel an overwhelming sense of disconnect because we use a lot of technology, I feel that the play is even more meaningful now because of the human connection and the emphasis on the everyday.

Chay Yew I think some plays don't need to be done again because they've become redundant. I don't think *Our Town* is redundant. There is this burning glimmer of truth about the way that we live that goes beyond race. That's actually inherent in the play. That's why we go back to it. Plays like these exist because it still speaks to the young and to the old, and that's why it always will be done.

Todd Bjurstrom If you look at a Rothko or something, some abstract work where you stand in front of it and you're looking at it and emotions stir up for some reason, and what does it mean? Well, who knows? What does it mean to you? I think that that's a real testament to how great this play truly is, that there's so much that's open for interpretation and there's so much that's open for discussion. Thornton Wilder doesn't give you the answers.

Kimberly Scott I think that there's a knowledge and a wisdom that comes upon death. One of the best things about death is that we get to lay down our prejudices and our stubbornness and our nonsense and even more so embrace the beauty and the wonder of humanity. I guess that's also why I believe that the in-between places between our lives, that there's definitely some rehearsal halls, some rehearsal rooms in that null space. There's some doors that are marked, "Rehearsal." Hopefully, there'll be a note waiting for me saying, "Rehearsal's in 15 minutes." I'll be very happy with that.

Chay Yew It's just the idea of writing something so microscopic and yet framed within something so macroscopic. It's hard to do because some plays are either very intimate, and it exists between three or four people and it doesn't go beyond that boundary, and some plays are epic for the sake of being epic. But this actually has a beautiful tension, I would say rubbing of borders, between oneself and the universe. That's why I think a lot of people are in love with the play in a very special way because we belong to this thing called the universe. And how do we define ourselves amongst all the planets?

It's very Buddhist in a weird way, too. Who are you? How do you function, knowing that you're actually not the beginning or the end, but a continuum? And how do you push forward, and what do you receive and what will you give?

Mahira Kakkar At the end, you're in the graveyard and you look up, and it's Ashland, so you can see all the stars. It's a canopy. That was part of the magic of doing it in an outdoor theatre. That was a shared moment for the audience and the cast every night. That felt like a little miracle.

Chay Yew Since the production was staged in a somewhat Brechtian style, the entire company came out on stage with the Stage Manager during his last monologue. They were looking up at actual skies when he mentioned the stars. At the end of it, after the Stage Manager says, "Good night," they all slowly gave a long exhale of breath, timed to the dimming to the final blackout. As much as Wilder brought the play out to the cosmos, with or without the possibility of "no living beings up there," the last breath brings us back to our world. The breath was affirmation and reminder of human life, the shortness of life, and I wanted the idea lingering into the audience at the end of the play.

Rex Young It was a release, a release of those characters, their soul, their spirit was being released. We borrowed them to tell the story and we were letting them back into the air. You just finished your show, this story, and you let it go together. I felt like it was letting those spirits out of the graveyard into the sky.

14

Deaf West Theatre and Pasadena Playhouse, 2017

For three decades, Deaf West Theatre in Los Angeles has offered productions which are performed simultaneously in American Sign Language (ASL) and English. The company's earliest work included *The Gin Game* and *Shirley Valentine*, while more recent efforts have ranged from David Mamet's *American Buffalo* to Jack Thorne's *The Solid Life of Sugar Water*. The company has garnered significant attention for its musical productions, including an original piece based on the myth of *Medusa*, as well as the shows which began in California but brought the company to Broadway twice in the 21st century: *Big River* in 2003 and *Spring Awakening* in 2015.

The Spanish Colonial Revival-styled Pasadena Playhouse began operating in 1916 as the Pasadena Community Playhouse and, by 1925, opened its own theatre, a classic proscenium house with a seating capacity of just under 700. It received the honorary designation of the State Theatre of California in 1937. Following the death of its founder Gilmor Brown in 1960, the Playhouse fell on hard times and closed its doors in 1969. It remained dark until 1986, when it was reopened as not-for-profit regional theatre. It would sustain damage in a 1991 earthquake and while much of the facility was fully repaired, a gash in the plaster of the stage house's interior back wall would remain, fully revealed to the audience of *Our Town* when, in accordance with Wilder's wishes, there was no curtain or scenery to obscure it.

When Danny Feldman became producing artistic director of the company in 2017, succeeding 20-year veteran Sheldon Epps, he began his tenure with *Our Town* produced in collaboration with Deaf West Theatre. Employing Deaf West's signature blending of ASL and English, the production was traditional, save that the role of the Stage Manager alternated among three Deaf actors—Alexandria Wailes, Russell Harvard, and Troy Kotsur—who would also play Mrs. Gibbs, Mr. Webb, and Simon Stimson, respectively. Hearing actor Jane Kaczmarek was on stage playing and voicing the role of the Stage Manager throughout. At times, hearing actors would SimCom, both speaking and signing simultaneously, a difficult process because it requires expressing one's self in two languages at the same time.

Russell Harvard, Alexandria Wailes, and Troy Kotsur in the 2017 Deaf West and Pasadena Playhouse Production of *Our Town*, directed by Sheryl Kaller. Photo by Jenny Graham.

The *Our Town* production design notably stayed in hues of blue, gray, and white, with costumes designs that reflected the time periods of the play. Director Sheryl Kaller explained the choice as a practical one, noting that signing would be most visible in that palette. Pared back even further than stipulated by Wilder, there were no tables used on stage.

In this chapter:
Deric Augustine, George Gibbs
Sandra Mae Frank, Emily Webb
Russell Harvard, Mr. Webb and Stage Manager
Jane Kaczmarek, Stage Manager
Sheryl Kaller, director
Troy Kotsur, Simon Stimson and Stage Manager
Sharon Pierre-Louis, Emily Webb, Rebecca Gibbs and Constable Warren
Alexandria Wailes, Mrs. Gibbs and Stage Manager

Jane Kaczmarek The first time I saw *Our Town* must have been '73 or '74 at Milwaukee Rep. It's significant because I went with a date, had no idea what the play was about, and found myself, by the third act, crying so hysterically, having no Kleenex, and literally using my hand, my arm, my cuff of my shirt, my purse, to sop up the mucus and tears that were flying out of my head. I think he probably thought I was a crazy person. It was the first professional play I'd seen, and it left me thinking, wondering, 'Can theatre really make people feel this way, think this way?'

Deric Augustine I would have loved to see *Our Town* back in the day, when the play was first done, and see how much of an impact it had on the country back then.

Sheryl Kaller I somehow knew that post-Obama, *Our Town* would have an unbelievable resonance with a group of people who are missing one sense. In other words, I feel like Obama being our first Black president opened us up to so much as a society, opened us up to so much hope, which is what *Our Town* is about, amongst the many things that it's about. I felt like that lid was going to close and as soon as I knew that it was changing hands, onto the other side, I knew what it was going to feel like, as a liberal, to be an other again.

Alexandria Wailes Deaf people have a very strong sense of community. Everybody knows each other. Nowadays, the Deaf community, we still do gather, but we are a little more dispersed all over the world, because of technology. We're not required to be physically in the same place to be a community. We can exchange information differently now than in the past, because we have mobile phones and whatnot.

Sheryl Kaller It's my personal philosophy about great plays, that I can have this idea which has everything to do with politics. I felt the politics were going to affect our day-to-day life. I think that in order to communicate with people that you don't know or you don't know anything about, or are a different color than you, or can't hear, or can't see, or can't walk, you have to pay a particular kind of attention to day-to-day life. I was more interested in what I imagined, looking at all those rallies with so much hate, that day-to-day life was going to change. That there was going to be more hate on the street. That there was going to be more dismissiveness. There was going to be, in all of our versions of Grover's Corners, trickle down from the top.

Sandra Mae Frank I'm the only Deaf individual in my family. Growing up, it was always tough on me because my parents did sign, but my sister did not. I have never really cared about that that much, but this play forced me to rethink family connection with language. With my personality, I feel more connected with my parents now. I try to text them now and let them know I love them. Just the culture is a little bit separate, and it's important to try to bridge that.

Alexandria Wailes Our production was a community of mixed languages, hearing and Deaf. We didn't capitalize on, "That Deaf family over there, don't interact with them." We looked at the town in terms of surviving and thriving and going through their lives.

Sheryl Kaller We did so much work at marrying the two languages that it was one language. It became their language. It became the Grover's Corners' language.

Alexandria Wailes I've been fortunate to do several Deaf West productions, and often the hearing people who become involved with Deaf West productions don't really understand what they've signed up for until they're in the rehearsal. They're like, "Oh, my god, I have to do all of this?" We're like, "Yeah, you do. Welcome to the party."

Troy Kotsur Grover's Corners is this small town where there's a few Deaf people who live there and so hearing people learn to start signing themselves. Back in the day, on Martha's Vineyard, many hearing people knew sign language because there were so many Deaf people there. So we felt *Our Town* was a small version of that, where the Deaf people are influencing the hearing people and they're learning signs. It was a good representation of what happened historically.

Deric Augustine If we do this play now as the way it was back then, a lot of younger people probably will see it and think, 'That really wasn't really entertaining.' That's why they have to switch it up a little bit, they have to create this new model of it.

Sandra Mae Frank I'm an English major, so I'm very familiar with English and I can read it and understand it and appreciate it as a beautiful language, but I want [ASL] to be equivalent. Sometimes language can be unequal. The audience has to really understand that it's not just something that we make up and translate in English-to-sign.

Sharon-Pierre-Louis I was the first actress who worked with Sandra Mae who knew ASL fluently. She was very happy about that because she said she felt in the past sometimes you had to focus more on the hearing actor catching up as far as the sign language, that culture aspect, and then getting together to make sure they're on the same page as far as the signs and the voicing.

Sheryl Kaller So much of society is understanding people who don't talk like you, who don't walk like you. It requires a deep dive in the intention of the line, not only the words.

Alexandria Wailes The comfort and fluency of signing, and a lot of times rightfully so, gets into supporting and fast-tracking the hearing cast members with their signing and speaking at the same time. When everyone shares one language, you don't have to do that. When you add a second language, or you're trying to meld or blend the two, that's a process. But often you make friends for life, because of this shared experience that you had of the stress, the trust, the support, and just getting through the experience together.

Sheryl Kaller Conceptually, with sign language, I believed that the hands should be the framing devices for everything. Tables define the space too much. I wanted the hands to do the sign of the table, so always when Alexandria was serving breakfast, we had her sign "table" and then serve. I also wanted to extend Mr. Wilder's idea of the only scenery we're getting is trellises.

Alexandria Wailes If you're looking at the time period, the early 1900s, how people signed then was very different than how we sign in the 21st century. The contact with the body, how high, how low – the signing space, how small, how big – so the actual technical aspect of American Sign Language has evolved over time. Gender identity, male and female, how they might sign differently. I was very mindful of making choices that honored the time period, because the sign is so present and physical and visual and dynamic, how you move in a space really informs the audience of who that person is and their personality.

Russell Harvard I signed the way they would sign in that time. It was sophisticated. Today, time is moving so fast, so our signing style is different. I call it vintage signing. I had that knowledge of how to differentiate between the two. It was more formal. You didn't rush like you do today with more half-signs.

I was teaching one of the cast members the difference between "thank you" and "good." "Thank you" is directed towards and "good" downward. Then I thought, wait a minute, the formal signing of good was downward with two hands; the opposite, bad, would be smacking, one with the other. Now, when we sign good, we throw away the other hand, we don't have time. Back then we had time to talk and now it's [snaps fingers repeatedly]. It's scary.

Sandra Mae Frank My right hand, my right pointer finger on my left wrist, where the watch is, that's how you sign time, but we couldn't sign that because of the time period. People didn't wear watches on their wrists. They had pocket watches, so we had to totally change the shape and location of the sign for time like we were pulling out a pocket watch.

Russell Harvard *Our Town* is different from the modern world. We created it so that everyone could communicate in American Sign Language, so that everyone could be understood, so that information could be shared.

Alexandria Wailes Sign translation isn't fixed. You can't just show up with everything already translated, and then go. I think there were a lot of people involved in this particular production who were caught off-guard. They were so surprised by how much work it takes to get to where we need to go. That really took a lot of our time, and it took time away from character work, from figuring out the physical space.

Sandra Mae Frank Deric, who played George, didn't sign. So sometimes I would give him some of my sign choices. His character was hearing, falls in love with Emily, who is Deaf, so naturally he would copy some of my character's signs. That took so long, getting the hands the same and similar choices, matching some stuff so it would show a relationship developing, a connection developing. It was an extra layer to the character.

Sharon Pierre-Louis It meant everything to me that Sandra's voice was heard. I took that as a great responsibility. Having a Deaf brother, I grew up watching how his voice was not heard and how he was put aside many times. So this was very close to my heart, that I do her justice and I do the play justice.

Alexandria Wailes I think for any director who's not a fluent signer working with Deaf people, it's as if you didn't know Spanish and you're working with a group of Spanish speaking actors. I think it would be with any language, it's not unique to ASL. But you need the brain space, you need interpreters, and you need the tools to best support your work as a director, and to be able to communicate with the cast.

Sandra Mae Frank With the body, it's more of location. I'm noticing fathers sign higher up, showing a strong man figure, and young girls are more of a low signer. Same with the voice. People speak with a deep voice, a strong voice, but when you're young, it's soft. Really, it's a characteristic, same with sign. Everything is involved. When actors speak, it's an extra bonus, but ASL has more of telling a story without adding much. You can tell a story with just your body. It's more powerful to me. It just pours out of the eyes and the body and the face.

Alexandria Wailes I'm generalizing, but a lot of Deaf people don't have the luxury of seeing and experiencing a lot of theatre, period, with people signing on stage. That's not our access to the world, because it's not out there very much. I think that for each and every time there's a production with sign language on stage, it's a shock, it's something you have to adjust to and understand how people communicate and sign in this through-line, because they haven't experienced it before.

Sheryl Kaller I wanted, in the wedding scene, for the actors to sing through the whole thing. I wanted them to move through the whole thing. We had to cut 90 percent of it, because no one knew where to look, even the smallest movements. I wanted to do shadow puppetry at some point during it, with hands, and that didn't work. It felt remedial. I also had to cut the singing at the funeral, a lot of it, because you can't hold umbrellas and sing at the same time.

Alexandria Wailes Our biggest challenge was for non-theatre-going Deaf audience members. They really struggled with the characters who were signing and talking at the same time on stage, because it's not natural to SimCom. This text is very specific language, so if you're not familiar with his writing, and familiar with this play, and with how people communicate, I think that something gets lost in translation. Both theatregoers and non-theatregoers understood most when ASL fluent people were on stage just signing. Those were the clearest moments.

*   *   *

Jane Kaczmarek Remember what Emily says to her mother: 'Look at me. Look at me. I'm here, Mama. I'm dead. Wally's dead, too. He died on a camping trip. His appendix burst on a camping trip.' All that. 'Look at me, look at me.' When you act with Deaf actors, you have to look at them, because they have to see what you're signing. They said there's an understood convention that, in a play, because the Deaf actor knows the lines that the other Deaf actor is signing without seeing them, you begin the scene looking at them and signing, and then it's understood that you can walk away and sign even though they can't see you. Because you can't have a play where people are just constantly looking at each other.

Alexandria Wailes I'm not a mother in real life, but I know as a mother you would protect your children and encourage them to be the best that they can be. Then for our production, with the son who's hearing and Emily is Deaf, that was an interesting relationship, and a continuation of that dynamic.

Sheryl Kaller You never go to the theatre where the Deaf people get more than the hearing people get. That was why the relationship of this play to a Deaf audience felt so significant to be able to do it that way. I think the hearing audience felt it, particularly when Russell translated going up into the moon, and he just did all this beautifully. Russell is a little more of a cynic than his character was—he has his head in the clouds a lot, that character.

Deric Augustine After the show Deaf audience members would come up to me and say I did a very good job, and I would say, "It's a lot of work, I'm sorry if I didn't come off as an expert sign ASL speaker." They would say, "You know what? You did a very good job, and I am proud to call you a member of our family, and thanks for taking the time to learn ASL and sign."

Sheryl Kaller I felt a huge responsibility to Deaf audiences. Even the sound effects—we did Foley work, so that Deaf people could see the sound effects.

* * *

The Stage Managers

Jane Kaczmarek It was an amazing experience for me to be a woman playing the Stage Manager. I think we all have this image, or I did, of Spalding Gray and Hal Holbrook and the lot playing this rather kind of disaffected guy in a vest and a cap, smoking a cigarette and telling, 'Okay, this is what you're about to see.'

Sheryl Kaller Because it was my heart on the stage and, for me, I felt I had never seen a woman say those words, it was a completely subjective choice, nothing other than I had never heard a woman say those words out loud.

Jane Kaczmarek Being a mother of three so affected what I saw as the Stage Manager and allowed me choices that I don't think a man could get away with. I came out of it really wondering how a man could ever play the Stage Manager, after the opportunities of what that role offers, or the insights a woman has, with a role like that.

Alexandria Wailes What we discovered during rehearsals, early on, was that the Stage Manager role has a lot to say. That information would not come across as clearly and strongly if a hearing person was signing and talking at the same time, SimCom-ing all of that information. So early in the production, Sheryl and DJ [Kurs], the Deaf West artistic director, agreed that we should have three Deaf actors who are already in the show do double duty, sharing the role of the Stage Manager. It was really the four of us, four voices of the Stage Manager. That brought a very curious, close look at storytelling and the idea of the intersectionality.

Jane Kaczmarek Deaf West was insistent that one of the Deaf actors played the Stage Manager, and Danny and the theatre felt it was very important to have a speaking person. So of course, we did it together. The Stage Managers rehearsed our scenes forever standing in front of a mirror and watching each other so that our sentences ended at the same time, so that the paragraph ended at the same time. You have to be so in sync with these things. The only way to really do that is by watching each other, and then trusting when you're on stage we've mastered that rhythm.

Sheryl Kaller We couldn't keep the Stage Manager neutral, and we tried frankly, but in Deaf theatre, you have to show your face, or Deaf people don't understand what anyone's talking about. It became like pay dirt, having a woman in that role, connecting to being a mother and losing a child, and a daughter getting married and all that. That happened by accident.

Alexandria Wailes We started off with me as Mrs. Gibbs, then going into [Russell as] Mr. Webb, then Troy, who was Simon Stimson. Three very integral members of the community in *Our Town*. It was interesting to segue between the thread that held the Stage Manager together, and its different manifestations, how we divided and conquered the role of the Stage Manager. I do believe that by Act III, the speaking Stage Manager, Jane, took more of a back seat. But it was already written in the script, because Emily in Act III has her realization and discovery about life, and how life is short. Those realizations she had to discover for herself. The Stage Manager is there making a proposition, saying, 'Here, now we're transitioning from life to death. How are you considering your life?' I think it was a fantastic analogy in terms of how we physically used that concept in two languages.

Jane Kaczmarek It was so thrilling as an actress to know that I had such a connection with someone who couldn't hear a word I was saying, and telling a story to people about, 'Slow down and listen to each other.' The very essence of doing *Our Town* with the Deaf community was the message of that play.

Alexandria Wailes I came up with some ideas on my own, in terms of translation. But this was before the actual division of the Stage Manager material happened, so that was a whole new thing. It was, 'Oh, wow, okay. Let's go back again, how do I make choices as the Stage Manager in those instances where I'm actually sharing that role with Jane?' It was important to me to show a separation between this omnipresent narrator, sharing important information, and Mrs. Gibbs, salt of the earth. I worked with Russell and Troy as well, because the three of us wanted to have a through-line of sign choices as the Stage Manager to support the collective of who we are, to support the audience's comprehension of who we were in that moment.

In Act I, it's heavy in exposition for the Stage Manager, so I made choices that were more straight to the audience, describing things matter-of-factly. In this town, this is what it looks like, this is how it's laid out. I'm creating a visual map in space, almost like a diorama of the space in sign language. It felt more presentational, like a museum educator almost. Very human in terms of the way of relating and engaging with the audience to try to draw them in.

Troy Kotsur I'd be the Stage Manager and then I would become Simon. I was struggling with that. How am I going to clearly do that? How would the audience understand the differences of my roles? I decided that I was going to provide a clue for them to understand—the purple handkerchief. I had a vest on and it was in my pocket, folded up really small. So, when I was the Stage Manager, I was just telling the story, very neutral, and then I would pull out this purple handkerchief and people knew when they saw that that I was going back to Simon. I was the professor, too, and I would hunch my body and put on the glasses. I tried to sign differently also, sign very fast and show it in my body.

Alexandria Wailes When I became Mrs. Gibbs, the shift was in my body, how I embodied that, I shifted down more. I'm a person who does housework every day, and cooks, and gets the kids ready for school, so the physicality is a big shift. That's a fine line of acting and the use of ASL together.

Jane Kaczmarek I think being the only hearing Stage Manager with those three marvelous actors, I wanted to remind them, 'We're all in this together. I'm here with you. You're here with me. We've got each other's backs on this.' We became a real quartet. Alexandria and I started. I would be speaking, and she would be motioning where this church was and that church was, and then we would look at each other and say, 'Okay, now we're going to take you over here.' It was like two best friends, two sisters, two old ladies in the town telling you the story together. It was a more convivial kind of storytelling. Then Alexandria leaves to go and becomes Mrs. Gibbs, puts her apron on and comes down the stairs, and I say, "And here comes Mrs. Gibbs coming down to make breakfast." I turn and look, and Troy has taken her place and is standing beside me. So we would look at each other, or I'd probably touch his shoulder like, 'Yes, now *we're* together.'

Alexandria Wailes I think that all three of us were deliberate about finding the way of the Stage Manager. The three of us look very different, however that sense of presentation and describing, gave us the permission to step out of the Stage Manager role, and then become the characters that we are in the story.

Sheryl Kaller That's the reason why those three actors were chosen to do it. I also saw a production once of *Our Town* where they turned it into an ensemble. No one made entrances and exits, and I dug it. In Act III, I had all three of them doing it together. We translated it in character, that last monologue. In other words, if Mrs. Gibbs was saying those words, how would she say them? If Simon Stimson was saying those words, how would he say it? That was the meta that we did in Act III.

Russell Harvard It was like interpretive dance. We tried to make an image more than just what the lines were, to simplify them with our hands. We didn't want to just do signing. We wanted to make it whole, three-in-one. We just played it in, no ego involved. Sheryl said just go and do it and let me see what you've got. DJ came in and gave us some feedback and then we showed it to Sheryl and she said, "I love it."

Jane Kaczmarek We went through every single line in that play with the ASL masters, changing words, changing lines, making sure that the sentiment was right of what the line really was, what we were trying to get across. That was poetry in itself. The line I remember so well that was altered for us for the production was, 'Does anyone ever realize life as they live it?' she says to the Stage Manager, something like that, at the end. And he says, "No. The saints and poets, maybe – they do some." It was pretty dry. They worked on it and saints became taking two hands and making a circle above your head like a halo. And poets, oh, my god. Poets was the gesture of your hands sliding up from your abdomen up to your heart and opening up with your palm to the audience. That meant words that come from your heart.

Russell Harvard In Act III, it made sense for me to do the last part, because we knew that Alexandria and Troy would be in the cemetery. So Alexandria took the first part and Troy had the second one. We had rehearsal time for the three of us to blend in and incorporate ideas.

Jane Kaczmarek I would sit backstage with Troy before we'd go on for the soda shop scene. We would sit, and we would kind of hold hands. It was just so comforting, and I felt so intimate with him in a way that I never had with another actor. I thought, 'This is amazing, because he's never heard a word I've said, and he's never spoken a word to me.' Yet, that bond was just so profound. Just sitting, waiting to make our entrance together. When it was time to go, I would tap his knee to say, 'Our entrance is coming up.' He looked so excited, alive, couldn't wait to get on that stage. It provided a lot of things on stage and off stage for me as an actress.

*   *   *

Sheryl Kaller I wanted to integrate the Deaf members of the central families into what the Stage Manager was saying. I had Alexandria take off her apron, put it down, cross over. We tag teamed it. I feel like Simon Stimson gets so little real estate that having him speak as an interpreter of Mr. Wilder gave Simon more weight. It was really important to me that Howie Newsome was Deaf and a man of color. To me, what *Our Town*, what Mr. Wilder is saying, is if we could all just take a moment—like with Howie Newsome—because with Howie Newsome, these people talk about things that are important to them.

Alexandria Wailes We had inside jokes that Mrs. Gibbs and the milkman maybe had a thing. Because the creative team knows my ethnicity—I'm half-Black—they were like, 'Of course, that's fine that George would be Black, or darker.' We certainly had some inside jokes like, 'How did that happen? Something's not right.' But again, that goes with a town that's small.

Sharon Pierre-Louis It felt more vulnerable in a way for me to play Constable Warren, because all of a sudden, I do the costume change and then I step on stage and it's just me. That's what I'm used to doing. I would keep hearing the little actor in myself talk versus when I voiced for Emily, I was so immersed in that there was not as much room at all really for me to think about myself or how I was feeling. With Constable Warren, it was almost—I don't want to say like being naked on stage—but all of a sudden it was more vulnerable for me to just step out there after voicing and being paired with another actress.

Alexandria Wailes My Mrs. Gibbs, the way that I worked, she was heart. She was a mother, she takes care, she gives, she protects. I thought of some things in my life, women in my family, the women that I admire who don't get the appreciation they deserve for being who they are. Unconditional love, selfless, completely selfless, giving and giving, that was my Mrs. Gibbs. The tough love, but all for bettering her kids, and her world. She was a dreamer, but she never got to go to Paris. That just broke my heart.

Deric Augustine I think that George is like any other teenage kid, excited to get out there and see the world and have fun, play sports, meet girls. And when your mother or your grandparents ask you to do something, 'I don't want to do that. I just want to go out and have fun.' Your father just breaks you down: 'As a man, you have to take care of your family. You have to listen to your parents. You have to do your chores. These are important aspects of life.' It was a learning situation for George, and I think you have to open yourself up to that, be vulnerable to we all make mistakes, especially at a young age. In my personal life I was raised very strict. My mother raised two boys and we had to listen to my mom. But George, let's make him not that he disrespects his parents, but let's make him more of that boyish teenager where he just shies away from his mother and he wants to do what he wants to do.

Alexandria Wailes When Mrs. Webb and I were sitting next to each other, shelling peas, and chatting, that's more like a moment of relief from the day's work, a little more gossipy, chatty. It's a choice of mannerism to convey that. Just like if you have a phone voice, that sort of thing.

Sandra Mae Frank I believe that Emily is a little bit more naïve than me. An 'everything's fine, everything's fine' type attitude, but without really understanding the rebellion or connections and just wanting something more.

Deric Augustine I don't think George got conceited or arrogant. I think that he got a boost of confidence in a way that kind of went over his head, if that makes sense. He's getting better at baseball, he's getting more attention from the ladies, so I think his confidence grew in a way that it came off as arrogance.

Sandra Mae Frank If Deric had to get my attention, say to make sure, 'Did that make sense?' or 'Did I just make that up?' or whatever, we would write notes. He would speak and I wouldn't look and I couldn't hear. I would just keep writing and writing and writing.

Simon Stimson

Sheryl Kaller I was obsessed with Simon Stimson, I still am obsessed with Simon Stimson. I felt like it was very important to the story as Mr. Wilder felt it was important to the story, that Simon Stimson and the music be collaborative.

Troy Kotsur I had a feeling that Simon himself was a conductor or composer. When they gave me that role, I was confused. He's a music conductor and he's Deaf, but I said, 'You know what? I'm going to go ahead and accept that.' I realized that maybe he lost his hearing after he had already gotten a love for music. Maybe he lost his hearing later on and maybe he was angry and that led to problems for him in his life. I remember the movement of the music and the rhythm. I remember when it was fast-paced or slow and all of that and showing the rhythm inside. You don't have to hear the music to feel the music and see the music.

Sheryl Kaller I think that it makes his addiction and his loneliness so much more profound when he is someone who loves music. When he is someone who is an artist in some way. We chose to make it less literal and more letting the Deaf people know there's singing going on. We did make sure there were certain signs that were understood.

Troy Kotsur It's a small town where everyone knows everyone. They knew, 'Oh, that's Simon. And he thinks that he has problems.' They knew that he was a drinker. He couldn't hide it, it's such a small town. Also, his movements. Whatever I did when I was in that character would show that. I tried to show in my body that I look drunk also show that he felt or angry. I did show that he has a love for music but also that he was isolated in his house.

Russell Harvard In that time, he probably didn't have the resources that he needed. We knew he was a town drunk. I think 1939 was when Alcoholics Anonymous came to life. Not everybody knew how to handle that situation. Editor Webb was helping him find his way back home and it was just about that—how to help him get home, not how to help him get better. Nobody knew what to do during that time.

Troy Kotsur When I signed when I was angry, I signed really big. I would sign some mistakes, that didn't make sense, that weren't clear, and that way the audience would know that I was drunk. Sometimes I would check with the person who was voicing—I would make sure that they're going to voice things a little slurred to show the drunkenness. I would also sign quicker, and I would sign erratically. I would take pauses and then sign a lot and then take a moment and then sign a lot. Not the normal pace that you would sign. A typical person, when you're signing, if you have an interpreter, the way that they voice it is the same as a hearing person's conversation. But if you would suddenly be quiet and then talk really fast, it would be awkward. You would realize, 'Wait, something's wrong with this person.'

Act III

Jane Kaczmarek So often the Stage Manager is just watching. I felt it was so important as a mother to allow a child to go through something that I know is going to be a mistake and incredibly painful, but knowing, as a mother does, you have to let them do it. You have to let them experience it, and that that pain is going to be absolutely shattering. But they have to do it. You're trying to discourage Emily from going back, that it's different now, you don't want to do this. But once she makes up her mind, I wanted her to have the most wonderful experience going back. I wanted to create for her for those few seconds the beauty of that time and that memory, so that even though it gets completely dashed, she'll be able to carry it with her for eternity. That it was worth it to go back for even those few seconds.

Troy Kotsur I couldn't even look to the left or right. I'm dead, I'm not allowed to move. That was a huge challenge for me because I rely on my eyes. I would try to catch their hand movements in my periphery and so I knew when their last line was. I can't look around and be like, 'Oh, are they done?' Because I'm supposed to be dead. Sheryl would make sure that there was a little bit of movement, so that they could cue me into knowing that it was my turn.

Alexandria Wailes My personal belief or philosophy about what happens when we leave this mortal existence, I do believe that if you're ready to go, then the transition, then the letting-go of the earth, the earthly bonds dissipate fast. Thinking, life, desire, material things, they dissipate. You can let them go if you're ready. If you leave not-ready, then that takes more time. Mrs. Gibbs, by Act III for me, I felt that she was closer to really being free and accepting. I think that the mama, she's like, 'Ooh, darn, I should have, I could have, I would . . .' But at the same time, she also had moments of being more nonchalant, matter-of-fact.

Sandra Mae Frank Using my own emotion, letting the audience see them, I think that's more important than holding them in. Just putting it out there, take the pain and deliver, and be vulnerable and use it to benefit my performance, and not hold back because the audience can sense it. Let it go and let the audience see it. They need that, too.

Deric Augustine Thornton Wilder is an amazing writer, and for Act III, it's a lot of pressure on Emily. I remember in rehearsals, I was like, 'I really wish George had a little bit more of a storyline in Act III,' but it gave Emily a time to shine. But that last moment, when I'm walking up to her [grave], there's just a burst of emotions and sadness and grief. You still have to play that every night. You have to get into that zone.

Troy Kotsur I can't imagine what it would be like to be in a grave forever not to be able to move that whole time. To see everything that's happening around you but you can't say anything or do anything, you feel helpless. But Simon, because he didn't have a happy life, I think he felt peaceful when he died. He wasn't comfortable with all the gossip going around town in life, he saw all the problems in everything and he felt like he couldn't hide. In the grave, he was finally able to hide.

Alexandria Wailes At the very end of the play, when Emily finally accepts her place, I tell her, 'Yes.' That entire time in Act III, the people who have gone were all facing out, straight out, but when Emily comes, my Mrs. Gibbs wanted and deliberately looked over as a welcome, like the welcoming committee. Having [Emily] with me gave me a little flash of remembering all the people who are still alive. I had a tear going down my face, I'm sure the people in the first row were the only ones who could see it.

Jane Kaczmarek When she goes through the birthday and the presents, I had a wonderful time, because she is signing throughout. When she finally says, "I can't. I can't go on," Sandra Mae walked out of the light of that scene and—they called it the Deaf accent—spoke. That sound is so shocking for hearing people to hear, because we hadn't heard her say anything through the entire play, that her mounting grief and awareness of what's happening comes out of her vocally, going through saying goodbye to everything.

Sandra Mae Frank I know that when there's a Deaf person [on stage], they don't speak until there's one moment and it creates such an impact for the hearing audience. I wanted to cause a stir because I'm very big on doing something different. I wanted to figure out which line, which time. When is the best time that I can do this to cause such a moment? I'll voice in real life if I'm very, very, very mad, but I don't typically use my voice. It makes everybody stop. It causes impact. At such a high emotional time, I thought that that would be the right place, just emotions pouring and then breathing.

Jane Kaczmarek I crossed over to her and put my arms on her shoulders, put my arm around her, and we started walking to the grave, and she hesitated, and then realized there really wasn't anything else. We continued, and I put her in her seat. She looked forward. And I took my hands in front of her and I pulled her hair back off her shoulders, and smoothed the hair down her back, as if I was preparing her in her coffin, and walked off. I think that all really came from being a mother and having two daughters.

Sandra Mae Frank I saw how she felt, how she responded. I like to watch and see. We kind of feed each other as actors, energy, emotion, and so that means onstage it's crazy. I just wanted to keep that, keep that emotion.

Jane Kaczmarek There is something about that play, about playing the Stage Manager, that I didn't realize until I did it—how the relationship really is different between men and women. In the first place, men can't do that. I mean, if a man started smoothing her hair on stage as the Stage Manager, it'd be a little like, 'Well, why is he touching her?'

*   *   *

Deric Augustine *Our Town* shows you how love is the key to pretty much everything: how family is important, how relationships are important, how language is important. I think that's why it has this much of an impact today. This newer generation, the people below the millennials, need to see this, because I think love and family and trust and language is a part of their culture, or our culture, and I think this play can show people that, 'Hey, man, family, and love is important. Right now, you guys are focused on the wrong things – social media, politics.'

Sheryl Kaller All the research that I did on Mr. Wilder, I found him a quirky thing in this fabulous way, so I wanted to add some quirk to the production as well. Why am I doing it today? Why am I doing it if not to experiment with things like that? He's not alive anymore, and he was a quirky guy. Even if he was as hopeless and as trapped and as lonely as Simon Stimson is, he still wrote the play.

Alexandria Wailes I do wish that we had more time to gel, because there was so much time and energy spent on creating, and then the run is short, we weren't able to really grow with the material that we had. I do think that now I would be curious to see other productions out there, to see how they capture the sense, the language they use, what political, social, religious layers are involved.

Sheryl Kaller If I would go back, and see it now, I think we would probably be able to find probably a baker's dozen pauses that I just stuck in where I felt the silence was louder than the words.

Jane Kaczmarek Another time I saw *Our Town*, I was doing a silent retreat. I was taking a meditation course for quite a while in Pasadena. The silent retreat was all day, and I was in a wonderful centered place leaving it. I stopped for a cup of coffee or something on the way home and I saw a flyer for a high school production of *Our Town* at San Marino High School, which is right next to Pasadena. I thought, 'God, I want to see this.' I went home, I found my old college copy of *Our Town*, and I went and saw this production, this high school production. I didn't know anybody in it. I must've looked like one of those kind of lunatics, you know? Drives around looking for productions of *Our Town*. But no matter.

It's so good as a high school production, because the message still comes through beautifully no matter what the skill of the actors. But that Emily, in this high school, was the best Emily I'd seen since Judith Light [at Milwaukee Rep]. That came as a surprise. I guess the message of all of that is that, no matter what the circumstances, you can always find some ray of light in any situation. Not even a production of *Our Town*, but just in life. Things change and time passes, but don't forget to see the sunflowers every day and hear the clocks ticking.

Russell Harvard I remember the final performance. Jane was a mess. She was sobbing, she was crying. This is her favorite play. She looked at me at the ending and at the beginning, crying, and I was like: 'We have to do this.' I had to mouth the words. But it was so beautiful.

Jane Kaczmarek You put this play down for a couple years, and you pick it up again and you think, 'Oh, my god. How did I not realize that 10 years ago?' True simplicity becomes transcendent. There's something about the sacred ordinary. This was so evident in this meditation class I was doing, about the sacred ordinary— that it's the things that are so small and taken for granted that are the truly sacred things in our lives. To be connected to those things is to truly know happiness.

Open Air Theatre, Regent's Park, 2019

Writing about the May 2019 production of *Our Town* at the Open Air Theatre in Regent's Park, *Time Out* critic Andrzej Lukowski suggested that the staging was "probably its biggest ever UK production."[1] That may be true of recent engagements— the Manchester Royal Exchange can seat up to 700 and the Almeida Theatre tops out at 325, while the King's Head Pub, where the show was mounted in 2013, only manages 125 patrons at a time. However, the 1991 production with Alan Alda at the Shaftesbury Theatre in the West End, which can accommodate 1,400, surpasses all of those. That said, at the Open Air, *Our Town* was open to the solar system and the universe without impediment, which does speak to an expansiveness far beyond the number of bodies that witnessed it from the theatre seats.

For *Our Town*, it was important to take careful note of the theatre seats at the Open Air, because, to a first-time visitor, upon entering, there seemed to be seats everywhere, even behind the open stage area. However, this was not an in-the-round staging. The permanent section of steeply raked green plastic-molded seating faced a smaller section of blue plastic-molded seats, interrupted with a few stray orange interlopers, arranged on a series of platforms supported by visible scaffolding. This was the set for the play. The effect was to suggest an almost 360-degree amphitheatre and it was not merely backdrop, but also a playing area, calling to mind the hills— "awful blue they are" in the words of the Stage Manager—that surround Grover's Corners, including the hill upon which the cemetery in Act III sits. The aisles and rows among the blue seats even delineated parts of town when called upon to do so. The acting company reposed in these seats when not specifically in scenes, in addition to performing scenes among them. But when "members of the audience" called out questions to Mr. Webb in Act I, they were actors out in the green seats.

While in recent years the Open Air has garnered acclaim for its musical productions, including revivals of *Little Shop of Horrors*, *Into the Woods*, and *Jesus Christ Superstar*, plays are hardly strangers. Even with the comparatively recent arrival of another London outdoor venue, Shakespeare's Globe, the Open Air, which dates back in its original form to 1932, still offers up its own Shakespearean productions, as well as American classics such as *To Kill a Mockingbird*, *All My Sons*, and *The Crucible*.

Tom Edden, Francesca Henry, Arthur Hughes, Pandora Colin and Karl Collins (foreground) in the 2019 Open Air Theatre, Regent's Park, production of *Our Town*, directed by Ellen McDougall. Photo by Johann Persson.

Performed in May and June, *Our Town* evening performances began while the sky was still bright blue (on clear days), but the audience departed under cover of night. There still a distinct chill during the earliest performances, with the first preview commencing while the air temperature stood at 58 degrees Fahrenheit, dropping to 53 by the time the Stage Manager wished everyone good night, not inappropriate for a New Hampshire spring. This is apparently not uncommon at the Open Air, as the souvenir stands offered recycled wool blankets at a very reasonable price, presumably locally made, not manufactured in one of the Cartwrights' mills.

In this chapter:
Pandora Colin, Mrs. Gibbs
Rosie Elnile, designer
Orlando Gough, composer
Francesca Henry, Emily Webb
Arthur Hughes, George Gibbs
Thusitha Jayasundera, Mrs. Webb
Ellen McDougall, director
Laura Rogers, Stage Manager

The play

Ellen McDougall The things that really resonated were the fact that [Wilder] had started writing it during the time that he spent in Europe in the '30s, and was able to say, despite everything that was going on around him at that point, that he still had faith in humanity. I think that shines through.

Arthur Hughes It reminded me of *A Christmas Carol*. Not the learning of a lesson for someone miserly, but the looking back over your life at what you had. The difference with *Our Town* is it's much more a looking at the beautiful things that you might have overlooked, not that you've abused like Scrooge did.

Ellen McDougall I think that [the Open Air leadership] were surprised how people don't seem to know it, because it's such an amazing play and it's so well known in America. It's strange to me that it hasn't crossed over because I think it is so universal as a text. I recognize that it has this reputation for being sentimental and nostalgic and small, but it's so clear that the thinking behind it, and what he's asking people to think about, is so dark. To think of it as just a small, sentimental play is a massive misreading of it. It's a puzzle.

Thusitha Jayasundera I had a terrible tragedy in my family in 2018. I'd lost my most beloved brother. I was having to straddle Sri Lanka and England and so I couldn't really work at the rate that I like to work. I had to look after my mum in Sri Lanka. I had to look after all of the many things that my brother left incomplete. My life had been turned on its axis and I wasn't going to go up for this audition, but I was curious about this play. I started reading it. Something about it resonated. I thought it was absolutely astounding. It talks about temporal existence in such an extraordinary way. It talks about the delicacy and the sacred ordinariness of life and power.

Francesca Henry At the moment in London, the plays are very in-your-face. The things I've been going in for are very critical looks at inner city London, which is where I'm from. So the scripts I have been reading have been very aggressive or offensive in the way they are written and what they are presenting the audience with, always ending with a huge climax at the end of every act, where the characters were dealing with a lot of emotion on the outside. To read this play in the context of what I've been reading at my other auditions, I wasn't really calibrated for the subtleties of the writing, for the subtleties of the style.

Orlando Gough Wilder is very, very, specific about what he wants. It's possible to do the play, I imagine, without doing any composing at all. You can just decide to go along with what he says. People sing those hymns and it's very straightforward.

What does he say? 'My play swears at music.' I could see what he meant by the dryness of the tone, of the piece. It's the kind of piece which feels that it doesn't need a kind of emotional support.

Ellen McDougall I think it's really tricky because it's very easy to clutter it. I can imagine that if you do that, you actually play into that reputation of it being sentimental and nostalgic quite quickly. I think there's a sense that if you, for example, have a set, set in the period, and costumes set in the period, what are you really asking us to look at?

Pandora Colin In much the same way as *House of Bernarda Alba* has a reputation for having quite a fraught backstage atmosphere, I wonder if the nature of *Our Town* means that you do find yourself being a community and all getting behind the ethos of the play. In *Bernarda Alba*, she's constantly divide and rule—she's playing all the daughters off against each other, and it is a really unhappy play. I wonder if the nature of *Our Town* means that everybody has this much more affectionate, collaborative atmosphere.

Thusitha Jayasundera In an early conversation, one of my co-actors, a family man, was talking about how moving he found certain bits of it that we had been rehearsing. I said to him without thinking, "I feel like it's sort of is a spell." It brings you back to the very fundament of your existence somehow without you even knowing it, or without going on some huge long conscious process.

Francesca Henry Ellen said the first time she watched the play she found it very frustrating. I was glad she'd said that because that was one of my first reactions reading it, having got the part as Emily, being quite frustrated by what she doesn't say and the gaps in her story. Ellen was like "That's okay, that's frustrating. I think that's a good place to start with this play." Then she read off this Thornton Wilder quote about humanity. That humans were finicky and difficult and pernicious and awful, but he was willing to give them another chance. In his plays he's always trying to give the audience another chance to look at themselves and the characters another chance to live it, and the actors another chance to look at what we could be. That made me give it the chance it needed.

Thusitha Jayasundera I was very interested to learn that people relocate it to all kinds of locales, but I found the particularity of this small-town American existence and the various trappings of that made it somehow feel completely universal to me. It helped in blowing the doors wide open and letting everything rush in. I don't know whether I had a particularly intellectual appraisal of it. It was just an extremely emotional truth, which it insisted on unearthing time and time and time again. You never tire of performing it because the act of performing it is a very regenerative one.

Arthur Hughes It felt like we were letting the actors on stage and letting the writing speak for itself. Felt like that's kind of the message of the play, that it doesn't need any extra frills. It is what it is. We were going to make a real point of that because the theatre we were doing it in is open air. You couldn't be more exposed.

Ellen McDougall I'm really conscious that Thornton Wilder wrote this in 1937. It's a long time ago in a very different context to where we are now in theatre. It's not just a text, in a way. It's a blueprint for a production and he understood why he proposes no scenery. I think that is embedded in what the writing is doing. It's not like taking another play from that time and slapping a concept on it, because it already is conceptual.

Pandora Colin The music immediately helped create the tone for rehearsals. We were suddenly all in the same world, in the way that music can do when you don't quite have a set or costumes or anything yet.

Orlando Gough Shape note singing seemed to be immensely appropriate because of its simplicity and its honesty, the way that it conjures up a kind of emotion which is quite restrained but very heartfelt, with very simple means. I did a bit more research about shape note singing and came to look at the hymns of William Billings who turns out to be one of the first formal composers in America. He writes these very beautiful hymns in four-part harmony. It's simple chords, but very dynamic parts with lots of quite big intervals, so that it's leaping up and down quite a lot. It has a combination of simplicity and sophistication which is really moving and emotional.

Ellen McDougall One of the points of departure that I felt was possible and useful was to do with, 'Who is in *Our Town*? Who are the cast? What does it mean to be doing it now?' When he wrote it, you wouldn't see such a difference if you had contemporary costumes from 1938 and then you are asking the audience to imagine 1901. Whereas now, going back to 1901 is a massive difference. I think that that feels quite exciting to me in terms of sort of owning that meta-theatrical quality of it.

Thusitha Jayasundera There is a little direction about the level of performance that Thornton Wilder thinks of as appropriate, which is unemotional, very pragmatic. It's not in any way a sort of a grandiose kind of projection of anything.

Pandora Colin For Mrs. Gibbs, her job is her home and providing for her family, and looking after her husband, who works too much, and her son on the sort of cusp of manhood. I would say she pretty much never thinks about herself, and always prioritizes her family. When Thusitha and I were doing it, we were just like, 'Yeah, what's the difference? This is what we do now.' I'm not saying all women are domestic goddesses or that I am either. But just that thing of the universally recognizable dance of getting your kids up and fed and out in the morning is exactly the same.

Ellen McDougall While he has positioned it in this very monocultural, small town in this very specific time, we are meeting that play from the position of 2019 and what our idea of a community might be. The first thing that happens in the show is when the Stage Manager comes out and says, 'Okay, you're going to see all these people in the play.' We have a lineup of all of the 18 people. You've got someone as old as nearly 80 and an 11-year-old and a person who uses a wheelchair and someone else with a physical disability and a multi-racial cast. There's this idea about going, 'This is who we are,' telling us this is an idea of a community.

Arthur Hughes It's always encouraging, I think, where you see especially more than one actor with a disability. I feel like if there's a reason for addressing it, then it should be discussed and addressed. But it was never really brought up in rehearsals in any discussion about the play at all. The only real discussion was logistical in a big old Open Air Theatre for moving around Gary's wheelchair. When we come out as the actors, obviously you see my hand, but then it was just: now I'm the actor playing George, and obviously the actor playing George has a hand like this, therefore George has a hand like that. And that's it.

Ellen McDougall I haven't connected their ethnicity with the characters they're playing. I suppose in that way that I was saying, it's a meta-theatrical thing, going, 'These are the actors in this show, and now they're going to step into these roles.' I very deliberately cast the two families as a combination of race identities that would be biologically impossible.

Francesca Henry There was a conversation about African American dialect, versus location dialect, because Ellen had cast his play color blind, within the families especially. What would have been my accent, with my racial background at that time, versus what would have been Arthur's? Wouldn't have matched. Do we have to be sensitive to that? Or is that too much, too twee, too contrived? That was an interesting conversation.

Arthur Hughes We came on at the start and we are introduced by name as ourselves. So before we become George Gibbs or Dr. Gibbs, we come out as ourselves and go, here I am, I'm a disabled actor. Here is Dr. Gibbs, he's a Black actor. Then we play these parts irrespective of that. I think that in the end, that was the point that was being made.

Ellen McDougall The context is for a London audience, so all our ears are not so tuned in as it would be in an American context to that specific location. I did feel that doing it in American was useful just because the way it's written on the page, you can see that it's written in a dialect. I think if you then try and do it in English accents, you always hear that jarring.

Laura Rogers I think originally she even went down the road of having a sort of drag Stage Manager, and she met with some drag acts, and, in fact, one of them said, 'This is completely wrong. I don't think this is a good idea at all.' You want a Stage Manager to be present and part of it, but almost part of the scenery rather than distracting from the play by being such a huge presence.

Ellen McDougall That role of the Stage Manager obviously shapes our understanding of that play and presents us that play. I auditioned a huge range of different both performance artists and actors for that role. I met a couple of queer cabaret performers who were male. There's just something about locating the center of the play in a male voice that to me in this day and age plays into an idea about a patriarchal power structure that I wanted to destabilize. I think it makes you tune in in a different way.

Laura Rogers It's a standalone part. They don't really have any interaction with anyone apart from a couple of times in the show. It meant that I was just able to do a lot of learning by myself and then slot in. In a way it was helpful that I'd never seen a production of it before. I couldn't take on any mannerisms from anyone else. I only had myself to rely on.

Thusitha Jayasundera I think it felt the most honest thing to do for Ellen's point of view of framing it to sort of say, all of these people who come from all corners of the earth who happen to be theatre actors in London, we need to sort of acknowledge that fact first, because it was quite a mixed racially mixed company. We need to declare that we are aware of this and then we need to sort of start telling you the story.

Laura Rogers It was quite daunting. I felt actually quite isolated at times. So, in fact, the tech week was great because I suddenly felt like, 'Oh, I'm part of this family.' Before that it felt like I was an outsider. But maybe that was also helpful for the part. I thought the Stage Manager's like a little piece of every part of the community, all made up into one person. I wanted it to bring the human element, but I think Ellen liked the idea that it's a very ethereal part, an otherworldly part. Is it a God-like figure or a ghost-like figure? Or just somebody that has happened to live in this community in the spirit of everybody else in that world?

Francesca Henry I found a lot of Emily's personality, her precociousness, is very similar to me at her age. I was very over-reaching, let's say. Which was completely normal in my culture—being a girl who wanted to go to school, make speeches, was nothing. I went to a very academic girls school. That was my thing, that was expected; for that to be so exceptional in her environment and so stifled. I find the conversation where they're shucking beans with her mother just excruciating. I don't think I'd ever really appreciated the academic freedom that I'd had, that I have, in such a visceral way, until you see the fear that that evokes in her mother. Her mother sees it as hubris.

Arthur Hughes I think George has a really grounded moral center. He always does the right thing, even when Emily's telling him, 'You're being a jerk at school.' He knows to come back. Even though he goes in and out of it, he does always come back.

Laura Rogers There's something very likable about [the Stage Manager], very warm and cool about him, that's engaging. I just don't think of myself as that person. In a way, I was thinking of myself a bit like Columbo. He always knows.

Pandora Colin I suppose Mrs. Gibbs is a bit softer than Mrs. Webb, and she's a bit warmer. She's not quite as funny from an audience point of view. I guess Mrs. Webb is funny because of things being a bit more black and white for Mrs. Webb, whereas Mrs. Gibbs is a little bit more flexible. I feel like she's as philosophical as anyone in that community at that time would be. Self-reflection wasn't really acceptable. We talked about that a fair bit—self-reflection or analyzing a situation or looking at dynamics, all that stuff, it wasn't such a part of how people were then. When they have those conversations around the table on the morning of the wedding, when she and her husband are talking, we talked a lot about how they are heartbroken and completely screaming and sad inside.

Thusitha Jayasundera We started rehearsing the stringing beans scene both with Mrs. Gibbs and then with my daughter. We fell into this trap of playing an underlying blue note, that sort of sign post of slight conflict about things which are informed by our existence now. It's like a Jacobean undertow, something that signals a subtext of something, which is not there in the script. I was thinking, why is this scene so difficult to play? Because we're completely overburdening it with all kinds of other trappings that it simply does not contain. When we had the courage to just play what was simply on the page and nothing more, there was this extraordinary epiphany, where it just flowed and all of the richness and all of the depth were contained within its simplicity.

Francesca Henry When I was practicing with Thusitha, I was saying how, when I was 12, I lived with my dad, not my mum. I'd mentally substituted her for my dad. I was very emotional. Because being 12 is that time when you start to separate your parents as an extension of yourself into being your own person. Emily understands that when she goes back. She watches her twelfth birthday and watches her mother as a woman, not as an extension of herself. I think about being 12, my parents had just split up, I was understanding them as people with feelings and a relationship which didn't involve me and so I did go back to my twelfth birthday and came to pretty similar conclusions as it takes Emily 24 years to.

Laura Rogers You don't get the adrenaline that you might have before another part. I've played Lady Macbeth at The Globe, and of course there is definitely an arc to that. I've played a lot of characters where you die or something tragic happens to you or somebody around you. So when you came off after the show, I didn't have that feeling of that big comedown that you might get if you've really put yourself through the emotional mill.

Pandora Colin Mrs. Gibbs has got that kind of imagination that we don't see so much in the other characters. But she just squishes it down, because this is her life. This is what they do. It's tragic that the one time she leaves Grover's Corners, she dies. We talked a lot about, 'Oh, god, poor Mrs. Gibbs.' She has these dreams of going to Paris, and he's sort of, 'Oh, stuff and nonsense.' It's not the greatest tragedy. It's just life.

Ellen McDougall One of the things that's curious is we noticed all of our instincts are to look for drama and conflict and complexity. We kept going: no, the whole point is it isn't that, it's daily life. It isn't that there's this ulterior motive with Machiavellian plots.

Francesca Henry Ellen doesn't like weddings and it's very funny how I, in rehearsal, was underplaying [Emily's] speech, underplaying the fear, underplaying the plea to her father because, to my mind, weddings are wonderful things. But Ellen's like, 'No, this is it. She's jumping off the cliff.' This is not 'I don't want to do gym class today.' This is, 'I don't want you to ever leave me. I'm never going to see you again. This is the end of life as I know it. This is me moving to Mars.'

Arthur Hughes "Why, I'm ashamed of you," wasn't just, 'Stop being selfish, think of what you want to do.' It's, 'Face up to being a man.' The stage direction is George looks over the scene and comes to himself. What is that? I had a list of bullet points. The first one was, 'What?' Second, 'Why is Ma crying?' Third, 'Is the wedding ruined?' Fourth, 'Have I done this?' Fifth, 'I need to fix it.' Sixth, 'Where's Emily?'

Thusitha Jayasundera I think it's about looking behind what's presented. It's about immutable truth that lay underneath, something that is structured in a very, very particular way. What I found was that if the play was done very tightly and as written, with the specificity, that allowed it to escape the bounds of what is on the page in the way that is intended. Because it is presenting something incredibly conservative on the surface. A life lived in very, very sort of tight and regimented bounds, gender placements and so forth. In order for the play to speak, that has to be absolutely played to the hilt and then the play is released.

Francesca Henry It's very rare that you get to see the start of something on stage, because it's not always dramatically interesting. You want to see the end, you want to see the fireworks. But in this play, you do get to see the start when they're talking over the fence, you see the start of what ends in the soda shop. In the soda shop you get to see the start of the rest of their lives. Every word on stage matters, but every word they say, every line, is an offer which neither of them can actually have the courage to pick up. It's like a slow climb, a slow cycle up a mountain. It's so truthful, it's so real. Everyone had that awkward moment with someone.

Ellen McDougall I think one of the reasons the play feels so contemporary and retains so much power for an audience now is that every single character, the writing of every single character, feels underpinned by love. Thornton Wilder loves all of those people for all of their flaws, for all of their ridiculous misplaced notions.

Francesca Henry If he goes to agriculture college, it's done. She can't wait three, four years, she'll be an old maid. Life will move on. If it's going to happen, it has to happen now. In that moment, the reason why they don't say 'I love you,' apart from the fact that it's so scary, is that the thing that's going through their mind is, 'I'm going to lose you. If you leave, I'm going to lose you. It's the right thing for you go but I'm going to lose you. I've just shouted at you. I've just been very mean to you, I've pushed you away. I might have lost you already. You've been mean to me. I think I've lost you.' Every nice thing that he says back to her, every piece of the old George she sees, is a confirmation: 'Maybe I haven't lost you.'

Ellen McDougall It is again about a community that celebrates difference. Not everyone is going to have the same experience. There is pain and there will be people for whom life doesn't add up. It reminds me of Jacques in *As You Like It*, for example. I think the genius of that play is that it's a comedy. Everyone gets married. It's all bloody great. Then there's one person who goes, 'I can't bear this. I'm leaving.' What that does, and it's the same with Simon Stimson, is go to the audience, 'It's okay if you don't buy in because you're also represented. Your pain is also represented somehow.'

Pandora Colin What's weird in that community is Simon Stimson not having children and the story of why that might be, why he's drinking, and why Thornton Wilder wrote that character. He was gay—that was what we decided. So that's the dark side to a community that insists that being married is the thing to do, that's the fallout. The victims of that are people like Simon Stimson and his wife. We figured that was Thornton Wilder's little note of autobiography in there.

Orlando Gough When we were talking about possible music for the play, Tom, the sound designer said, "You know, why not 'Blackbird' by The Beatles?" He had heard it sung at a wedding, and I heard it sung at my father's funeral. We talked about this idea of a song that you could hear at a wedding and then it could also be appropriate for a funeral. "Blackbird" went away because it seemed too far away from Grover's Corners. It was too British.

Francesca Henry I think the first few times I did it, fear was one of pervading emotions because, when I think of death, when lots of people think of death at my age, it's scary. Death after a difficult childbirth, scary. Death where you have to meet ghosts, scary. Death where your mum can't speak back to you, scary. But I don't think that the text supports fear in any way. It's quite the point that she's not scared either before, during, or after. Regret, a lot of sadness, but not fear.

Arthur Hughes I don't think it hit me straightaway about taking life as it comes. It just hit me on a particularly nice afternoon when we were out and I was just listening to these words being said. I always think I'm lucky doing what I'm doing, but there was a resonance in hearing Laura do one of these speeches and really taking it in.

Pandora Colin Because Mrs. Gibbs says quite a lot, 'Just be patient. Just wait,' we were trying to have a gentle feeling of expectation of something. There was a thing that they're waiting for. So that is partly why we're not talking to each other, is because there's that expectation, 'If we just sit here and wait patiently, it's going to come to us.' It's a state of anticipation that kept our focus forward.

Laura Rogers It's like the audience know in a *Columbo* show who's done the crime, and the enjoyment is watching Columbo finding it out and piecing it together. The Stage Manager knows already what's going to happen at the end of the show and is guiding the audience. The enjoyment comes from seeing the audience work it all out. The audience don't really know why they're watching it. It only becomes clear at the end why they've needed to see that life.

Pandora Colin In Act III, everything about how they don't understand and they can't see, I really felt like Mrs. Gibbs says it with great affection. Not, 'Oh, it's so awful.' I didn't want it to be filled with angst. I think she's just looking back rather affectionately and saying, 'Aren't we funny, and isn't it a shame? But that's who we are.' It's with love for humans rather than disdain or judgment.

Arthur Hughes It was that third act of going back, of being taken by a mystical guide, suddenly the realism of the play is gone. That sense of getting a chance to look over your life again. It starts quite easy. Everything is just so. Everything is as it is. Before I got to the final act I was like, 'What's going to give? Where is the drama here?' It was all quite, I don't want to say mundane because it's written nicely, but then it is that final act, it's turned on its head. That is what gave me the thought of *A Christmas Carol*, because I imagined Scrooge flying over London and looking over the life he's led and he's going to lead, seeing Emily and the Stage Manager visiting places in her past.

Thusitha Jayasundera There's a kind of a meditation on the brevity of life, on the specialness of it, meditation on eternity. That last act was an incredibly important thing to be witness to every single night. It gave me a lot of comfort and I think a lot of psychological space to quietly grieve. Whatever I was feeling in that moment, I felt could become very happily encompassed by what he was writing about. I felt like I was given permission to feel what I was feeling. It did seem extremely expansive that way, extremely humanitarian.

Pandora Colin I'm going to keep coming back to this play and reading it as a sort of guide to life forever, now that I've found it. I'm not a religious person, but it's like a little book of prayer, or a guide to life.

The park

Rosie Elnile The first ideas that we had for this show didn't make it into the final design. My initial response to it, was that it felt kind of archeological from a design perspective. I had quite a strong instinct, which for various reasons didn't happen, that there should be very old things, very old costumes or sets, sat right up against very new things. Because the thing that I find moving about the piece was this idea of humanity or the earth existing in a blink of an eye. What those thoughts translated into in the context of Regent's Park was really trying to use the natural world. This is obviously written into the text, but it felt really inappropriate to me to put in a set of any kind.

Ellen McDougall The opportunity that being outside offers is that thing he says: "The life of a village against the life of the stars."[2] Secondly, we start just before dusk. By the time we're in Act III, it will be darkness and which will mean that when we go to the twelfth birthday, we have to light that artificially, but it means that it necessarily has a different theatrical language to Acts I and II, which feels useful. Then we end with an idea about stars and darkness and the big sky.

Thusitha Jayasundera My feeling was always that the less distracting the surround was and the more forceful the training of the audience's attention was upon what was being described in the play, the more successful it's likely to be. I mean, you're competing against one of London's most beautiful Regency parks. In the first act, I felt like there would inevitably be a kind of a split focus because even with the most prodigious powers of attention, when you're in the outdoors, your attention operates in a different way. But then the evening performances were often very magical because the moon was out. The real thing is wonderful to be around, full stop. But this is a play that works on the imagination and it isn't about literal representation of any thought.

Rosie Elnile That space needs certain things in order to function. It needs height, to an extent, and it's a huge space to perform *Our Town* in. So to have a completely empty stage, which is as the stage directions dictate, wouldn't have worked. The idea was to create as much as possible, rather than an audience looking at a set, quite a sense that the audience and the actors were in a circle, so we were one.

Pandora Colin The idea was that when you're sitting in your seat, you're not your character anymore, you're part of the company. You just give your focus to the play. That was the goal. Sometimes it's hard to have that level of concentration all the time. Either your eyes might wander, or you'd be looking at the person in the scene, but perhaps the audience member just beyond them in your eye line would be on their phone doing some shopping or talking quite a lot, or asleep. During the milkshake scene, you would look at audience members and see couples cuddling each other, and looking at each other, remembering. Every single performance, at least one or two couples would have those moments either remembering when they had been in love when they were teenagers, or when they had first got together. It was really, really moving.

Laura Rogers Being outside you really can get a relationship with the audience. You see everybody's faces and you use them as the other character in the show. It opens out, you're talking to a whole group of people and they're communicating back to you as well. I think that was incredibly helpful for the part of the Stage Manager.

Rosie Elnile We had orange seats within the seating bank as well, and that was wanting to show some idea that things are replaced or things change, or, as time passes, things become different. We had an idea, in a very conceptual way, that isn't really relevant to the text, that maybe some of these seats are broken and they'd been replaced by these other seats, which felt important because there's a thing in the text that the town that they speak about is very white. It's at one very specific moment in American history. There's one small mention of Native

Americans, indigenous Americans; it felt really important that I showed in the set somehow that things change.

Francesca Henry The final act was beautiful outside and in that moment when all of the pieces settle in and the play really sings, doing that in the dark, outside, at sunset, with the birdsong and having her realize the error of her ways and the beauty of life, it's such a natural setting. It did half the work for me to be honest.

Rosie Elnile Thornton Wilder really gives you a map of how to design what he's written. Apart from what we did with Emily's birthday party, which is slightly different, I felt like Ellen trusted him implicitly and I didn't trust him. It's not like I don't trust him because I think inherently the text isn't saying something beautiful about humanity. I just think that the text is saying something beautiful about humanity in the '30s. I think any piece of art that you write is always about the time that it's written and it's about the person that makes it.

Orlando Gough I have to admit sometimes being frustrated at how prescriptive Wilder is. I write quite a lot of music for Shakespeare plays. Shakespeare was incredibly benevolent about what you could do with one of his plays and very, very unprescriptive. Wilder seems to me almost the opposite. It's like he's got a complete vision of the entire play in his head. Everything. Everything, from beginning to end. Of course, the problem with that is when you come to do a version of it 70 years later, there's just nowhere to move. It's like being in a box. Sometimes there's a slight temptation to just kind of bash at the box a bit.

Thusitha Jayasundera There's something very unifying from an audience point of view, watching us watch the play. I think there's something very relaxing about seeing actors in repose while another actor takes on the telling of the story. It has a kind of a relaxing and involving effect upon an audience. It invites a kind of storytelling mode as opposed to. 'Here's the prosc arch, behind here is where we keep all our theatrical stuff that you don't get to see, and we'll just pull it out and present you with miracle after miracle.' Everything is just declared. There is a an 'OK, we're just going to be getting this story around the campfire' sort of feeling.

Laura Rogers When we did the show in the evenings—not obviously in the matinees because it was summer and so it was light all the way through—but in the evenings, the interval coincided with it getting dark. To do that final act in darkness was completely magical. People that I know who'd come to it, who knew nothing about the show, in the interval were a bit like, 'Oh, okay, this is just a play about mundane lives and nothing is going on, nothing is happening.' Then they come back after the interval and it's dark, and suddenly it takes on a completely different vibe and they suddenly found themselves being totally moved and crying.

It had just crept up on them and they hadn't even noticed until the end, and they're like, 'What just happened to me? I can't believe that's just happened. How did you do that? Why did you do that to me?'

Francesca Henry Because it's outside you could see the audience. Lots of them start off on their phones, lots of them start off texting, taking photos of the trees, of the stage, a lot of Instagram—snap, snap. I think something about being outside took away the theatre etiquette, made people feel like they were at the cinema or something. The point of this play is, 'Stop looking at life through your screen.' Watch the journey that the play took people from, from that beginning to, 'Look at yourself, be in the moment, stop being silly, appreciate your now.' That people found quite moving. I think they were quite disappointed with themselves that they were so blind at the start.

Pandora Colin I think it works perfectly, for the most part. Because Editor Webb talks about the universe so much, and nature, and the birds, Tom Edden timed it, or the birds timed it, a couple of times perfectly where he's giving his talk and he goes, "And we all notice a good deal about the birds." Then they'd all squawk. That happened quite a few times. It was just gorgeous.

The present day

Ellen McDougall To me, the politics in the UK is an extreme version, but also a similar pattern, to what is happening across the world. We're putting up walls instead of breaking them down. For me, that line in the play—there are so many, but one of the lines in the play—that absolutely speaks to that is towards the end when the Stage Manager talks about the Civil War and says, 'These people had never seen more than 50 miles of this country, but they had this idea that the United States of America was something to fight and die for.' The idea of unity across difference is absolutely held up in that moment as something that we've lost right now. That line resonates so powerfully to me, but it doesn't have to be saying, "Europe." We hear it. To be honest, it speaks to me of the politics of America as well. I don't know, but I keep hearing this phrase, "Make America Great Again," and nowhere in that phrase is the idea of United States. It's gone. The brand is now America, not the United States.

Rosie Elnile I wouldn't say that it's a Brexit *Our Town*. I think Brexit is a symptom of something much bigger within British culture at the moment. I don't think that Brexit is the cause of what's happening at the moment. I think it's a symptom. It does feel like it was an *Our Town* that was an attempt to talk about shared humanity in a time in Britain when we're finding it quite difficult to see each other's humanity.

Arthur Hughes I think some parts of the world now, especially here and in the US, I guess there's more small-mindedness, and maybe there has been, certainly in my lifetime. I find the world view's getting smaller and smaller. I think about 'Grover's Corners is enough treat for anybody. We're happy with our lot and we don't need to go and see other things.' It always used to get a big laugh in the show, that scene. It wasn't a big joke laugh, it was a knowing laugh. People who come to see the theatre in London probably have a less small-minded approach. But that was a laugh at the situation, the way some people think these days. 'We don't need anything else outside of where we live. We're just fine, thank you very much.' I find that a worrying thing at this moment in society, in some parts of society.

16

Sing Sing Correctional Facility, 2013

The placid community of Grover's Corners has been found everywhere in the world, in the unlikeliest of places, at the unlikeliest of times. Still, there is no small amount of cognitive dissonance upon learning that the play was produced in the late spring of 2013 at Sing Sing Correctional Facility, a maximum-security prison an hour north of New York City. A marker outside the prison gate attests to Sing Sing's somewhat notorious place in the history of incarceration: "Original cell block built in 1825. Prison terminology 'Up The River,' 'The Big House,' and 'The Last Mile' coined here."

A not-for-profit organization called Rehabilitation Through the Arts (RTA) has produced 25 shows at Sing Sing, ranging from works by August Wilson to the musical *The Wizard of Oz*. RTA's successful work at Sing Sing has led to the establishment of similar programs under the company's aegis at several other correctional facilities in New York's Hudson Valley. It is one of many such programs operating in prisons in the US and internationally, using theatre as an activity which requires teamwork and coordination among the incarcerated population to advance empathy, socialization, self-confidence, and talent. The program at Sing Sing is sufficiently popular that there is a waiting list of men hoping for the opportunity to participate.

To produce the plays, outside volunteers come to the prison twice weekly for rehearsals, which last only a couple of hours each, based on the regimentation of time in a prison environment and which can be subject to cancellation without notice, based upon events within the facility. Rehearsals take several months. Show directors are outside professionals, and female actors are brought in on a limited basis for roles that cannot reasonably be gender-swapped to male. In the case of *Our Town*, the cast was entirely male, save for the roles of Emily, Mrs. Webb, and Mrs. Gibbs. Rebecca Gibbs became Robert, Mrs. Soames became Mister, and so on. The production's director, Kate Powers, directed for RTA previously and subsequently to *Our Town*, and has extensive experience leading theatre classes and productions within correctional facilities.

Our Town was mounted in the general visiting room, a long, low-ceilinged space, with industrial lighting and linoleum-tiled floors, with a small array of vending machines along the eastern and southern walls. It resembles nothing so

Kate Kenney (foreground) and the company in the 2013 Rehabilitation Through the Arts production of *Our Town* at Sing Sing Correctional Facility, directed by Kate Powers. Photo courtesy of RTA.

much as a school cafeteria in need of refurbishment, albeit with guard stations and assorted warning signs about proper behavior.

All that was set up specially for the play were some low risers, lifting the acting area a few inches above the audience seating, and rows of folding metal chairs arranged on three sides of the stage, with most directly facing the broadest part of the platform. There were costumes for the main characters, no small freedom in a facility where both the population and the officers wear strictly regulated uniforms. The Stage Manager opted for a beige tuxedo, complete with tails, the mothers wore aprons, George had his baseball hat.

There are three performances of any production at Sing Sing, two solely for the prison population, and one for invited guests of RTA. Entering the space after a full body scan, hand-wanding, and the checking of all personal items, the public is taken in small groups through a set of double gates, with one locked behind them before another opens. At the time *Our Town* was produced, family members of the men in the production were not permitted to attend; that policy was subsequently changed.

Because of strict limits on when the men needed to be in their cells for the evening, Powers determined that the play had to be performed without intermissions if there were to be no cuts. The transition from the first act to the second was simple, but when the second act moved to the third, directorial innovation revealed itself. Once George and Emily left their wedding, the cast went about arranging chairs for the cemetery, but the audience became aware of two lines of men proceeding up the two main aisles to the stage. They each carried a chair and walked with a deliberate pace, dressed in prison green, staring straight ahead as they passed among the crowd. When they reached the stage, they proceeded to its rear. They placed their chairs, evenly spaced along the wall and sat, staring straight ahead the whole time. They would remain that way until the end of the play.

The western wall of the visitor's room consisted primarily of high windows, with wire woven within the glass. The timing of the latter two acts was such that the wedding and the very start of Act III benefitted, first from the orange glow of the sun setting across the Hudson River, throwing the room into the hues that film makers call "magic hour" because of the brief, extraordinary light that will soon resolve into darkness. It did so for *Our Town*, almost as if designed, draining the light and life from Grover's Corners and allowing the overhead fluorescents to assert their cold industrial whiteness on the scene in the afterlife.

There was a simple printed program for the play, the cover featuring art created by a member of the prison population. While there was a cast list, there were no biographies. The audience knew nothing about the actors they watched in the play, save for what they can infer from the men living in a maximum-security prison. For the one public performance, they are simply actors, portraying characters, with nothing of their past or future. They are only in the present for two uninterrupted hours, living in Grover's Corners.

In this chapter:
Jermaine Archer, Stage Manager
Kenyatta Hughes, one of the dead
Kate Kenney, Emily Webb
Samuel "Minister" Morris, Joe Stoddard
Kate Powers, director
Marcelle Smith, George Gibbs
Omar "Sweets" Williams, Dr. Gibbs

Play selection and casting

Kate Powers When I first started going into that facility and working with those men, they would never tell me directly if I had said something wrong or if I was doing something they didn't like, because they wanted to be sure that I was coming back. They didn't want to appear ungrateful. I showed up one night before auditions thinking that we were going to have a fun night. We were going to read the first act with the men and start to talk about the themes and the ideas of the play a little bit.

We got there and the tension was just palpable. The room was roiling with some folks openly unhappy. It was unusual. The steering committee, which was comprised of five of the guys in the group, was having a conversation with a group, saying that this is the play that had been selected. A small, vocal cohort of guys, probably about seven or eight of the men, were incandescent with anger. 'Why are we doing this play? Why are we doing this white play? What does this white play have to do with us?'

Sweets Williams It seemed plain, it seemed vague, it seemed bland. I wasn't interested in it at all.

Minister Morris It really didn't have no connection, when we read it, to me. I'm thinking Black issues, Black America, so when they finally said this was going to be it, I objected. "When are we going to tell a story from a Black perspective? Were there any Black plays?" So they noted my objection, and Kate was like, "Give it a try." And I'm like, "No, I'm not going to give it a try. I don't see myself in *Our Town*." We would go back and forth. Then she pulled me to the side and said, "Could you consider if we make it *our* town, you don't have to look at it from Thornton's perspective. Let's try to make it *our* town, *our* perspective."

Marcelle Smith For the most part, when someone watches plays or especially guys in here, they get what they want to get out of it. It's entertainment. They look for the funny parts, things that they've seen happen before or things that they can relate to.

Jermaine Archer A lot of people felt like: we don't talk like this. This is not our play. This is not a play about us. It was written by white people for white people, and maybe we need to change some of the language. Of course, Kate was like, "Absolutely not. This is a classic. Trust me. They will get it." We were like, "Listen, we need to update some of this language. We don't need to dumb it down, we don't need to ghettoize it, but we need to change some of this because people are not going to enjoy this."

Kate Kenney Some of them made some very good points, but at that point most of them hadn't actually read the full play. They'd read parts of it, and said, "It's really boring," or, "Nothing happens, it doesn't mean anything to me."

Jermaine Archer I like action and I didn't see any action in it. I didn't like that there was no set, there were no props. I didn't like the fact that we were going to have to trust our audience's imagination. I really did not think our audience would get it. I said, "Yes, the Friday night audience may appreciate it. But what about our guys on the inside? I think they're going to tune out." I didn't want to lose our core audience, the people that we do this for every year.

Kate Powers I said, "Just read it one more time. Look at the life of the individual and the life of the stars, that question of what's eternal within you and how do you live our life every minute when you're locked in a place where you want 25 years to fly by just like that. If you still think it doesn't have anything to say to us as a community, then I'll drop it."

Kenyatta Hughes One of the things I always harken back to is when I was maybe nine or ten years old. I was riding in the car with my dad and he was playing Men at Work. He was singing along, having a ball. I asked him why he listened to so much white music, by which I meant music by white artists, but on some other level something more. He told me, "Son, there's no such thing as white music or Black music, there's just good music and not good music." From very early on, I understood that art, if it resonates on a certain level, it can be universal.

Kate Kenney The people who were leading the opposition still auditioned for the play. They said, "I want to be an actor in this even though I don't like this play. If this is what we're doing, then I'll do it, but I still don't think it's a great play." Over time, each one of them had a different journey. One of the most outspoken people at the very first rehearsal has been in my classes for years after, and he still says this is his favorite play.

Jermaine Archer When I first read it, I thought it was morbid. But as I rehearsed it, and as I memorized it, I don't think it was used for shock value. I think it was just reality. It's a reality that none of us wants to face. Death is a reality. We're all going to face it one day, and there are so many people that choose to ignore it. Let's just prepare for it.

Rehearsals

Kate Powers In that environment, I want to make sure before we get on our feet that everybody really understands what the story is we're telling, and has had some ownership of that. We read slowly and we stop and we talk a lot. The conversation around human beings being shut up in little boxes came up a lot. A group realization over the course of a couple weeks of table work about, 'Well we're human beings shut up in little boxes. How are we the same as these people? How are we different than these people?' I brought in a lot of photographs of African American and Native American people doing pretty much all the professions in the play from approximately 1900 to 1910. One of the men, a Black man, said, "I never knew Black people dressed like this."

Jermaine Archer I loved the part. Every other play I played a villain. That's the first time I said 'I'm happy, I think this is the best role I'm going to play.' To me, it was Mr. Roarke from *Fantasy Island*. You don't know if he's real, you don't know if he's alive, you don't know if he's a representation of God. Some people see him and some people don't. Even though I wasn't sold on the play, I was sold on that role.

Kate Powers We watched that documentary *OT: Our Town*, about the school in Compton. In that documentary, they ask some of the very same questions that some of the men in RTA were asking. "Why are we doing this play? What does this play have to do with us? How do we move towards, or evade, emotional engagement with other people?"

Sweets Williams I never experienced walking with my wife. You don't see that in Black neighborhoods. You don't see a doctor coming around. You go to a free clinic, you go to the welfare center. So you're not used to these type of things. I associated it with Mister Rogers. That's the best place I could put *Our Town*. That was my growing-up. That's my youth. That's my father. That's my getaway. There was no race for Mister Rogers. What you take from Mister Rogers, you take from *Our Town*. You leave from there feeling better than you came.

Kate Powers One of the men said, "You have to understand, our wedding jitters are different." I said, "In what way are they different?" He said, "Well we have to marry the women who are willing to have us. Not necessarily the women that we might choose out in the world."

Jermaine Archer He shows people who they are without being disrespectful. I love that he takes someone's world and shifts it a little bit and said, 'Look, you see what's going on?' Without making you feel bad about it. When I take Emily back to Grover's Corners, and just show her, 'Look, you see that?' instead of saying, 'You could have been spending your time better.' It was more of a gentle, grandfatherly moment.

Kate Powers One of the things that's challenging in there is physical contact between the professional actresses who are coming in and the men. It needs to be extremely limited. George and Emily could hold hands in this *Our Town*, but they certainly couldn't kiss at the wedding. How do we seal the deal at a wedding if you can't have a kiss? Marcelle Smith, who was playing George, said that he thought it would be really good if they could jump the broom. So that's what we did.

Kate Kenney The modern impulse is reach out and have that physical connection, but the constraints of the play as well as the constraints of the prison say you can't do that. How do you channel that emotion? How do you make it count? At the end of the soda shop scene, we did end up walking out holding hands.

Marcelle Smith They're looking at the moon, and they look at each other, and look back at the moon. 'Oh, this is cute right here, I like this.' Two young kids. I remember that time. I remember that time where I was scared to talk to the girl, I didn't know what to do. Throw a piece of paper at her, or something like that. Don't even know what to say. It was like George. He didn't really know what to say, so that little part of me came out.

Kate Kenney In performance, I think to some extent there's a tension that builds, and then when that happens, when they actually touch hands, the audience reacted like it was a modern-day movie and the characters are making out. There was such a vocal, immediate physical reaction to what seems like a very simple moment, but the audience watching it saw how momentous it was.

Marcelle Smith Once he had his focus, that was it. Nothing else mattered. The only thing mattered was for him to be happy and for her to be happy. Even in the soda fountain scene, where he gets the drink for her and he doesn't have any money to pay for it, but it doesn't matter, because what I wanted to do got done and it was accomplished.

Kate Kenney Doing the soda fountain scene with Marcelle we were talking about how men and women sometimes try to impress each other or make themselves look like a desirable partner. He was saying, "When I was 15 and I wanted to impress this girl, I stole a car, and drove it off and had a little joyride and crashed the car, because I was 15 and didn't have a license. I woke up in handcuffs, but it gave me this status." Then here's George, who wants to impress this girl, and he's like, 'Well I've got a farm, what's that other guy you've been talking to got? I can be a good provider for you.' Since Marcelle was no longer 15 when this was happening, he said, "What I did was stupid, because that didn't prove to that girl that I could take care of her. It just made me look like a big shot, but I didn't have anything to offer her. George has something to offer Emily."

Marcelle Smith You've got every one of those characters inside here. You got a Stage Manager. You always have somebody walking around, telling what's going on about everything. He's always watching, and you don't even see him. Then you got the one guy that's in love with his girl. He's daydreaming, and you've got to tell him, "Yo, you're slacking in school, man. Yo, you forgot to do this, man. Get your shit together." You've got the people who are dealing with their loss, and then you've got people that help them cope with that. This is a Grover's Corners, wherever you go.

Kenyatta Hughes I think because it is a closed community, it's a little bit different. There's no difference in motivation or of content. Everything that's in the outside community is in the inside community. People want to know other folks' secrets. There's a certain voyeuristic quality, unfortunately. But we don't necessarily want to share of ourself.

Kate Powers We changed the latitude and longitude, we changed the names of the towns to be towns that you could see out the windows of the cell blocks. We were 53 percent Protestant, 24 percent Catholic, and 20 percent Muslim, the rest indifferent. When the Stage Manager is talking about the Catholic church is here, and the Baptists are down in the hollow by the river, we said, "And the mosque is up the hill." I didn't feel like I was violating Thornton Wilder.

Minister Morris I think that was recognition of the diversity of the group of men inside. We had Muslims, Christians, and different people. I like to think that my objection, saying that this ain't Flatbush, and Kate saying this is our town—so we had Muslims or we had Christians in there. Just putting something that we could recognize and accept. Guys had a sense of belonging more. Why can't we inject ourselves inside the play, to really suit that to be our town, rather than the place where Thornton set it?

Kenyatta Hughes The narrator, when he spoke of certain things, placed the town in a context that was more reflective of the cast that made it up. Not about necessarily ethnicity or cultural upbringing, but also about the circumstance of being incarcerated and the fact that the people who were viewing it, whether it was the audience that was part of the prison population or it was the guests that were coming in on that Friday from outside, to just make Sing Sing an actual player, a character, in the play.

Jermaine Archer I was able to say, 'These are things you're missing out in life. I don't need bombs exploding and guns, and cars screeching to show you this. I can show you in real, mundane, everyday life. You need to look at this and you really need to understand that this is real. If this looks familiar to you, this is what's going on in your life as well.'

Kate Kenney That issue of crying. Many of the men are really concerned with their status there and the façade. Sometimes it's a safety concern, having that level of vulnerability. They're reluctant to go there. Both Jermaine and Marcelle, we both had exchanges of, 'Oh, you're getting teary which makes me teary.' In those moments there's no difference between working with the men on the inside and working with a professional actor on the outside, because, when you can get to that point where you're actually just being human beings connecting with each other, there are no other boundaries.

Jermaine Archer I didn't know anyone that can go from zero to 90 that fast. We would be talking, and then it was, "Okay, let's do the scene." The next thing you know her face is red, she's crying. It messed me up the first time she did it. It was difficult to look at her and to see. She's crying and I don't see an actor. I see a little girl crying. We had to do that scene over and over before I could get comfortable with it to not break character, to not want to hug her.

As soon as the scene was over, the color would come back to her face. Tears would stop flowing. As the Stage Manager, it wouldn't have affected me because I do this all the time. This is my job. I show up, I show people their lives, I disappear. As Jermaine Archer, it was very difficult in the moment. Then, reflecting on it? I have three daughters and looking at her was like looking at one of my daughters. I would want to be able to comfort them and I'm in prison and I can't.

Minister Morris Love is something that I always dreamed about. In adolescence, you really don't experience certain things. I ain't experienced much. Puppy love. Me and my girlfriend had a daughter, but that was out of pleasure more than love. So you think about the aspects of love as a scene. Then you read and you're like, 'I wonder what love really is?' Like Emily and George.

Kate Powers It's always rewarding as a director to watch an actor take a risk. The ways in which they sometimes run towards the thing that scares them. But in an environment like a men's maximum security prison, those risks are riskier. Letting down one's guard in there is a bigger deal. If you're going to have a serious conversation about death, and about grief, and about what is fleeting, and what is eternal, that requires more vulnerability. The things the men in that room know about grief and loss that I don't know are deep.

Jermaine Archer I decided at first that he was God. No one else can see him but the person he's talking to. He has God-like attributes. Later on, I decided I don't know who Thornton Wilder wrote him as, but in my mind, he's going to be Mr. Roarke forever because I didn't understand Mr. Roarke, but I was able to appreciate him.

Kate Powers One night we had a Grover's Corners town fair. We just spent one Friday night playing the kinds of games that you would play at a Fourth of July picnic. We learned that Constable Warren was a cheater when it came to certain of those kinds of games. Part of the way that he moves through that town is the police way, but he's also responsible in a paternal way for this community. We wanted to make sure he didn't come off in that environment looking anything like the more negative connotations of police.

Jermaine Archer Guys laugh at me when they hear house music coming out of my headphones. I like to think that's when I wasn't too cool to dance. I used to go to the club and actually dance. Before we would get into fights in the club. I believe going back to those unimportant days in prison, mundane days, just a regular every day, those were the good old days. Before we were consumed by the streets. I believe in prison we miss those unimportant days more than we miss what we would call our glory days, because that's when we were innocent.

Kate Powers I remember Jermaine saying to me very late in the process, he said, "Man, at the beginning I really didn't know what you were talking about, about this no scenery thing. I didn't know how it was going to work."

Jermaine Archer The night before opening night, we were doing a run through dress rehearsal, and I happened to exit stage right, and I walked around where the audience would be. The entire production, the entire floor, all the way back by the windows, and I looked. I got the picture. And I was like, 'Wow'. Because I'm in the picture, I don't see it, but when I came out of it and walked around, I said, 'Now, I see what Kate sees.'

Minister Morris As soon as I can I get involved with programs with young people, it's like raising the dead to life. I'm sitting there one time with another brother, and I say, "Look at the dead. Brothers are playing real good dead people," but what I was saying was, 'Well, how do you raise the dead?'

Marcelle Smith That's the RTA. We always help everybody out because the play's not just you. It's everybody. If somebody else messes up, or you don't help them out, it doesn't really matter how good you were.

Performance

Marcelle Smith It's distracting when prisoners come. Sometimes they laugh, and you're trying not to laugh. You try not to look at them, because you know if you look at them, you're going to break character and you're going to start laughing.

Kate Powers The men have told me this, I never witnessed this part myself, but there have been performances of things where people have started shouting things like, "Early go back. Early go back." Meaning they would rather go back to the cell block than continue to sit there and watch the play.

Sweets Williams People die every day at a maximum facility. A guy that you're close with dies, your friends die. You can't go to the funeral, as opposed to being in medium. When someone dies up here, everyone hurts. They've been there for 30 and 40 years. It's a family member, it's an uncle, it's a cousin. Whether you see them like that or not, that's what they are.

Kate Kenney I remember looking out over this crowd of the guys who were all in green, and the men behind me who were in their state greens. Being so aware of being there with all of them, and so aware that they were really, really listening.

Jermaine Archer There was one point on Friday night, as they were setting up for Act III, where I was so caught up in the moment that I let more time go by than was scheduled. I was supposed to be speaking while they were bringing the chairs on, and I was just so taken into the moment, I was looking at it like, 'This is amazing.' I was an audience member for a minute.

Kenyatta Hughes I began to put myself in a certain mindset before I entered and then try and maintain that mindset throughout, because I had come to make certain decisions about what I wanted it to be about. It didn't necessarily mean the same thing to everyone who was doing it. I think I may have discussed it a little bit with certain individuals. There's guys there who were like, 'Look, this is evidence that there's no spirit. There's a body because rigor mortis has begun to set in and that's why he can barely move.' Different individuals did whatever they found that worked with them.

Kate Powers Every production I've been involved in, there are things that the outside audience laughs at and there's things that the inside audience laughs at and then there are things that everybody laughs at. One of the things that the men found particularly engaging was the two mothers. They thought the two mothers were very funny. They spoke back to them, not in a harassing kind of way but in a, 'You tell it, mama, you tell him what's what' way. They were really interested in the soda fountain scene and I think some of these men, probably in spite of themselves, had these very big grins on their faces while George and Emily were at the soda fountain. I remember after George said, "So I guess this is an important talk we've been having." There was a big laugh and then one guy said, "You better kiss her."

There was a lot of laughter when we were making that shift from the wedding into the cemetery, when all of the dead men started coming from every direction, moving the chairs that had been the congregation at the wedding. Initially, I think it was a bit that they looked funny, 'What's going on, why are they moving in that strange, slow way?' Also it was a bunch of guys who were still in their state greens. They weren't in something that was demonstrably a costume. What was fascinating to me was as they started to realize who those men were representing and what they were doing there, that laughter stopped. It fell off a cliff.

Kenyatta Hughes The thing that gave me a grounding was the idea of prison as a cemetery. Giant catacombs above ground instead of under, with all these different mausoleums stacked on top of each other and these people inside it who are, for all intents and purposes, dead to the world. They're like ghosts reaching out, trying to communicate with the living world, hoping that someone will respond to them and acknowledge that they're even speaking.

Kate Powers Those nine guys, who comprised what we called our dead men walking, were wearing their state greens with an audience which was another 250 men in state greens. Suddenly, the cemetery was just huge.

Jermaine Archer Act III, taking Emily back, one of the most powerful moments. The cemetery moment, watching the guys bring out the chairs, which basically were their tombstones. Watching them in character walking. Then, sitting there and they're not moving. That was powerful in this setting, because we feel like we're dead. When you're in prison, you're civilly dead. We're not physically dead, we know we're still breathing. But I'm dead until I get out of here. No one knows me. Watching that was a profound moment for the audience to see. That's us. Except we have a chance to come back.

Kenyatta Hughes The similarities between being incarcerated and being deceased was something that I really latched onto, trying to find a space in myself that would allow me to sit and be as externally lifeless as possible while being internally active and hoping for some amount of recognition from those who are still alive.

Sweets Williams Hardcore killers, rapists, murderers, robbers, everyone leaves with tears in their eyes. Some people mask pain real good. Some people break down fast. You can never prepare somebody for pain. You're breaking the rules. You're in a hard place where you must be hard at all times.

Minister Morris Have you heard the expression, "If you can make it at the Apollo you can make it anywhere?" That's the same thing inside. If you could get the audience to feel what you are trying to portray then you know the cast did a good job.

Marcelle Smith Outside, your audience isn't 200, 300 convicted felons. They got this mask on and don't want to shed a tear because of the sad moments and don't want to laugh too hard. They got the iron face on just watching. When you see the audience feel it, it makes you feel it even more. It makes you go into that character even more. I think that's how it would feel on the outside, performing a play for an audience that came specifically to see that play.

Kenyatta Hughes It's a very different thing when you watch a play that's composed of actors that you don't know. Even if you like them, in the abstract idea, I don't really know you as a person. As opposed to these are individuals, some of whom have literally shared the same cells, shared a six by nine room, in some cases 23 out of 24 hours, for months on end. So when they see these men whom they've spent years with and experience particular types of hardships with, they're more inclined to acknowledge that vocally. Maybe yell someone's name or clap on an entrance, even though the entrance might not demand such a thing. There's another performance going on, where the audience is actually part of the cast.

Marcelle Smith I always liked when the outside audience came in. That was always a better feeling for me, because I get the chance to show somebody that I'm not just this ID number, or this person that did something this many years ago.

Sweets Williams I don't think if you recorded it on live camera, I don't think you can relive that day. You had to be there. Not only did the cast feel that, the whole entire visitors' room, the guests, the officer of the guards, I think everyone felt the same thing. It was a pretty somber moment.

Minister Morris A good thing, when you're in population, and you're walking down a hallway, and guys will tell you, "Oh, he was a good undertaker." They remember lines from the plays. They're very attentive and they give very good feedback, as well as staff. There are correctional officers there who attended, the deputy of security, and they listen, for security purposes, but just the fact at what we're doing. They follow the story. They're after the same things.

Marcelle Smith I would get, "Yo, that's crazy man. You meet somebody, you grow up with them, you get married and then they die off. That shit's hard." Or, I would just get, "Do you feel like a little kid up there, man? I remember them days, man. I remember them days." I knew they got it.

Kenyatta Hughes It's a play that seems to be about nothing at all, but only to drive home the point that we seem to think that everything is nothing at all. The play itself, arguably, doesn't resonate until the punchline hits. It's like a *Seinfeld* episode. This is a play about nothing until it's revealed that it's everything. Your family, your friends, every moment of each day that you're experiencing while you're waiting for something to happen, everything is happening right now.

Jermaine Archer I was able to look and there were few guys, a few, who showed their emotions but most of them had to savor it inside, and they couldn't release those tears because you're sitting in a maximum security prison surrounded by convicted violent felons. In this environment you don't want to be the guy that someone saw crying at an RTA play. There were a couple of guys in the audience who are not taking it in, or who are rebelling with outrageous comments and laughing because that's their defense mechanism. They don't want to feel. But many of them, when it was over, they came to us, they said, "That was the best play y'all ever did. Y'all finally did a play for us." That blew my mind because I underestimated our audience. I never again underestimated the inside audience because they got the play quicker than I got it.

You had two guys in here, one of them was in his 70s, the other one is in his 60s. One of them has 150 years, so he's never going home. To someone like him, the play takes on a whole different meaning because when you see death you realize, 'I'm going to be carried out of this place. What's it going to be when my time comes?' It forces him to face that reality, and I believe he's one of the guys who said, "You finally did a play for us I know that my time is going to come one day. And I'm able to face it now." The biggest fear of a convicted felon is dying in prison.

Reflection

Jermaine Archer That play changed my life because I always cared about time. That's the one thing on everyone in prison's mind: time. It's hard to live in the moment in prison, every single moment is very difficult, for safety reasons. I don't need to experience the deprivation, the degradation, the humiliation and violence. I don't need to kick that to 100 percent. Sometimes, I have to log off and just exist. But at the same time, I realize I got 22 years to life, and I don't have any timeouts. So I need to live as much as possible.

Kate Kenney My feeling is that it had more of an impact on me as a human being and as an actress, and more of an impact on the men who were a part of RTA specifically, than many of the other plays. It's a play that comes up over and over again, year after year, in my classes, in rehearsal processes that I go through with the men.

Marcelle Smith I've been incarcerated over 22 years now. And it's like, wow, you never really pay attention to certain things, so you want to pay attention to everything. It goes back to your purpose. Was I supposed to be here? Was this a part of the plan for me? How did this form into a plan? Nobody plans to be incarcerated, especially not for all of this time. But I think about it now. I still have my health. I'm still all right. It didn't break me down physically or mentally, so this is a learning process.

Kenyatta Hughes By the time we'd come to *Our Town*, I had come to a certain appreciation of the things I had often taken for granted. As a result, I don't know that *Our Town* necessarily drove home any particular lessons or offered me any particular revelations. Folks say the phrase, "You're preaching to the choir." Although my response to that often is, "Even the choir has to go to church."

Marcelle Smith No matter who, or what, masks we have on in here, we all went through those same things in life. So no matter what, you're going to be able to relate.

Sweets Williams I just wish it was longer and more detailed about other things. I want to see Emily have a sister or a child we didn't know about come back and take a walk. You can never have enough of *Our Town*. You want to see Doc Gibbs' grandson come and take over the doctor's office. A *Part Two*.

Jermaine Archer I mentor a lot of young people in the prison. I'm kind of like a father figure, an uncle figure, to some of the guys. No matter how much I try to show it or explain it to them that life is going on, we need to enjoy these moments. We need to make the most of this time. You don't want to do 25 years and then pick up again and think you're going to start living again. They don't get it. I feel like the Stage Manager because I'm watching them waste time. I feel like the Stage Manager a lot because I go around, I don't tell people what you should do. I just tell you what you can do.

Marcelle Smith Everybody looks at you different—prisoners, being in a program like that, doing plays. They don't look at you as somebody that could transgress against them. They're like, 'Oh wow, that's Marcelle, he do the plays. He a cool dude.' Now you know a few things about me. It's the same thing with the officers.

Kate Powers The men said, over and over, variations on, "We're shut up in little boxes, too. We're literally shut up in little boxes." The difference between them and Emily, as several of them described it, was that when they come home, they've got a chance to do it differently. Whereas Emily has really lost that opportunity by the time she gets to that part of the play.

Kate Kenney At the end of the process, we used to sign these posters for everyone of the artwork. The men would write on it for each of the outside people involved. One of the men, who wasn't even a cast member, but was backstage crew, he wrote very simply on it, "You made me cry. You proved I have a heart." It stuck with me, because he must have been walking around thinking, 'People have called me heartless,' or 'I am heartless,' or 'I'm stone-cold, and yet this play touched me in that way.'

Marcelle Smith What I got from it was that a lot of times people say, "In life you figure out what you're willing to die for." I don't believe that's right. You're going to find things in life that you want to live for.

Kenyatta Hughes The poet Naomi Shahib Nye has a line in a poem that says, "There's a way not to be broken that takes brokenness to find it."[1] That's the thing: we are broken, but unfortunately, much of the time, or for a long time, for many of us, we don't necessarily know that we are broken. Instead we think that the things that we are experiencing are a result of being broken, some of it being trauma perhaps, some of it being inability to interact and fully connect with one another. That I am not complete. I think that that's something the play speaks to, for the audience member. If they can take that lesson that that they too have missed these things, they've overlooked the important and valuable. They can, in time, begin to reassemble those broken pieces because they're all still there.

Minister Morris I should think, in retrospect to the rest of it, that if I see anything in it, returning for me obviously ain't the same than when I went in. I can't look at myself at 17, I couldn't figure myself out at 17. I don't know at that point where I am with that boy, because this is where you're going to be at for the next 33 years. For me returning, looking at everything all over again, it's a blessing that I'm able to be outside of walls and walk again, but I looked at it when I left. I ain't that child, or the individual that committed that crime, homicide, at 17 years old. That is a dead-and-gone individual, now a resurrected man with college degrees and certificates.

Marcelle Smith A few scenes I had with Kate, I started thinking as we're doing it, 'Wow, you're never really in the moment until you find that purpose. Once you find that purpose then you're in the moment.' Now every day has a purpose. Now it's no longer, 'What am I going to do tomorrow?' It's, 'I know exactly what I'm going to do tomorrow. I know what I'm going to do the next day after that and the next day after that, because I found out what my purpose is. Why am I doing this? What am I doing this for? Does it benefit me or does it benefit somebody else?' If it benefits somebody else, maybe it benefits me, too.

Minister Morris *Our Town* is not just a place, one place. *Our Town* could be anywhere you make it. It could be in China, in Germany. It's our town. The people make the town. Their experience, their lifestyles, and what they're going through. The environment makes the town. Every fraction of this earth, 96 million square miles, they've got so many different towns in it, from the richest places to the poorest places of the world. They survive, they endure, but they make it their town.

Sweets Williams I'm not living in a ghetto anymore. I live in *Our Town*. I live in Grover's Corners. When the play ended, it wasn't a white or Black town. It's everybody's town. I always take some of that with me everywhere I go, and give more to people. I try to be patient. I try to be kind, for the most part, because that's the right way to be. *Our Town* teaches you that way. If you model your life after *Our Town*, you won't go wrong.

17

Epilogue: 11 O'clock in Grover's Corners

In the process of conducting the interviews that comprise most of this book, many words and phrases recurred: Universal. Mundane. Boring. Favorite. White. Greatest. Cheesy. Sacred. But perhaps the most surprising was, "I'm ashamed to admit it."

That last phrase came up in close to half of the interviews in one way or another, primarily among theatre professionals, because they were confessing to the fact that while they had certainly heard of *Our Town*, although it had permeated the collective consciousness, they had never actually read it or seen it. A few of those admissions made it into the text, but not anywhere near as many times as I heard it. It's not an exaggeration to say that for every person who told me how they had loved the play deeply since their very first encounter with it, others told me how the play had escaped them—or how they had managed to avoid it. However, every single person I ever asked could sing "Love and Marriage" from the *Our Town* television musical when the title was offered up, though not one knew of its origin.

Most everyone else came to *Our Town* with some notion of what it was, rightly or wrongly, even though, in a number of cases, by the time they finished their journey with the play, their perspective had changed significantly. Although I didn't speak with every cast member from every production, no one came away indifferent to the power of the play; even those few who were relatively nonplussed acknowledged its power over their castmates, colleagues, and audiences.

This journey with *Our Town* has also forced me to eat my own words. In an article for *American Theatre* magazine on the proliferation of *Our Town* nationally in 2018, I foolishly wrote of high school productions, "Unless the young actors have already lost loved ones, can they fully appreciate and enact the agonizing third act?"[1] I learned from these conversations how very wrong I was and, sadly, how many young people's lives have been touched by loss, from disease, from gun violence, from suicide. I was also shown, although I had not opined on the matter, how difficult it must be for every parent to watch their children or their children's friends tell this story, since it forces parents—however benevolently and indulgently they may have arrived at the play—to contemplate the loss of their children. How remarkable that this is foundational in one of the most popular plays in academic production for the past eight decades.

I can't say how many times I have seen *Our Town* over the years. I believe my first was the 1988 production at the Long Wharf Theater in New Haven. I can recall with great specificity the two times I have been brought to tears by *Our Town*. The first came when I saw David Cromer's production for a second time in New York, not long after the unexpected loss of a longtime friend. During Act III, Michael McKean, my neighbor in New York, sat right next to me in an aisle; I was afraid he would think I was having a breakdown. He told me later that he didn't even realize I was there, as he was so engaged with his role; if the Stage Manager responded to every person visibly moved by *Our Town*, the play might never finish a performance. The second time I sobbed at Wilder's creation, silently, was when I saw it performed by the men at Sing Sing, which so gutted me that I began crying at the start of the wedding scene and didn't stop until the play ended.

I have seen *Our Town* many times since those experiences, but particularly in the last year, without tears, perhaps because my analytical brain was in control, straining away, superseding my emotional core. At the same time, a play I have always admired has revealed itself and been revealed to me by the wisdom of others in unexpected ways; I would not have said 18 months ago that *Our Town* was one of my favorite plays, but now it certainly is. I look forward to being able to receive it again soon, I hope, more with my heart than with my head.

As I wrote at the start, Thornton Wilder was rather explicit in what he wanted us to take from *Our Town*. It is not hidden or oblique. If anything, it is a charge to each and every audience about how to think about how they approach life, to appreciate life and appreciate others while we have them. It is a secular theology, to use an oxymoron, that imagines an afterlife devoid of religious precepts, in service of urging those who experience the play to make the best use of their own life. That this message reaches every single person who works in service of telling Wilder's story and advancing his philosophy becomes evident the more one speaks with those who have had that opportunity.

It does seem that no matter what their circumstances, those who tell the story of Emily, George, and Grover's Corners all arrive at much the same destination with the play—the same appreciation, the same respect, the same awe. Where they set off from and how they reached that destination is what varies widely and that is the process and power of making theatre, a place where a story launched in 1938, about a small town in 1899, 1901, 1904, and 1913, can still not just be enacted and enjoyed, but remain relevant almost a century later.

Having been born in New Haven, I lived only miles away from Thornton Wilder for the first 13 years of my life, though he was often away from home, given his penchant for travel. I wish I had known the play and understood the play at that age, as I surely would have wanted to write to Wilder and perhaps even ask if I could meet with him; unfortunately, my passion for theatre didn't begin until a year or two after he passed away. Had I been sufficiently aware and assertive in the early 1970s, what might I have written, what would I have wanted to say to him about *Our Town* and what he asked of us, of me?

"I try. I'll keep trying."

April 2020

Sources, Permissions and Notes

Sources

All interview material is from sessions conducted by the author between February 2019 and April 2020, unless otherwise footnoted, except for quotes from Paul Newman in Chapter 5, drawn from a 2006 video interview by Tony Vellela for his video series "Character Studies," and used with his kind permission.

Material in Chapter 16 on the Sing Sing production benefits from reading transcripts of interviews by Peter Kramer of Lohud.com, conducted in June 2013, which, while not quoted, provided an excellent refresher to the author's own recollections.

The interviews represent a mix of in-person meetings, phone calls, and video chats; the majority were one-on-one. Joint interviews were conducted with the actors who shared the same roles at, and with company leaders of, TBR and LSU, in Chapter 8; with pairs of actors in the Theatrical Outfit company, as well as the two directors, in Chapter 11; with Anne Keefe and Alison Harris for Chapter 5 on Westport, Carlota Sosa and Rafael Romero in Chapter 12 on Miami New Drama, and Anna D. Shapiro and Jessica Thebus for Chapter 9 on Lookingglass.

Quotes from interviews have been edited and condensed for clarity and length. In cases where lines from *Our Town* are referenced, the text has been aligned with the actual dialogue, except in instances where the speaker was obviously paraphrasing and condensing dialogue in order to make their point.

In cases where there are direct quotes from the play, or where people were recounting things they said or that were spoken to them, the text uses double quotation marks. However, to distinguish intentional paraphrases or internal dialogue and thoughts related by those interviewed, those are enclosed by single quotation marks.

Texts of *Our Town* referenced in this book include: *Our Town* by Thornton Wilder, Coward-McCann, 1938; *Three Plays by Thornton Wilder*, Bantam Classic, New York, 1961; *Our Town* by Thornton Wilder as anthologized in *Thornton Wilder: Collected Plays & Writings on Theater*, The Library of America, New York, 2007; and *Our Town* by Thornton Wilder, Harper Perennial Modern Classics, 2013.

Permissions

Quotes from *OUR TOWN* by the interviewees are not culled from the play's text, but are transcribed from the interviews. In instances where quotations from interviewees referencing *OUR TOWN* are paraphrased, they were intentionally left uncorrected.

OUR TOWN, A Play in Three Acts by Thornton Wilder. Copyright ©1938, 1965, 2003, 2013 by The Wilder Family LLC. Reprinted by permission of The Wilder Family LLC and The Barbara Hogenson Agency, Inc. All rights reserved.

Dialogue between Emily and Mrs. Gibbs and Emily and Simon Stimson from the first edition, later deleted from successive printings of *OUR TOWN, A Play in Three Acts* by Thornton Wilder. Copyright ©1938 by Coward-McCann and the Wilder Family LLC. Reprinted by permission of The Wilder Family LLC and The Barbara Hogenson Agency, Inc. All rights reserved.

Excerpts from "A Preface for *Our Town*" by Thornton Wilder. Copyright ©1938 by The New York Times Co. Reprinted by permission of The Wilder Family LLC and The Barbara Hogenson Agency, Inc. All rights reserved.

Excerpt from "Preface" to *Three Plays: Our Town, The Skin of Our Teeth, The Matchmaker* by Thornton Wilder. Copyright ©1957 by The Wilder Family LLC. Reprinted by permission of The Wilder Family LLC and The Barbara Hogenson Agency, Inc. All rights reserved.

Excerpt from *OUR TOWN, A Play in Three Acts*, Readings, "L'Envoi" Appendix 11. Final Thoughts by Tappan Wilder, Harper Perennial Modern Classics, Copyright ©2013 by The Wilder Family LLC. Reprinted by permission of The Wilder Family LLC and The Barbara Hogenson Agency, Inc. All rights reserved.

Excerpt from "*Our Town* – From Stage to Screen." Correspondence from Thornton Wilder to Sol Lesser. Copyright ©1940 by The Wilder Family LLC. Reprinted by permission of The Wilder Family LLC and The Barbara Hogenson Agency, Inc. All rights reserved.

Excerpts from Thornton Wilder's letters to Aaron Copland and Isabella and Isabel Wilder from *The Selected Letters of Thornton Wilder,* Edited by Robin G. Wilder & Jackson R. Bryer. Letters copyright ©2008 by The Wilder Family LLC. Compilation of the letters and added text copyright ©2008 by Robin G. Wilder & Jackson R. Bryer. HarperCollins Publishers. Reprinted by permission of The Wilder Family LLC and The Barbara Hogenson Agency, Inc. All rights reserved.

Excerpt from *Thornton Wilder A Life*, by Penelope Niven, Copyright ©2012 by Penelope Niven. HarperCollins Publishers. Reprinted by permission of Jennifer Niven and The Barbara Hogenson Agency, Inc. All rights reserved.

Excerpts from Thornton Wilder's letters to Gertrude Stein from The Thornton Wilder Papers, Yale Collection of American Literature. Reprinted by consent of The Wilder Family LLC and The Barbara Hogenson Agency, Inc.

Excerpt from Thornton Wilder's letters to Jed Harris and Dwight Dana from the Thornton Wilder Papers, Yale Collection of American Literature. Reprinted by consent of The Wilder Family LLC and The Barbara Hogenson Agency, Inc.

Excerpts from an unpublished Act Four of *Our Town* in the 1942 radio script, *Contact*, from The Thornton Wilder Papers, Yale Collection of American Literature. Reprinted by consent of The Wilder Family LLC and The Barbara Hogenson Agency, Inc.

To learn more about Thornton Wilder, please visit www.ThorntonWilder.com

Notes

Chapter 1

1 Thornton Wilder, *Our Town: A Play in Three Acts*, Harper Perennial Modern Classics, New York, 2013, p. 103.

2 Thornton Wilder, "A Preface for 'Our Town,'" from *Thornton Wilder: Collected Plays & Writings on Theater*, The Library of America, New York, 2007, p. 657.

3 Thornton Wilder, "Preface to *Three Plays*," from *Thornton Wilder: Collected Plays & Writings on Theater*, The Library of America, New York, 2007, p. 686.

4 Thornton Wilder and Tappan Wilder, "Appendix 11: *L'Envoi*," from Wilder, *OUR TOWN: A Play in Three Acts*, Harper Perennial Modern Classics, New York, 2013, p. 187.

5 "The Big Read Blog (Archive): Edward Albee on 'Our Town,'" produced by Josephine Reed, posted by Adam Kampe, National Endowment for the Arts, March 9, 2011, retrieved online from: https://www.arts.gov/big-read/2011/edward-albee-our-town.

6 Samuel Beckett, *Waiting for Godot*, Grove Press, New York, Evergreen Edition, 1956, p. 57.

Chapter 2

1 Penelope Niven, *Thornton Wilder: A Life*, HarperCollins Publishers, New York, 2012, p. 426.

2 Thornton Wilder to Gertrude Stein, from *The Letters of Gertrude Stein and Thornton Wilder*, Edited by Edward M. Burns and Ulla E. Dydo with William Rice, Yale University Press, New Haven, CT, and London, 1996, p. 175.

3 Ibid., p. 179.

4 Ibid., p. 206.

5 Jed Harris, *Watchman, What of the Night*, Doubleday & Company, Inc., New York, 1963, p. 82.

6 Rosen, "Plays Out of Town: *Our Town*," *Variety*, Los Angeles, Vol. 129, Issue 7, January 26, 1938, p. 58.

7 Peggy Doyle, *Boston Evening American*, January 26, 1938.

8 Mordaunt Hall, *Boston Evening Transcript*, January 26, 1938.

9 Unbylined, "The Stage, Wilbur Theatre, 'Our Town'", *The Boston Globe*, January 26, 1938, p. 11.

10 Elinor Hughes, *Boston Herald*, January 26, 1938, p. 8.

11 Unbylined, "'Daughter' 18G, 'Caesar' 8G; Hub O.K.," *Variety*, Los Angeles, Vol. 129, Issue 8, February 2, 1938, p. 59.

12 Unbylined, "'Town' Changes Hub Verdict; Disputes," *Variety*, Los Angeles, Vol. 129, Issue 9, February 9, 1938, p. 55.

13 Letter from Alexander Woollcott to Thornton Wilder, January 26, 1938, Thornton Wilder Papers, Yale Collection of American Literature (hereafter YCAL). Beinecke Rare Book and Manuscript Library, at: https://archives.yale.edu/repositories/11/resources/1402.

14 Letter from Woollcott to Wilder, January 28, 1938, Thornton Wilder Papers, YCAL.

15 Unbylined, "Gossip of the Rialto," *The New York Times*, February 27, 1938, p. 149.

16 Wilder to Stein, February 1, 1938, from *Letters of Gertrude Stein*, pp. 207–8.

17 Arthur Pollock, "Frank Craven Acts as Guide through the Life of Man in 'Our Town,' Thornton Wilder's Play at Henry Miller's Theater," *Brooklyn Daily Eagle*, February 5, 1938, p. 20.

18 Wilella Walford, *New York Post*, February 5, 1938.

19 Brooks Atkinson, *The New York Times*, February 5, 1938, p. 18.

20 John Chapman, "'Our Town' Proves Challenging, Imaginative Stage Experiment," *Daily News*, February 5, 1938, p. 21.

21 Richard Watts Jr., "The Theaters," *New York Herald Tribune*, February 5, 1938, p. 6.

22 Eleanor Roosevelt, "My Day," United Features Syndicate, March 2, 1938, retrieved online at: https://www2.gwu.edu/~erpapers/myday/displaydoc.cfm?_y=1938&_f=md054890.

23 "The Kate Smith Show," CBS Radio, April 6, 1938, script reproduced in *Kate Smith Speaks: 50 Selected Original Radio Scripts, 1938-1951*, by Richard Hayes, Bean Manor Media, Oklahoma, 2013, unpaginated.

24 Unbylined, "'Town' Changes Hub Verdict; Disputes," *Variety*, Los Angeles, Vol. 129, Issue 9, February 9, 1938, p. 55.

25 Unbylined, "'Mice and Men' Gets Award of Drama Critics," *New York Herald Tribune*, April 19, 1938.

26 Wilder telegram to Jed Harris, July 12, 1938, Thornton Wilder Papers, YCAL.

27 Dwight Dana letter to Wilder, July 21, 1938, Thornton Wilder Papers, YCAL.

28 Harris letter to Wilder, September 21, 1938, Thornton Wilder Papers, YCAL.

29 Harris telegram to Wilder, June 23, 1942, Thornton Wilder Papers, YCAL.

30 L.N., "Fred Stone Returns to Broadway in 'Lightnin'—Thornton Wilder Makes Stage Debut in 'Our Town,'" *The New York Times*, September 16, 1938, p. 18.

31 Amos G. Wilder, *Thornton Wilder and His Public*, Fortress Press, Philadelphia, PA, 1980, p. 82.

32 Unbylined, United Press wire service report, January 22, 1939.

33 Wilder in a letter to Isabella Wilder and Isabel Wilder, October 17, 1944, reprinted in *The Selected Letters of Thornton Wilder*, Edited by Robin G. Wilder and Jackson R. Bryer, HarperCollins Publishers, New York, 2009, pp. 423–424.

34 Unbylined, "18 USO Shows Set for Europe," *Variety*, Los Angeles, Vol. 158, Issue 9, May 9, 1945, p. 44.

35 Raymond Massey, *A Hundred Different Lives*, Little, Brown and Company, Boston, 1979, p. 295.

36 Associated Press as printed in the *Christian Science Monitor*, February 13, 1946, p. 13.

37 Unbylined, "U.S. Gives Nod to 40 Plays for Germany," *The Billboard*, Vol. 58, Issue 32, August 10, 1946, p. 4.

38 Unbylined, "Theatre Used to Sell Democracy to Youth in Germany; 'Edison' Scores," *Variety*, Los Angeles, Vol. 164, Issue 13, December 4, 1946, p.17.

39 Unbylined, "Court, Liverpool: 'Our Town,'" *The Stage*, London, Issue 3,395, April 26, 1946, p. 1.

40 Unbylined, "Despite its Good Press, London 'Town' Slow B.O.," *Variety*, Los Angeles, Vol. 162, Issue 10, May 15, 1946, p. 65.

41 Elissa Nadworny, "The Most Popular High School Plays and Musicals," NPR, updated, July 31, 2019, retrieved online from: https://www.npr.org/sections/ed/2019/07/31/427138970/the-most-popular-high-school-plays-and-musicals.

42 Richard F. Shepard, "Old Hits, Like Annuities, Pay and Pay," *The New York Times*, December 25, 1967, p. 31.

43 Howard Taubman, "'Our Town' is Integrated in Los Angeles," *The New York Times*, December 14, 1968, p. 62.

Chapter 3

1 Penelope Niven, *Thornton Wilder: A Life*, op. cit., p. 528.

2 Ibid., p. 538.

3 Thornton Wilder, Act 4 of *Our Town*, Thornton Wilder Papers, YCAL MSS 108, Box 81, folder 2097a.

4 Les., "Radio Reviews: Contact," *Variety*, Vol. 147, No. 6, July 15, 1942, p. 38.

5 Unbylined, "Federations Set for Charity Drive," *The Brooklyn Daily Eagle*, November 9, 1939, p. 26.

6 Unbylined, "Jewish Charities Merge for Drive," *The Sun*, New York, November 13, 1939.

7 "Our Town," *Campbell Playhouse*, produced by Orson Welles, CBS Network, broadcast May 12, 1939.

8 "Our Town," *Lux Radio Theatre*, NBC Blue Network, May 6, 1940.

9 *Our Town*, produced by Sol Lesser, screenplay by Thornton Wilder, Frank Craven & Harry Chandlee, directed by Sam Wood, released by United Artists, May 24, 1940.

10 Thornton Wilder and Sol Lesser, "Our Town from Stage to Screen," *Thornton Wilder: Collected Plays & Writings on Theater*, pp. 680–1.

11 Niven, *Thornton Wilder*, pp. 483–4.

12 "Our Town," The Theatre Guild on the Air, ABC Network, broadcast September 29, 1946.

13 Raymond Massey, *A Hundred Different Lives*, Little, Brown and Company, Boston and Toronto, 1979, p. 303.

14 Burgess Meredith, *So Far, So Good*, Little, Brown and Company, Boston and Toronto, p. 64.

15 *Variety Television Reviews, Volume 3, 1923–1950*, Garland Publishing, New York and London, 1989, unpaginated.

16 *Our Town*, Television ten-minute version, Thornton Wilder Papers, YCAL.

17 *Variety Television Reviews, Volume 1, 1946–1956*, Garland Publishing, New York & London, 1989, unpaginated.

18 *Variety Television Reviews, Volume 6, 1957–1959*, Garland Publishing, New York & London, 1989, unpaginated.

19 Land., "Radio Reviews: Camel Caravan," *Variety*, Vol. 147, No. 6, July 15, 1942, p. 38.

20 *Our Town*, CBS Network, January 23, 1947

21 Thornton Wilder to Aaron Copland, April 9, 1950, reprinted in *The Selected Letters of Thornton Wilder*, Edited by Robin G. Wagner and Jackson R. Bryer, HarperCollins Publishers, New York, 2008, p. 488.

22 Sid Smith, "'Grover's Corners' Illustrates 'Our Town,'" *Chicago Tribune*, July 30, 1987, retrieved online from: https://www.chicagotribune.com/news/ct-xpm-1987-07-30-8702250666-story.html.

23 David Richards, "Artful 'Corners,'" *The Washington Post*, July 31, 1987, p. C1.

24 Alvin Klein, "Tom Jones Looks Back," *The New York Times*, August 26, 1990, p. CN12.

25 David Richards, "The Musical that Will Not Die," *The Washington Post*, July 21, 1996, p. 112.

26 Jennifer Dunning, "Movement Enhances 'Our Town's' Poignancy," *The New York Times*, November 7, 1994, Section C, p. 12.

27 Chris Jones, "Life, Death and the Tricky Stuff in Between," *Chicago Tribune*, June 26, 2011, retrieved online from: https://www.chicagotribune.com/entertainment/ct-xpm-2011-06-26-ct-ent-0627-middleton-review-20110626-story.html.

28 Laura Collins-Hughes, "An 'Our Town' with Sex Offenders in 'America is Hard to See,'" *The New York Times*, February 2, 2018, p. C2.

28 Casey Llewellyn, *O, Earth*, manuscript, 2016, p. 56.

30 Peter Bradshaw, "Dogville – Review," *The Guardian*, May 20, 2003, retrieved online from: https://www.theguardian.com/film/2003/may/20/artsfeatures.londonfilmfestival2003.

31 Unbylined introduction, "Revisiting Hours: 'Dogville' and Our Great American Nightmare," *Rolling Stone*, August 17, 2018, retrieved online from: https://www.rollingstone.com/movies/movie-features/stream-this-movie-dogville-711678/.

32 Christopher Orr, "The Movie Review: 'Dogville,'" *The Atlantic*, August 24, 2004, retrieved online from: https://www.theatlantic.com/entertainment/archive/2004/08/the-movie-review-dogville/69537/.

33 Thomas Mallon, "George Saunders Gets Inside Lincoln's Head," *The New Yorker*, February 6, 2017, retrieved online from: https://www.newyorker.com/magazine/2017/02/13/george-saunders-gets-inside-lincolns-head, published in the print edition of February 13 and 20, 2017 under the headline "Go to His Grave."

34 Joe Fassler, "The Leftovers, Our Town, and the Brutal Power of Ordinary Details," *The Atlantic*, June 24, 2014, retrieved online from: https://www.theatlantic.com/entertainment/archive/2014/06/the-brutal-power-of-the-ordinary-details/373327/.

35 Helen E. Hokinson, "Does this Play Have Scenery," *Life*, February 28, 1938, p. 28.

36 Julian B. Tuthill, "Summer Theater Reviews: Too Much Johnson," *The Billboard*, Cincinnati, Vol. 50, Issue 35, August 27, 1938, p. 19.

37 George S. Kaufman, "Local Boy Makes Good," published in *Greatest Revue Sketches*, Edited by Donald Oliver, Avon Books, New York, 1982, p. 294.

38 Kenneth Tynan, "Requiem for a Nun," *Curtains* by Kenneth Tynan, Longmans, 1961, p. 277.

39 Art Buchwald, "Buchwald's Column: Our Town," *New York Herald Tribune*, September 13, 1962, p. 19.

40 Dutton Foster, *Our Rotten Town*, Playscripts, New York.

41 *Death of a Streetcar Named Virginia Woolf*, devised by Tim Ryder and Tim Sniffen, written by Tim Sniffen, manuscript, 2016, p. 57.

42 John Geoffrion, *Our Town . . . with Zombies*, manuscript, 2019, p. 36.

43 "Two Girls for Every Boyd" by Dan O'Shannon & Tom Anderson, *Cheers*, NBC TV, Season 8, Episode 9, broadcast November 23, 1989.

44 "Fashion Show" by Eileen O'Hare, *The Nanny*, CBS TV, Season 3, Episode 15, broadcast January 8, 1996.

45 "A Star is Born" by David Kendall, *Growing Pains*, ABC TV, Season 3, Episode 7, broadcast October 27, 1987.

46 "Betrayal" by Jill Gordon, *My So-Called Life*, ABC TV, Season 1, Episode 17, broadcast January 12, 1995.

47 "Their Town" by Sagan Lewis, *St. Elsewhere*, NBC TV, Season 6, Episode 17, broadcast April 20, 1988.

48 "Children's Hospital: A Play in Three Acts" by Rob Corddry & Jonathan Stern & David Wain, *Children's Hospital*, Cartoon Network, Season 3, Episode 9, broadcast July 28, 2011.

49 "The River's Edge" by Roberto Aguirre-Sacasa, *Riverdale*, The CW, Season 1, Episode 1, broadcast January 26, 2017.

50 "Hogcock/Last Lunch" by Tina Fey and Tracey Wigfield, *30 Rock*, NBC TV, Season 7, Episode 12, broadcast January 31, 2013.

Chapter 6

1 Lyn Gardner, "Our Town review – Wilder's hymn to ordinary lives is remade for Manchester," *The Guardian*, September 22, 2017, retrieved online www.theguardian.com/stage/2017/sep/22/our-town-review-thornton-wilder-manchester-royal-exchange.

Chapter 7

1 Gabriel Nathan, "Our Norristown: On Producing Our Town at a Psychiatric Hospital," published in *Thornton Wilder in Collaboration: Collected Essays on His Drama and Fiction*, edited by Jackson R. Bryer, Judith P. Hallett and Edyta K. Oczkowicz, Cambridge Scholars Publishing, Newcastle-on-Tyne UK, 2018, pp. 338–9.

Chapter 9

1 "Anna D. Shapiro and Jessica Thebus on 'Our Town,'" Lookingglass Theatre Company, February 5, 2009, retrieved from YouTube at https://youtu.be/sln1hLwSuk0.

Chapter 10

1 Wilder, *Our Town*, Harper Perennial Modern Classics, op. cit., p. 31.
2 Ibid., p. 83.

Chapter 11

1 Wilder, *Our Town*, Harper Perennial Modern Classics, op. cit., p. 3.
2 Moisés Kaufman and the Members of the Tectonic Theatre Project, *The Laramie Project*, and Moisés Kaufman, Leigh Fondakowski, Greg Pierotti, Andy Park, and Stephen Belber, *The Laramie Project: Ten Years Later*, Vintage Books, New York, 2014, p. 73.

Chapter 15

1 Andrzej Lukowski, "*Our Town*: Review," *Time Out*, London, May 23, 2019, retrieved online from: https://www.timeout.com/london/theatre/our-town-review.
2 Thornton Wilder, "A Preface for 'Our Town,'" from *Thornton Wilder: Collected Plays & Writings on Theater*, The Library of America, New York, 2007, p. 659.

Chapter 16

1 Naomi Shahib Nye, *Cinco de Mayo*, retrieved online from https://www.pbs.org/newshour/arts/weekly-poem-cinco-de-mayo.

Chapter 17

1 Howard Sherman, "Why *Our Town* Springs Eternal, But Especially Now," *American Theatre*, Theatre Communications Group, March 2018, p. 46.

Thanks and Acknowledgments

First and foremost, to every single person who spoke with me for this book, who shared so much more with me than could possibly be included here. Your candor, talent, and wisdom are the only reason this book exists. My thanks as well to their many colleagues and collaborators on these productions, who contributed to their journeys with this play.

I offer my thanks to many people who helped on this project: my editor Dom O'Hanlon, who, while not the first person to ask me if I'd ever thought about writing a book, was the first person to ask who could actually offer me publication and was willing to take the chance. My appreciation as well to Meredith Benson.

For turning a theatre administrator from a social media theatre kibitzer and blogger into a part-time professional writer about theatre, I am indebted to Alistair Smith of *The Stage* in London.

For allowing me to expound on *Our Town* in print for the first time, Rob Weinert-Kendt at *American Theatre* magazine.

For crowdsourced help on social media at the very start of this project: Monica Bauer, M. S. Burton, Tripp Burton, Christopher Caggiano, Jill Cornell, Paul Gabbard, Michael Guillot, Troy Heard, Jules Odendahl-James, Cindy Marie Jenkins, Liz Richards Krebs, Kate Langsdorf, Shaun Leisher, David Loehr, Nick O'Leary, Barbara Pitts McAdams, Gregory Maupin, Duncan Pflaster, Linda Powell, Karen Brown Saine, Nicole Serratore, David Sheward, Heidi Tandy, Filonna Thomas, Autumn Tustin, Lisa Viall, Daniel P. Wilson, Myra Wong.

Lisa Gulino at Crowne Plaza Executive Center in Baton Rouge for help with accommodations in my visits to that city; Michael J. Moritz, for recording equipment counsel and acquisition; John Gromada, for technical support with said equipment and related software; and Sue Frost and Randy Adams of Junkyard Dog Productions for the frequent use of their conference room as a location for many of the interviews in this book.

Laurence Maslon of New York University for sharing a copy of George S. Kaufman's *Local Boy Makes Good*; Benjamin Dreyer of Random House (and author of *Dreyer's English*) for a small but essential early piece of factual detail from an unimpeachable source; Dr. Stacy Wolf of Princeton University for early counsel and encouragement; and Jacqueline Lawton, my invaluable sounding board on my various writing.

Glenn Holsten and Meg Sarachan of FreshFly in Philadelphia for allowing access to their archive of footage of rehearsal, performances, and interviews connected with the Montgomery County Emergency Services production of *Our Town*.

Mark Harris and Christopher Oscar Peña, for their help reaching members of the Westport/Broadway *Our Town* cast; DJ Kurs at Deaf West Theatre for help in reaching the Deaf West/Pasadena Playhouse cast and for ongoing counsel; Ryan Oliveti of Theatrical Outfit for his help as liaison to the *Our Town/The Laramie Project* acting company; Cathy Taylor of Cathy Taylor Public Relations in Chicago for her help as liaison to the Lookingglass Theatre Company; Andy Locke and the staff of the Open Air Theatre in Regent's Park for their hospitality; and Sarah Hughes for helping me to connect with UK-based agents and actors.

Thomas Mailey and Dee Johnson from the communications office of the New York State Department of Corrections; Renee Mulligan and the officers and staff of Fishkill Correctional Facility in Beacon, New York; Dr. Lesley Malin and the officers and staff of Sing Sing Correctional Facility in Ossining, New York; and Katherine Vockins and the staff and board of Rehabilitation Through the Arts, for making it possible for me to interview *Our Town* cast members who remained incarcerated at the time of writing.

Patrick Hoffman, Doug Reside, and the staff of New York Public Library's Library of Performing Arts at Lincoln Center in New York; Melissa Barton and the staff of Yale University's Beinecke Library in New Haven; and Jane Klain and the research staff at the Paley Center for Media in New York, for helping someone who hadn't plunged into a library in almost four decades, let alone genuine archives.

My departed friends Mel Gussow, A. R. Gurney, and Mike Kuchwara, who would have been surprised and I like to think delighted by this book, for their many kindnesses to me, which began just after I graduated college.

Heather and Alan Ayckbourn, for their generous friendship.

Mark Lamos and the extraordinary cohort of artists he brought to Hartford Stage from 1985 to 1993, for the best unaccredited graduate degree in theatre one could ask for.

Barbara Hogenson and, with very special appreciation for her dedication, of The Barbara Hogenson Agency, Alan Brodie and Victoria Williams of Alan Brodie Representation Ltd., and Abbie Van Nostrand of Concord Theatricals for their invaluable help on matters literary and legal.

Tappan Wilder and Rosey Strub of The Wilder Family LLC for their encouragement, support, interest, knowledge, and guidance.

Karen Blass, Mike Flaumenhaft, Steve Grinder, Steve Kaplan, Melina Lillios, Deborah Schwartz, and Bob Sherman, for being with me in the provinces north of

New York in the late 20th century, in our growing-up and in our marrying and in our living and in our losses.

Catherine "Kaki" Marshall, for always understanding.

Lauren Doll, for everything.

Index

CPSIA information can be obtained
at www.ICGtesting.com
Printed in the USA
LVHW051735280121
677758LV00006B/108